Order & Ardor

Order & Ardor

THE REVIVAL SPIRITUALITY OF *Oliver Hart & the Regular Baptists in Eighteenth-Century South Carolina*

Eric C. Smith

Foreword by
Thomas S. Kidd

The University of South Carolina Press

Published by the University of South Carolina Press
Columbia, South Carolina 29208

uscpress.com

Printed in the United States of America

Library of Congress Cataloging-in-Publication data
can be found at http://catalog.loc.gov/

ISBN 978-1-61117-878-4 (cloth)
ISBN 978-1-61117-879-1 (ebook)

For Candace

Thy people shall be willing in the day of thy power.

Psalm 110:3

CONTENTS

FOREWORD

Thomas S. Kidd

The eighteenth-century Baptist pastor Oliver Hart was one of the founders of southern evangelical Christianity. Along with Sandy Creek Baptist leader Shubal Stearns of North Carolina, Hart was arguably the most important Baptist leader in the eighteenth-century South. Hart was no bit player. He was a titan in a movement—evangelical Christianity—that came to define the South as the Bible Belt. Hart's ministry takes us back to a time when many northern Christians in the American colonies worried that the South was benighted and bereft of churches. Hart's revivalism and organizing abilities helped to address the South's lack of Christian zeal and begin the tectonic shift toward the "Christ-haunted South" of the nineteenth century.

Hart's prominence makes it remarkable that Eric C. Smith's book is the first full scholarly treatment of Hart. It would be hard to think of an eighteenth-century American religious leader as prominent as Hart who has suffered from such neglect. Smith's timely book will go a long way toward rectifying that problem.

As Smith notes, southern evangelicalism in the eighteenth century is also understudied. Until recently, many of the studies about colonial southern evangelicals focused on prerevolutionary Virginia, not the lower South. Thankfully, books like Samuel C. Smith's *A Cautious Enthusiasm: Mystical Piety and Evangelicalism in Colonial South Carolina* (University of South Carolina Press, 2013) and Thomas J. Little's *The Origins of Southern Evangelicalism: Religious Revivalism in the South Carolina Lowcountry, 1670–1760* (University of South Carolina Press, 2013) have begun to map out the contours of South Carolina's evangelical movement in this era. Smith's book on Hart is a natural next step.

The work that previous generations had done on evangelicals of the lower South focused on the Separate Baptists and the Sandy Creek (N.C.) tradition of Shubal Stearns, and for good reason. The startling radicalism and missionary zeal of the Separate Baptists is an alluring topic, against which the orderly piety of Regular Baptists like Hart seems a little staid. But Smith makes a persuasive case that the Regular Baptists were not so different from the Separates as earlier scholars might have suggested. As moderate evangelicals, leaders like Hart emphasized both "order and ardor," in Smith's nice phrase. In doing so, they were probably more typical of white evangelical Christians across the eighteenth- and nineteenth-century South than the Pentecostal style of the early Separates.

Smith locates Hart in the context of the emerging spirituality of the Great Awakening, with its focus on conversionism, revival, activism, outpourings of the Holy Spirit, and evangelical ecumenism. The book reveals the breadth and depth of Smith's consultation of archival materials on Hart, which are far-flung and extensive. One of the most important historiographical conclusions Smith makes here is to adjust our view of Regular Baptist piety and activism, which (he correctly argues) has been contrasted too starkly with that of the Separate Baptists. Although I am still struck by the path-breaking ways of the Separates and the Sandy Creek group, Smith shows that many of the Regular Baptists embraced a strong, if moderate, brand of revivalism that often complemented rather than clashed with the Separates' piety. After Smith's work on Hart, it will be hard for scholars to keep repeating the outdated conclusion that Regular Baptists, who predated the Great Awakening, were somehow opposed to revivalism because of their Calvinist beliefs.

As Smith shows, Hart's emphasis on church order hardly prevented him from engaging his congregation and his household on an emotional level as penitents broke through to conversion. In remarkable diary entries from a 1754 revival in Charleston, Hart manifested the strain of spiritual egalitarianism that so marked the leaders of the Great Awakening. For example, he took seriously the emotions and experiences of young women, even servants. One woman, Margaret, who apparently lived with and worked for Hart's family as a servant or slave, "got comfortable" with a sense of God's forgiveness to her. As Hart spoke with Margaret, he "found her quite clear, with regard to the Lord's visiting her with his love last night. . . . She had these words, *I have loved thee with an everlasting love* [Jeremiah 31:3], set home with so much light, and evidence, that she could not avoid taking comfort from them."

Although Hart saw himself as a facilitator of revival in his church, he was also eager to have women like Margaret speak about their experience of grace. He asked Margaret to tell "Betsy" and "Nancy" about what the Lord had done for her. As she did, Hart was moved to record the conversation. "'Oh Miss Betsy!' said she, 'Jesus Christ is sweet, he is precious, had I known his sweetness,' said she, 'I would not have lived so long without him'; and then turning herself to another, said, 'Oh, Oh! Miss Nancy, Christ is sweet! And since he hath had mercy on such a vile wretched sinner as me, I am sure none need ever to despair.'" The gathered throng melted into tears.

Hart's egalitarianism had its limits, of course, as it did for virtually all white evangelical pastors in the colonial era. Hart exemplified the typical moderate evangelical accommodation on slavery, for example. He was pleased to see slaves converting to Christianity, but he owned slaves himself, and saw no contradiction between biblical morality and chattel slavery. In this, Hart was just following other evangelicals such as the great English evangelist George Whitefield, who expressed initial reservations about American slavery but went on to own slaves and a plantation in South Carolina. Hart seems to have developed some scruples about slavery upon his return to the North during the Revolutionary War. But readers expecting Hart to "connect the dots" between his spiritual egalitarianism and the right of all people to be free will be disappointed.

But this limited egalitarianism is what makes Hart such an influential figure in southern evangelicalism. The passion for unbounded revival, carried out in the context of church and social hierarchy, lies at the core of what made southern evangelicalism so enduring. Anyone seeking to understand white evangelical faith in the early American South could hardly pick a more representative figure than Oliver Hart.

PREFACE

I first met Oliver Hart in the pages of a textbook by Tom Nettles, professor of historical theology, in preparation for Nettles's History of the Baptists course at The Southern Baptist Theological Seminary in the summer of 2009. Hart's achievements astonished me: he organized the South's first Baptist association of churches, established the first Baptist ministerial education fund in America, raised up an entire generation of Baptist preachers for the South, helped produce the influential *Charleston Confession* and *Summary of Church Discipline*, campaigned for the patriot cause in the American Revolution, and more. This trail-blazing Baptist seemed to be equal parts tireless activist, studied theologian, and godly pastor. Out of the dozens of dynamic Baptists I met in that course, Hart captured my imagination more than any other. As I continued my studies, I realized how little attention had been paid to the man who seemed to stand at the headwaters of Baptist life in the South. When the time came in 2011 to select the subject of my PhD dissertation, I immediately knew that I wanted to tell Hart's story.

What I did not realize at the time was how prevalent the theme of revival had been in Hart's ministry, and what an important role Hart played in the eighteenth-century evangelical awakening. Yet the longer I spent with Hart, the more convinced I became that revival was the integrating theme of his life and spirituality. Like the diaries of his hero George Whitefield, Hart's personal writings pulsate with the spiritual energy of the Great Awakening. It was an intriguing discovery, because the Regular Baptist "Charleston Tradition" that Hart represents is widely perceived as having left revivalism to their dynamic Separate Baptist cousins. Before long, my thesis became clear: Hart, the stalwart Regular Baptist of the South, wholeheartedly embraced the revival of the Great Awakening in a spirituality of both order and ardor.

This book is the product of many hours of reading and reflecting on the letters, diaries, and sermon notes written by Oliver Hart's own hand. I would not have had access to these eighteenth-century documents without the assistance of several competent and courteous library staff members. Many thanks go to Graham Duncan of the South Caroliniana Library in Columbia, Julia Cowart of the James B. Duke Memorial Library in Greenville, the research staff at the Historical Society of Pennsylvania in Philadelphia, Jason Fowler who at the time served at the

James P. Boyce Centennial Library in Louisville, and Bill Sumners of the Southern Baptist Historical Library and Archives in Nashville.

I am amazed and humbled that so many esteemed historians have been willing to interact with this material on its way to publication. Michael Haykin is a model of warm-hearted Christian scholarship. He encouraged me to follow my interest in Oliver Hart at our initial meeting and then patiently taught me the art of historical research and writing, one dash of his purple-inked fountain pen at a time. Greg Wills, from whom I have learned so much about the Baptists of the South, graciously gave of his time to talk with me about my major argument and sharpened my thinking on numerous levels. It was Nathan Finn who urged me to keep chasing the theme of revivalism in Hart, and also to broaden the scope of my project to rethink the entire Regular Baptist movement in terms of revival. James Patterson taught me historical theology while I was an undergraduate at Union University. He happily and unexpectedly reentered my life to provide invaluable editorial advice as I was submitting the manuscript for publication. Thomas Kidd, whose writing has so influenced the way I think about writing evangelical history, not only offered his own expert analysis of the manuscript but also did me the tremendous honor of writing the foreword. Each of these scholars made his own unique contribution to the final product of this book. It is immeasurably better because of them.

Two other historians also deserve mention for their quiet but decisive influence on me along the way. At a point when I was not at all sure if I could ever write anything, I had the privilege of sharing a meal with the esteemed Baptist historian Timothy George. After kindly inquiring about my research, he asserted, “We need a book about Hart’s theology and his spirituality. Write it!” Since that moment, I have never looked back. If Timothy George charged me to write a book, who was I to argue? David Dockery served as president of Union University during my undergraduate days there. My respect and appreciation for him have grown steadily in the years following my graduation, not least because he is the first person I ever heard speak about the giants of Baptist history. I now realize what a precious gift he bequeathed to me and to Union by rooting us in our Baptist past, and I am so grateful. George and Dockery are both first-rate scholars, devoted churchmen, Baptist statesmen, and sterling representatives of the “order and ardor” spiritual tradition of Oliver Hart. I hope that, in a small way, this study will honor these men and express my gratitude to them.

It is my joy to serve as pastor to the dear people of Sharon Baptist Church in Savannah, Tennessee. They have encouraged me to pursue these studies, tolerated my frequent historical allusions from the pulpit, and best of all have loved me as a member of their family. Several other faithful friends have supported me throughout this project, especially Jared Longshore, Ryan Griffith, Devin Maddox, and Ray Van Neste. They never cease to refresh my spirit.

Much has changed in my life since I first met Hart in that summer Baptist History course. Nine years later, God has given me three children who have enriched and enlivened my life in ways I could not then have imagined. I am overjoyed to be the daddy of Coleman, Crockett, and Clarabelle. This book is dedicated to their wonderful mother and my precious wife, Candace. Her love and support stand behind this work, along with anything else of value I ever produce. At the start of this journey, we strolled together down Charleston's historic lamp-lit streets, as Oliver and Sarah Hart may have walked more than two centuries ago. I look forward to going back.

Finally, a word about perspective seems in order. I am not only an evangelical Christian but a Baptist pastor in the South who attempts to minister each week within the same tradition as Oliver Hart. I personally affirm Hart's approach to theology and spirituality and unabashedly admire the testimony of his life. It would be silly to pretend that I approach my subject with total objectivity. At the same time, I have no desire to present Hart as a flawless subject. To do so would be dishonest to the historical record and a betrayal of what he believed about himself. Therefore, alongside his many sterling qualities and accomplishments, I have also tried to draw attention to the more regrettable aspects of his story, most notably his participation in eighteenth-century slavery. To acknowledge the inconsistencies and imperfections of Hart's life allows the contemporary reader to see Hart for who he is, and hopefully to identify with him as a real human being like ourselves. It also affirms what Hart so frequently confessed about himself throughout his life, that he was a sinner in need of divine grace, depending on the perfect merits of Another.

Introduction

Oliver Hart and Regular Baptist Revivalism

When Oliver Hart sat down to record a few lines in his diary before bed on Sunday, August 25, 1754, the hour was late. According to his usual practice, Hart had preached twice at the Baptist meetinghouse in Charleston, South Carolina, where he had served as pastor for almost five years. But on this Sunday, Hart returned home to find his house "crowded, mostly with Young People." The youth of Hart's congregation were in deep spiritual distress, and had come that their pastor might lead them to experience the new birth, as they had done almost every night the previous week. Hart wrote that "the Lord Enabled me to [preach] with a good degree of Freedom; many were Affected: Blessed be God the work among our young people seems to go on gloriously!" It was one of many similar gatherings that took place among the Charleston Baptists throughout the fall of 1754. An unusual seriousness had gripped the youth of the church. Night after night, they assembled to hear Hart preach, to pray in groups, and to receive direction on finding "comfort" in Christ. Some of the meetings were accompanied by "melting down into tears," others by "crying out." Hart believed it was a heaven-sent revival. "Blessed be God! I have more Reason to believe that some of our Young people are Concerned for their Souls, and it may be that the Revival may prove to be more Extensive than first Expected. Lord grant that many may be Awakened to a sense of their Misery, and Enabled to fly to the Rock of Ages for Refuge." Hart's experience represents well the Great Awakening's persistence and power in the American colonies. Historian Thomas S. Kidd has persuasively argued that a "long First Great Awakening" in the eighteenth century produced a new evangelical movement in America, marked by "persistent desires for revival, widespread individual conversions, and the outpouring of the Holy Spirit." Hart fits precisely this profile of revival spirituality.[1]

Yet the Regular Baptists of the colonial South are not remembered for their support of the revival. The Regulars traced their origins to the Particular Baptist movement in sixteenth-century England, so called for their belief that Christ's death accomplished redemption for a particular, or elect, group of people (their General Baptist counterparts were Arminian in their theology, and asserted that Christ died in the same way for all people). The Regulars had been established in America generations before the evangelical revival reached its peak in 1740. A second group of American Baptists emerged in the mid-1750s as a direct result of the Great Awakening called the Separate Baptists. They were more emotional and informal in their worship style, and less enthusiastic about confessions of faith and an educated ministry than the Regulars. The Separates were well suited to evangelistic ministry on the frontier, where they experienced explosive growth in the latter half of the eighteenth century. Because of their colorful persona and numeric surge during the period, the Separates are remembered as classic revivalists and are typically credited with bringing evangelical religion to the Baptists of the South. As the story goes, they only won over the staid and skeptical Regulars to the revival over the course of many years, through their indisputable success. While the Baptists of Virginia appeared to follow this pattern, Oliver Hart's diary indicates that the picture looked considerably different in the lower South, particularly in South Carolina. Here, a rich legacy of Regular Baptist revivalism had existed since the turn of the eighteenth century.

Regular Baptist revivalism in the South can trace its roots to the indomitable William Screven (1629–1713). Originally from Somerton in Somersetshire, England, Screven had immigrated to Kittery, Maine, by the year 1668. There, he learned the trade of shipright and joined a Baptist church in Boston. He also began preaching to his neighbors in Kittery, eventually forming a Baptist church there in 1682. The same year, Screven was brought to trial for "offensive speech" and "rash and inconsiderate words tending to blasphemy." When Screven refused to repent of his unlawful public preaching, he was fined £10 and barred from conducting "any private exercise at his house or elsewhere" in the province of Maine. Yet Screven and the Kittery Baptists had no intention of remaining silent. Screven described the group as "having a desire to the service of Christ . . . and the propagating of his glorious gospel of peace and salvation, and eyeing that precious promise in Daniel the 12th, 3d: 'They that turn many to righteousness shall shine as the stars forever.'" Knowing their witness would be stifled in Maine, Screven removed the church to South Carolina, where the religious toleration policy would allow them to spread the gospel. There, on the banks of the Cooper River, Screven settled an area he called "Somerton." Then in his sixties, Screven ranged widely from his new base of operations, preaching all over the Carolina lowcountry. His aggressive evangelical presence irritated area ministers. Anglican commissary Gideon Johnston (1671–1716) reported a conflict involving "a ship carpenter, the Anabaptist teacher at Charleston . . . concerning some of the town Presbyterians seduced by him." Joseph Lord (1672–1748), a Harvard-trained Congregationalist minister, complained to the governor of Massachusetts about "a certain Anabaptist teacher (named Scriven), who came from New England." While Lord was out of town, Screven "had taken advantage of my absence to insinuate into some of the people about us, and to endeavor to make proselytes." Screven had scheduled for two women to be received into the church "by plunging," but Lord convinced one of the prospects "of the error of that way." Through Screven's considerable labors, along with those of another Baptist revivalist, Gilbert Ashley (d. 1699), the Charleston church grew to ninety members by 1708. At the time of his death, Screven had also begun a new work in Winyah, later Georgetown Baptist Church. Screven's energetic ministry in the early eighteenth century foreshadowed the evangelical dynamism of later Regular Baptists during the Great Awakening.[2]

Screven's revival legacy continued in Isaac Chanler (1701–1749), who migrated to the Ashley Ferry in South Carolina in 1733 from Bristol, England. A Particular Baptist, Chanler strongly advocated the Calvinism of the *Second London Confession* (1689), publishing a book on the subject in 1744. Chanler found the Baptists living at Ashley Ferry to be deeply dissatisfied with the Charleston Baptist Church. At the time, the church was promoting Arminian views of salvation and jettisoning the treasured ritual of laying hands on the newly baptized. The Ashley Ferry group formed a new congregation of twenty-seven members in 1736, calling Chanler as pastor. The church flourished under his leadership. Within three years, around twenty adults entered church fellowship by profession of faith. In the spring and summer of 1737, Chanler baptized several new converts, while some twenty-one members decisively sought spiritual renewal and "submitted to the holy ordinance of laying on of hands with prayer, for the obtaining of fresh supplies of the Holy Spirit of grace." When the revivalist George Whitefield (1714–70) came to Charleston in 1740, he stayed in Chanler's home, calling Chanler "a gracious Baptist minister." Whitefield preached to large audiences at the Ashley Ferry meetinghouse and saw many conversions. He urged Chanler and other area ministers to form a transdenominational meeting to promote revival after he left. In a published sermon from these meetings, Chanler celebrated the revival as God's work and praised Whitefield effusively as God's instrument. Later, Chanler entered a print debate to defend Whitefield's ministry against the attacks of Anglican Commisary Alexander Garden (c. 1685–1756). Chanler's open support of Whitefield also brought him into sharp disagreement with Thomas Simmons (d. 1747) and the General Baptists at Charleston. From 1733 to 1749, Chanler proved himself to be "very laborious in ministry," revitalizing Regular Baptist churches across South Carolina. He assisted the Baptists at the Welsh Neck settlement on the Pee Dee River, ordaining Philip James (1701–1753) as their pastor in 1743. He also preached among the Baptists of Euhaw, Edisto, and Hilton Head when they were without a minister, and supplied the empty pulpit in Charleston until his death in 1749. As historian Thomas J. Little has observed, Chanler is another significant Regular Baptist figure who led the way in "expanding the reach of evangelical religion in the South Carolina lowcountry in the 1740s."[3]

A lesser-known Regular Baptist revivalist of the same period is William Tilly (1698–1744). Tilly had immigrated to Charleston from Salisbury, England, in

1721. After receiving a call to ministry at the Charleston Baptist Church, Tilly was ordained at Edisto Island (later Euhaw), South Carolina, in 1731. Like Chanler, Tilly welcomed Whitefield upon his arrival in the South. Whitefield mentions in his journals that Tilly travelled to his Bethesda orphanage in Savannah, Georgia, on July 31, 1740, to pay him a visit. Whitefield admired Tilly as "a warm and lively Baptist minister." He invited Tilly to preach for him on several occasions, and Tilly allowed the Anglican evangelist to serve him Communion. Tilly stands as another important illustration of the enthusiastic support that Whitefield and the awakening received from the Regular Baptists of the lower South.[4]

The southern, Regular Baptist revivalism of Screven, Chanler, and Tilly reached its apex in Oliver Hart, who arrived in Charleston from Philadelphia on December 2, 1749, the day Chanler was buried. Through his leadership in the Charleston Baptist Church and his broader efforts at galvanizing Regular and Separate Baptists of the South for revival, Hart established a remarkable legacy of vibrant, evangelical leadership during the mid-eighteenth century. After his death, younger men Hart influenced, such as Edmund Botsford (1745–1819) and Evan Pugh (1732–1802), labored with the same evangelical energy in the region, extending the Regular Baptist revival legacy into the nineteenth century.

Until recently, Regular Baptist revivalism has been largely overlooked in American Religious studies. More broadly, as Thomas J. Little has documented, historians have neglected the South's role in the Great Awakening altogether. Scholars for many years assumed that the southern colonies were resistant to the rise of evangelical Christianity until late in the movement, in contrast to New England and the middle colonies. Samuel S. Hill states, "If one wanted to pinpoint the salient beginning [of southern Christian evangelicalism], he would turn to the 1750s or perhaps the years just after 1800." Similarly, Christine Leigh Heyrman asserts in her influential work *Southern Cross: The Beginnings of Bible Belt Christianity* (1998), "Evangelicalism came late to the American South, as an exotic import rather than an indigenous development." Little rightly identifies the source of this misperception as the almost exclusive academic focus on religion in colonial Virginia rather than in the lower colonies of South Carolina and Georgia. Yet the assumption that Virginia's religious milieu was representative of the entire South fails to take into account the religious pluralism of South Carolina in the period.[5]

Today, historians are increasingly acknowledging the early and powerful influences of the Great Awakening in the colonial lower South. These include Sylvia Frey and Betty Wood's *Come Shouting Zion: African American Protestantism in the American South and the British Caribbean to 1830* (1998), Thomas S. Kidd's *The Great Awakening: The Roots of Evangelical Christianity in America* (2007), Samuel C. Smith's *A Cautious Enthusiasm: Mystical Piety and Evangelicalism in Colonial South Carolina* (2013), and Little's *Origins of Southern Evangelicalism: Religious Revivalism in the South Carolina Lowcountry, 1670–1760* (2013).As these scholars have discovered the extent of the Great Awakening's influence in the colonial South, they have found many Regular Baptists among the revival's supporters. One goal of this monograph is to build on their insights, taking an in-depth look at the revival spirituality of one of those Regular Baptists, Oliver Hart. Doing so will contribute to a greater understanding of the Regular Baptist movement and, more broadly, of the Great Awakening in the lower South.

This book also addresses a popular thesis pertaining to Regular Baptists and Southern Baptist identity. Many scholars incorrectly understand Southern Baptists to derive from the confluence of two distinct spiritual streams: Regular Baptists, assumed to be Calvinistic, insular, and revival-leery; and Separate Baptists, portrayed as quasi-Arminian, evangelistic, and revivalistic. On this reading, the vastly different Charleston (Regular Baptist) and Sandy Creek (Separate Baptist) traditions united to become the people called Southern Baptists. The historians chiefly responsible for this narrative are William L. Lumpkin and Walter B. Shurden.

In *Baptist Foundations in the South: Tracing through the Separates the Influence of the Great Awakening, 1754–1758* (1961), Lumpkin argued that Separate Baptists were responsible for bringing revival spirituality to the Baptists of the South:

> No group heralded religious revival so enthusiastically or so extensively in the period of 1755–1775 and none benefitted by it so generously as the Baptists. Borne upon a tide of exciting religious conquest and following a definite plan of regional expansion, they not only ministered to multitudes but also laid sure foundations for future denominational strength in the three decades after the middle of the eighteenth century. It must be noted, however, that the Baptist awakening was not in any primary sense the concern or achievement of the "regular" Baptist groups already resident in the South prior to 1755. It was, rather, the work of a handful of rugged, single-minded, enthusiastic colonists from Connecticut who, for their "irregularity," were known as "Separate" Baptists. These settled at Sandy Creek in central North Carolina in 1755 and immediately introduced the phenomenon of revival to the southern frontier.[6]

Lumpkin insisted that it was Separate Baptists "Shubal Stearns and Daniel Marshall, who brought revival to the South and laid the foundations for the Baptist denomination in that region." In contrast, Lumpkin presented the Regulars as distant and suspicious toward revival spirituality, chiefly concerned with "dignity and orderliness in worship; they were not used to the noisy and emotional preaching of the Separates." He opined that Regular Baptists "could never have won the South. They lacked the enthusiasm, the vision, and the leadership required for so formidable an undertaking." Lumpkin further mused that it was "in the providence of God" that the Regulars and Separates did not unite until after the revolution. This allowed the Separates "to give full attention to the evangelistic task without the organizational and doctrinal encumbrances," so that "the Awakening was permitted to run its full course in the hands of the Separates until it was interrupted by the Revolution." Lumpkin credited the revivalism of the Separate Baptists as the primary shaping influence of contemporary Southern Baptists.[7]

Shurden popularized Lumpkin's interpretation in "The Southern Baptist Synthesis: Is it Cracking?" (1981), originally delivered in the Carver-Barnes Lectures at Southeastern Baptist Theological Seminary. In this address, Shurden proposed that Southern Baptists were formed by the convergence of Regular and Separate Baptists, or the "Charleston" and "Sandy Creek" traditions. Shurden classified the Charleston tradition as chiefly concerned with "order," meaning the theological order of the *Second London Confession*, ecclesiological order as manifested in the *Summary of Church Discipline*, liturgical order in worship, and ministerial order through their concern for theological education. "In brief," Shurden said, "the Charleston Tradition consisted of pietistic Puritanism, Calvinistic confessionalism, and a commitment to an educated ministry. Permit me a generalization, and I would dub these folk 'semi-presbyterians.'" On the other hand, Shurden associated the Sandy Creek tradition with the "ardor" of revival piety. "Stearns and company were a highly emotional, deeply pietistic kind of people," Shurden wrote. "Unlike the city slickers from Charleston, they did not praise God by praising God; they praised God by reaching women and men. They had a mourner's bench and they expected public groaning, not polite amen's." He branded Sandy Creek with "revivalistic experientialism, anti-confessionalism, exaggerated localism, and a commitment to personal evangelism. Permit me another generalization, and I would dub these people, 'semi-pentecostals.'" Shurden's synopsis reinforced the perception of sharp discontinuity between the spirituality of the Regular and Separate Baptists.[8]

The context of Shurden's lecture is significant. As he presented his paradigm, two competing visions of Baptist identity vied for control of the Southern Baptist Convention. A "conservative" or "fundamentalist" group affirmed the inerrancy of Scripture and demanded fidelity to the denomination's confessional documents. A "moderate" or "liberal" group emphasized the soul-freedom of the individual and championed the coexistence of theological diversity in Baptist life. Shurden's alignment with the latter group is plain in "The Southern Baptist Synthesis." "We have always been a diverse people. That statement is not made simply as a plea for tolerance, though that in itself would justify it. It is made as a historical fact," he said. For Shurden, establishing discontinuity between Regular and Separate Baptist traditions was essential in his argument for diversity in the contemporary Southern Baptist Convention. "It is the togetherness, the diversity, the synthesis, which we must receive and confess and forgive. Above all, we must *know* it. Or there will be no hope for the denomination's future."[9]

Shurden's denominational vision did not live on in the Southern Baptist Convention, but his historical paradigm for Baptist identity did. In the nearly sixty years following the publication of Lumpkin's and Shurden's work, the discrete categories of Regular Baptist order and Separate Baptist ardor have been widely adopted at the academic level. For example, historian Donald G. Mathews in his influential study *Religion in the Old South* (1977) wrote that, in comparison to the fiery Separates from New England, the Regular Baptists of Charleston were "quiet, well mannered folk who were not active proselytizers." Baptist historian H. Leon McBeth, author of the popular textbook *The Baptist Heritage: Four Centuries of Baptist Witness* (1987) also passed on the Shurden Synthesis and commended the work of both Lumpkin and Shurden. Bill J. Leonard did the same in *Baptist Ways* (2003), asserting that "Other 'Regular' Baptists affirmed Calvinism but feared that revival enthusiasm undermined 'decency and order' while promoting unorthodox Arminianism." Other Baptist historians who have utilized the thesis include Jesse C. Fletcher, Albert W. Wardin, and Wayne Flynt.[10]

Southern Baptist denominational leaders have also often employed the Lumpkin-Shurden thesis in public discourse about Southern Baptist identity. In a 2009 article, college president Emir Caner called Lumpkin's work "the premier text if one wants to understand Separate Baptist thought and practice within the eighteenth century." Caner wrote that the Sandy Creek movement "surged forward with gumption and zeal while the more Calvinistic wing of Baptists, the Regular Baptists, lagged behind, fettered by philosophical presuppositions and doctrinal formalism." With Lumpkin, Caner explicitly identified Sandy Creek Baptists with revival spirituality. "Like their influential counterpart and mentor George Whitefield, the formalism and rigidity of a Reformed systematic theology was not primary in their preaching," he said. Southern Baptist seminary president Paige Patterson has also frequently promoted the Lumpkin-Shurden thesis. Patterson delivered the sermon at the two-hundred-fiftieth anniversary of the Sandy Creek Baptist Church, where *Baptist News* reported him to describe the "Southern Baptist river as flowing from two tributaries, one having its beginning in Charleston, South Carolina, the more Reformed tradition of Baptist life, and the other at Sandy Creek." Patterson continued, "I am a Sandy Creeker. If I could manage to have honorary church membership in any church in the Southern Baptist Convention, it would be Sandy Creek. . . . We Sandy Creekers still believe we are in the era of evangelism, missions and great revival."[11]

The Lumpkin-Shurden thesis has made its way down to the popular level among Southern Baptists, as well. In a 2006 Southern Baptist Convention controversy over personal prayer languages, pastor Dwight McKissick appealed to Shurden's description of the Sandy Creek tradition to support the practice. McKissick was so vocal about the Sandy Creek precedent that the *Florida Baptist Witness* published an interview with Shurden and other historians to mediate the dispute. Some local churches today interpret their congregational spirituality based on the Lumpkin-Shurden thesis, as First Baptist Church of Waynesboro, Georgia, does on its website.[12]

Though pervasive in its influence, the Lumpkin-Shurden interpretation of Baptist identity has not gone completely unchallenged. Lumpkin's work gave the impression that the Calvinism of the Regular Baptists led to ineffective evangelism, while an almost Arminian doctrine among the Separates produced an emphasis on individual conversion and a vigorous missionary piety. In response, several historians have argued for greater theological continuity between the two groups. Tom J. Nettles, Gregory A. Wills, and Thomas K. Ascol have all contended that both Regular and Separate Baptists held to a basically Calvinistic understanding of salvation, and both also practiced evangelism.[13] Still others have suggested that the Regular Baptists of Charleston were more influenced by revival spirituality than the Lumpkin-Shurden thesis allows. John F. Loftis identified Shurden's "lack of attention to development" as a major weakness of his thesis. He insisted that "in order to understand how these traditions formed an identity for the Southern Baptist Convention, an analysis of how these traditions evolved was necessary." Loftis offered a more nuanced picture of Regular Baptist revivalism, suggesting, "theologically, Regulars held their Calvinistic heritage in tension with the developing revivalistic theology epitomized in Whitefield."[14] This book argues that, for the Regular Baptists of South Carolina, there was no tension between their Calvinistic theological heritage and the revivalism of the Great Awakening. As the examples of Screven, Chanler, and Hart demonstrate, many Regular Baptists possessed a rich, revival spirituality long before the Separate Baptists ever arrived in the South. The central thesis of this work is that Regular Baptist Oliver Hart shared the revival spirituality of the Great Awakening and that revival played a greater role in Regular Baptist identity than is often suggested. The Lumpkin-Shurden thesis cannot account for this and should be revised or abandoned.

Baptist historian Loulie Latimer Owens has called Oliver Hart "a man history seems determined to forget." Despite numerous, enduring contributions to Baptist life, Hart has been overshadowed by contemporaries like Isaac Backus (1724–1806) and Richard Furman (1755–1825). Though Hart receives mention in most textbooks of American Baptist history, no substantial monograph has been devoted to his life. In the latter half of the twentieth century, Owens published several pieces related to Hart, the most important being her forty-one-page *Oliver Hart, 1723–1795: A Biography* (1966). Owens intended her treatment of Hart as a popular introduction, but her research is thorough, and she includes a comprehensive bibliography for further scholarly inquiry. In 1982, Baptist historian Robert A. Baker wrote two chapters on Hart in *Adventure in Faith: The First 300 Years of First Baptist Church, Charleston, South Carolina*, utilizing a number of Hart's original documents. Taken together, Baker's and Owens's work provide the most comprehensive portrait of Hart's life available today. In the ensuing years, various Baptist studies included Hart as a supporting cast member. In 2005, Tom J. Nettles devoted one chapter to Hart in his three-volume work, *The Baptists: Key People in Shaping a Baptist Identity*, focusing on Hart's theological commitments. Finally, Kidd and Little have both drawn attention to Hart's participation in the Great Awakening, Kidd with *The Great Awakening* (2007) and in *Baptists in America: A History* (2015); Little in *Origins of Southern Evangelicalism* (2013).[15]

While all the above resources helpfully introduce various aspects of Hart's life and thought, none supply the extensive treatment he warrants. No one has yet engaged the full breadth of Hart's diaries, letters, sermon manuscripts, and other handwritten materials scattered throughout various historical archives. A major goal of this study is to move toward filling this research gap by providing a detailed introduction to Hart's life and spirituality, through an inductive analysis of primary source documents. Hart was a devoted diarist and letter-writer throughout his ministry. His earliest diary, recording his experience in the 1754 Charleston Baptist revival, is kept at the James B. Duke Memorial Library at Furman University in Greenville, South Carolina. This collection also houses his extensive correspondence with Richard Furman from the years 1777–94.The remainder of Hart's diaries, covering the years 1769–70, 1775, 1779–82, and 1788, are all part of the Oliver Hart Papers at the South Caroliniana Library at the University of South Carolina in Columbia. The greatest value of these diaries lies in what they reveal about the patterns and priorities of Hart's personal spirituality and pastoral ministry. Further perspective on Hart's preaching ministry comes from ten of Hart's unpublished sermon manuscripts, as well as a meticulous record of sermons preached in the years 1773–94. This same collection contains extensive correspondence between Hart and a variety of friends and family. Other primary source material useful in this study includes five published sermons and a circular letter by Hart, the published minutes of the Charleston Association and the Philadelphia Association, as well as the *Summary of Church Discipline*, which Hart coauthored. Finally, a number of published works about Hart's friends, including James Manning (1738–91), Samuel Jones (1735–1814), Edmund Botsford (1745–1819), Samuel Stillman (1737–1807), Hezekiah Smith (1737–1805), and Richard Furman, contain copies of Hart's correspondence.[16]

Contrary to the prevailing perception of Regular Baptist spirituality, Oliver Hart's piety pulsates with the life of the Great Awakening. Indeed, detailed biographical study shows that Hart's entire life was profoundly shaped by evangelical revival. Very early, Hart embraced an international evangelical Calvinism that united Christians from across denominational lines during the era of the Great Awakening, committing himself to a revival piety that stressed the ways in which the exercise of grace "necessarily calls for the continued influence of the Holy Spirit." In 1754 Hart wrote about how such "divine influences" miraculously transformed his congregation during an awakening among the youth of the Charleston Baptist Church. As we shall see, these diary entries properly belong to an important genre of religious literature in the Atlantic Protestant world: the eighteenth-century "revival narrative." No less than in the 1754 Baptist revival, during which time

Hart experienced firsthand the intensity of religious renewal among his listeners, Hart's spirituality was marked by the evangelical activism of the Great Awakening. His efforts at evangelism and revivalism—in addition to the forming of gospel partnerships—together with his support of ministerial education and his involvement in colonial American politics broadened and extended his spiritual authority. At the same time, Hart's evangelical activism encouraged him to work outside traditional denominational channels; he and many other Regular Baptist revivalists shared the evangelical catholicity of the awakening. Therefore this book is much more than a study of Oliver Hart and the formation of Southern Baptist identity; it is a study of the rise of evangelical Christian ascendency in early America.

CHAPTER 1

Shaped by Revival

Richard Furman stepped into the pulpit of the Charleston Baptist Church on February 7, 1796, to deliver a sermon in honor of Oliver Hart, who had died just a month before. Hart had left an unsurpassed legacy among Baptists in the South. From 1750 to 1780, he had established the Charleston Baptist Church as the "Mother Church" of Southern Baptists. He was the chief architect of the Charleston Association, the first effort to organize Baptist life in the South. He had initiated a fund for the education of the Baptist ministers of the South, the first cooperative effort to fund theological education among Baptists in America. He had also personally mentored such notable leaders as Samuel Stillman, Edmund Botsford, and Furman himself, shaping future generations of Baptists in the process. As Furman recounted Hart's fruitful life, he drew his listeners' attention to the formative influence of the Great Awakening. At the time of Hart's conversion, "the power of religion was greatly displayed in various parts of this continent." Furman mentioned the revival ministries of George Whitefield, the Tennent family, Jonathan Edwards, and Abel Morgan, most of whom Hart heard in person as a young man. Ever since, Hart had "professed to have received much benefit from their preaching, particularly from Mr. Whitefield's." Indeed, Hart's life and ministry cannot be understood apart from the shaping influence of the eighteenth-century Protestant revival.[1]

Oliver Hart's story begins with the spiritual pilgrimage of his grandfather, John Hart (1651–1714). Born in Whitney, Oxfordshire, England, Hart began his life as a Quaker, and in 1681 he sailed for the New World to join his friend William Penn's experimental colony, "Pennsylvania." There at the Poquessing River, Hart farmed, served in the local government, and provided spiritual leadership for the community. He hosted meetings in his home, visited the poor and sick, preached, and even published "An Essay on the Subject of Oaths" (1692). Hart's religious views began to evolve, however, under the influence of a schoolteacher named George Keith (1638–1716). Keith challenged the Quaker's foundational "inner light" message, which taught that all people, regardless of conversion experience or faith in Jesus Christ, bore the presence of God within them. Keith instead called the Quakers to look away from themselves for salvation, to the objective work of Jesus Christ. This was a standard evangelical critique of the movement. George Whitefield would one day write after attending a Pennsylvania Quaker meeting, "I heartily wish that [the speaker] would talk of an outward as well as an inward Christ; for otherwise, we may make our own holiness, and not the righteousness of Jesus Christ the cause of our being accepted by God. From such doctrine may I always turn away." When Keith printed his views in 1691, the Friends excluded him from fellowship. To their dismay, Keith took many out of the Quaker movement with him, including John Hart. Hart resisted the written pleas of William Penn to reconsider his decision and began preaching to a Keithian gathering in his house. Still, he continued to question his beliefs. As he grew dissatisfied with his Keithian position, he found himself increasingly attracted to the doctrinal stability of the local Baptist movement. In 1697, he completed his meandering religious journey by receiving immersion in a local creek. In 1702, the nearby Pennepek Baptist Church invited Hart and his house church to join them. They appointed Hart assistant minister, a position he held until his death twelve years later. His last words were, "Now I know to a demonstration that Christ has saved me."[2]

Fewer details are known of Oliver Hart's father, also named John Hart (1684–1763). John made his home in Warminster Township, Pennsylvania, where he married Eleanor Crispin (1687–1754) in 1708. Together, they had ten children, among whom Oliver was the fifth. John Hart held a number of civil service positions, including sheriff, justice of the peace, and coroner. He was also a devout Christian, following his father to the Keithians and then to the Baptists of Pennepek. In 1746, John Hart led his family, with fifty-six members of Pennepek, to form a new church near their home in the upper Southampton area, where he served for many years as deacon and clerk.[3]

Both the Pennepek and Southampton churches Hart attended with his family belonged to an important network called the Philadelphia Association, formed by five Baptist churches in the Delaware Valley in 1707. Baptists were committed to local church autonomy, so the association held no actual authority as a governing body. The churches simply chose, "by their voluntary and free consent, to enter into an agreement and confederation . . . for their mutual strength, counsel, and other valuable advantages." The Philadelphia Association provided theological accountability for churches, served as an advisory council, promoted cooperation for missions and other benevolent causes, and helped connect churches and ministers. Theologically, the churches of the Philadelphia Association championed the Calvinistic doctrines of the Particular Baptist tradition and formally adopted the *Second London Confession* in 1742. Hart never departed from the theological heritage he received from his seat in the Pennepek Baptist meetinghouse. Furman remembered Hart as "a fixed Calvinist" to whom "the doctrines of free, efficacious grace, were precious." William Rogers also called Hart "an uniform advocate, both in public and private, of the doctrines of free and sovereign grace." Though Hart would blaze new trails for Baptists in the areas of organization and cooperative ministry, theologically he remained content to follow the well-trodden paths of his forefathers.[4]

In addition to his Particular Baptist background, nothing so profoundly shaped Hart's spirituality as the evangelical revival that swept through Pennsylvania in his adolescence. The American colonies had known revivals in sporadic, localized manifestations from their earliest days, but beginning in 1734, a new "concern about the great things of religion began," the intensity and scope of which had never been experienced. When Jonathan Edwards (1703–54) published his account of the Northampton, Massachusetts, revival in 1736, it proved to be the catalyst for an awakening that transcended denominational lines and geographical borders, and would completely transform the religious scene in the North Atlantic world. This included the Warminster County of Hart's youth, which became a hotbed of revival activity. Just a few miles from Hart's home, the Presbyterian minister William Tennent (1673–1746) trained a generation of revival preachers at his Log College at Neshaminy Creek. Among Tennent's pupils were his four sons, Gilbert (1703–64), William Jr. (1705–77), John (1707–32), and Charles (1711–71). All four Tennent sons would lead revivals, though Gilbert stole most of the headlines, chiefly through his controversial sermon, *The Danger of an Unconverted Ministry* (1739). Hart later said that he "frequently heard most of [the Tennents] preach with great pleasure, and, I hope, some profit." Hart likely heard Tennent through the influence of his childhood pastor at the Pennepek Baptist Church, Jenkin Jones (c.1686–1760). In addition to being a precisionist Baptist, Jones was also an ardent supporter of the Great Awakening. He regularly invited leading, non-Baptist revivalists like Tennet to preach to his Baptist people. Hart considered the Tennents "a race of men, devoted to the service of the sanctuary; who, for their abilities, zeal and usefulness, need not give any place to any family, that ever graced the American continent . . . the happy instruments of converting thousands of souls."

Hart also listened to another Log College graduate in these days, John "Hell-Fire" Rowland (d. 1745). Rowland was a powerful preacher, though his lack of restraint opened him to charges of "enthusiasm." In Rowland's funeral sermon, Gilbert Tennent admitted that, "Being young in years and of a warm temper, he was thereby led into some indiscretions in his honest and earnest attempts to do good." One such occasion came at the Baptist meetinghouse in Philadelphia, where Jenkin Jones had invited both Rowland and Tennent to preach. Rowland's impassioned oratory brought the people to such desperation over the state of sinners that Tennent was compelled to run to the pulpit stairs and cry out, "Oh Brother Rowland, is there no balm in Gilead?" Rowland, "startled by the effect upon his hearers of his fearful words, began to unfold the way of recovery." The incident, which touched off a considerable controversy in the church (covered in chapter 5), further reveals the charged revival environment in which Hart was spiritually nurtured.[5]

Above all others, George Whitefield left the deepest impression on Hart. Baptist historians never fail to draw attention to Whitefield's decisive role in the conversions of key Separate Baptist leaders, but Hart stands as an example of the grand itinerant's influence among the Regular Baptists as well. On his first trip to Philadelphia in 1739, Whitefield befriended Jenkin Jones, and thereafter received the Baptist minister's support whenever he returned to the area. The following spring, on May 9, 1740, Jones invited Whitefield to preach to over two thousand people at the Pennepek meetinghouse. Hart likely heard Whitefield then, and on many other occasions between 1739–41, when Whitefield preached to crowds in the thousands near Hart's home. Though he had grown up in a devout Christian home, the teenaged Hart had never experienced the phenomenon of "the new birth" he heard Whitefield extolling. Hart later lamented that "my youth was spent in vanity and a listlessness to all that was good." Yet sometime in the years 1740–41, just as the Great Awakening was cresting in Pennsylvania, Hart experienced a profound, evangelical conversion. He submitted to baptism by Jenkin Jones on April 3, 1741.[6]

Hart had received the new birth, but he had not yet sensed the call to preach. As a young adult, he learned a carpenter's trade and settled into the Warminster community as his father and grandfather had done before him. He also took an active role in the local church, participating in the formation of the Southampton Baptist congregation in 1746. The church soon recognized in Hart a unique earnestness about spiritual things that indicated to them a possible call to gospel ministry. Accordingly, the church licensed both Hart and Isaac Eaton to preach on a trial basis on December 20, 1746. One opportunity to test his calling came on February 21, 1748, when the pastor of the Southampton Baptist Church, Joshua Potts, came down with the measles. The church clerk noted that Hart "performed to satisfaction." This, along with other satisfactory performances, was enough to convince the church. Two months later, they "gave a full call to Oliver Hart and Isaac Eaton, to preach in any place where Providence might cast their lotts [sic], or need required." The same year, Hart married Sarah Brees (1729–72).[7]

So it was that Hart arrived at his night of destiny. On September 9, 1749, Hart attended the Philadelphia Association's annual meeting as a messenger for the Southampton Church. Jenkin Jones stood to read a letter containing a plea from the Baptist church in Charleston, South Carolina. The letter inquired "if there was any minister sound in the faith" who could come settle among them. After the meeting, Jones and other leaders in the association urged Hart to answer the call. He agreed. The members of the Southampton church again gathered for a special meeting on October 18 and ordained Hart for the work in Charleston in a service of solemn prayer and fasting. One month later, he boarded the *St. Andrew* in Philadelphia, leaving behind Sarah, expecting their second child, and one-year-old Seth. Shaped by the revivalism of the Great Awakening, Hart sailed for Charleston to discern if this was indeed where Providence had "cast his lott."[8]

The Charleston church was the oldest Baptist congregation in the South. Originally formed in 1682 in Kittery, Maine, the congregation had relocated soon afterward to Charleston under pastor William Screven. There the Kittery group, committed Particular Baptists, combined with a collection of General Baptists already in the area to form the Charleston Baptist Church. Screven was a remarkable leader and kept the two groups united throughout his term of service. Yet for the church to survive beyond his lifetime, Screven knew they must secure a suitable successor. Near the end of his life, Screven urged the church, "You, as speedily as possible, supply yourselves with an able and faithful minister. Be sure you take care that the person be orthodox in faith, and of blameless life, and does own the confession of faith put forth by our brethren in London in 1689, etc." Screven's admonition proved to be a mighty challenge for the people. Baptist historian Morgan Edwards later commented, "Had they attended to this counsel, the distractions, and almost destruction of the Church, which happened twenty-six years afterward, would have been prevented." Screven's two immediate successors both died shortly into their tenures. Under the next pastor, Thomas Simmons, the doctrinal tensions present in the church from the beginning erupted into open conflict.[9]

The church's long period of decline began in 1736, when two groups separated from the Charleston Church. The first group, comprised of Particular Baptists, established a new congregation at Ashley Ferry under the leadership of Isaac Chanler. A second group, General Baptists, began a new church at Stono River. Adding to this upheaval, Thomas Simmons shifted theological positions from a Particular Baptist stance to that of a General Baptist, thoroughly frustrating his largely Particular Baptist congregation in the process. He further aggravated the trouble in 1740 by vocally opposing the popular revival efforts of the Calvinistic Whitefield. The church voted to suspend Simmons in 1744 but this decision split the church, which still contained some General Baptist supporters of Simmons. It also launched a legal dispute over the meetinghouse property, which, to the bewilderment of the Particular Baptist majority, resulted in their losing ownership of lot 62. The church's morale continued to dwindle in 1746, when a group from the Edisto Island area broke away to form the Euhaw Baptist Church. Baptist historian Basil Manly Sr., who succeeded Hart as minister of the First Baptist Church of Charleston, believed that the church was reduced to three communicants at this time.[10]

Such was the Charleston church's condition when they solicited the Philadelphia Association for "any minister sound in the faith." For two years, they had survived on occasional sermons by Chanler, who lent his services from Ashley Ferry. Yet even this source of nourishment was suddenly cut off when Chanler died unexpectedly on November 30, 1749, at age forty-eight. The church was burying Chanler on December 2, 1749, when the *St. Andrew* pulled into port, carrying Hart. The

Charleston Baptists viewed Hart's timely arrival as providentially orchestrated, believing Hart to be the leader Screven had prayed for decades before. They officially called Hart as pastor on February 16, 1750. As Manly later interpreted the events, "The Lord had provided an instrument by which he designed greatly to promote the cause of truth and piety in the province, in the person of Rev. Oliver Hart."[11] A glimpse at that unique province will illuminate his thirty-year ministry there.

During 1769, a ship captain visiting colonial Charleston, Captain Martin, was struck by the city's complexity. He captured his impressions in a composition for the *South Carolina Gazette*, offering a sense of the unique assignment Hart accepted in moving to Charleston:

> Black and white all mixed together
> Inconstant, strange, unhealthful weather
> Burning heat and chilling cold
> Dangerous to both young and old
> Boistrous winds and heavy rains
> Fevers and rheumatic pains
> Agues plenty without doubt
> Sores, boils, the prickly heat and gout
> Musquitoes on the skin make blotches
> Centipedes and large cockroaches
> Frightful creatures in the water
> Porpoises, sharks and alligators
> Houses built on barren land
> No lamps or lights, but streets of sand
> Pleasant walks, if you can find 'em
> The markets dear and little money
> Large potatoes, sweet as honey
> Water bad, past all drinking
> Men and women without thinking
> Everything at a high price
> But rum, hominy, and rice
> Many a widow not unwilling
> Many a beau not worth a shilling
> Many a bargain, if you can strike it
> This is Charlestowne, how do you like it?[12]

If Charleston so astonished a worldly English sailor, one can only wonder at the effect it produced in a Baptist carpenter from Pennsylvania!

Charleston was the fourth largest, but by far the wealthiest, of all colonial cities, its free citizens worth nearly six times that of Philadelphians, seven times that of Bostonians, and eight times that of New Yorkers. When Josiah Quincy of Boston visited Charleston for the first time in 1773, he exclaimed, "In grandeur, splendor of buildings, decorations, equipages, numbers, commerce, shipping, indeed in almost every thing, it far surpasses all I ever saw, or expected to see, in America." Charleston had built its wealth on the rice and indigo industries, as Hart indicated in an early letter home to his father. "We have had a very Wet and fruitful season.—the planters, or farms here go much upon Indico, which proves a very profitable Commodity; if peace was to Continue, in all probability this would be the richest province upon the Continent by far: Oh that it may be Rich in good Works!" Evangelical preachers found that Charleston's material prosperity tended to produce spiritual indifference. When Whitefield warned Charlestonians of the dangers inherent in amassing wealth, he "seemed to them as one that mocked." As Hart shared in a letter to Samuel Jones, he contended with the same problem. "Religion is grown extremely unfashionable in these Parts. The God Mammon is much more rever'd, than the Lord Jehovah. What shall we eat? What shall we drink? And wherewithal shall we be cloathed? are Enquiries much more attended to, than, What shall we do to be saved?" he wrote in 1769. Though riches always carried temptations to sin, Hart viewed money itself as a neutral commodity, capable of both good and evil. He counted some of the city's wealthiest and most influential residents among his circle of friends, mentioning in his letters Henry Laurens, Thomas Heyward Jr., Daniel Legare, William Henry Drayton, and John Rutledge.[13]

Charleston's excessive wealth contributed to a culture of hedonism that further set it apart from other colonial cities. "At my first coming, the people of Charleston seemed wholly devoted to pleasure," wrote Whitefield in 1740. Historian Walter B. Edgar has suggested that no other colonial city could match the "frenetic social life" of Charleston. This included horse races, dances and balls, plays at the Dock Street theater, and a host of other diversionary activities. As one might expect, Charleston's idol of pleasure clashed with the devoted piety that evangelicals like Hart sought to promote. Sundays in Charleston were more often passed in "visiting and mirth" than in prayer and devotion, featuring drinking, card playing, horse racing, hunting, and fishing. Contending with Charleston's worldliness posed a constant challenge for evangelical ministers like Hart. He repeatedly decried stage plays and other public vices, most enduringly in his published sermon, *Dancing Exploded: A Sermon Shewing the Unlawfulness, Sinfulness, and Bad Consequences of Balls, Assemblies, and Dances in General.*[14]

Another contributing factor in Charleston's hedonism was the ongoing threat of death that loomed over daily life. Lowcountry rice fields not only produced wealth but swarms of mosquitoes that transmitted yellow fever and malaria, severely weakening the immune system of the general population. Charleston became notorious for "air so unhealthful" that its residents "had fevers all year long from which those attacked seldom recover." Childhood mortality rates may have climbed as high as 80 percent during the colonial period. Hart experienced this cruel reality firsthand, burying five children and a wife in his thirty years there. The volatile weather also posed a constant danger to Charlestonians. The "excessive sultry" heat of Charleston summers became downright oppressive at times. In July of 1765, Hart confessed to Samuel Jones that he was responsible for two sermons every Sunday, "but whether my strength will be equal to this, through the two following hot months, God only knows." More frightening than the heat were the violent storms that bombarded the coastal city. In 1752, Hart learned about the "boisterous winds and heavy rains" mentioned in Captain Martin's poem, when "a great and terrible" hurricane struck the city and, "[his] house was washed down and all [he] had almost totally destroyed." Another entry in 1760 recounted "a most violent whirlwind of that kind commonly known under the title of typhoons," which devastated numerous ships and houses. As other evangelicals were apt to do, Hart viewed the storms and other disasters as the chastising "judgments of God" against the city. To his dismay, "poor sinful Charles town" rarely "learned righteousness" in the aftermath.[15]

Hart likely found the racial makeup of Charleston to be its most exotic feature. The lucrative rice and indigo plantations required a large labor force of African slaves, so that the city was roughly half black and half white throughout the colonial period. So predominant was the black population in Charleston and its environs that one contemporary wrote that colonial South Carolina "looked more like a negro country." Everywhere the sounds of the slaves' Gullah dialect filled the city. Though numerous slaves translated into greater productivity for plantation owners, slave uprisings also posed a constant threat to Charleston residents. Hart's own relationship to slavery was complex; he ministered freely to enslaved and free blacks in Charleston, yet he also owned slaves, a topic to be explored in chapter 4.[16]

Churches of virtually every denomination sought to establish a Christian witness in Charleston's challenging spiritual context. The Anglican itinerant Charles Woodmason wrote of South Carolina in 1766 that "such a mix'd medley of religions is hardly anywhere to be found as here—not even in Philadelphia, or Amsterdam." These churches included the Anglican churches of St. Michael's and St. Philip's as well as those of the French Huguenots, Scots Presbyterians, Independent Congregationalists, Quakers, Lutherans, and Baptists—plus a Jewish synagogue. The many steeples arising out of the city formed such a striking picture to ships entering the harbor that some dubbed Charleston "the holy city." Characteristic of the transatlantic awakening, Hart worked with evangelical ministers from across the denominational spectrum to advance the revival there.[17]

Hart may not have possessed much pastoral experience when he stepped off the *St. Andrew* in 1749, but he apparently looked and sounded the part. Furman described him as "somewhat tall, well proportioned, and of a graceful appearance; of an active, vigorous constitution. . . . His countenance was open and manly, his voice clear, harmonious and commanding." More than a striking appearance, Hart brought the revival ardor of the Great Awakening to the Charleston Baptists. He started with the Charleston pulpit. For evangelicals throughout the transatlantic awakening, preaching the gospel was paramount in promoting revival. Hart preached every Sunday morning and afternoon, delivered a regular doctrinal lecture in a church member's home on Sunday nights, and organized a "Religious Society" in 1755, which he addressed on Monday, Wednesday, and Friday nights. He labored to preach sermons that were thoroughly biblical. He early recognized the importance of a "more copious knowledge of the Word of God," and in 1754 resolved to read ten chapters of the Bible every day. The fruit of this discipline is evident in his surviving sermons, which demonstrate a loving familiarity with the whole of the Bible. Hart's careful records show that he preached texts from across the canon of scripture, and the manuscripts of his sermon outlines are crammed with voluminous Biblical citations. Hart believed that a ready command of scripture enabled him to speak to his listeners with the very authority of God. "Let every thing you deliver be back'd with Scripture, and be careful to advance nothing, but what you can confirm with a *Thus saith the Lord*," he insisted.[18]

Hart specialized in doctrinal sermons that taught his listeners the great, stabilizing truths of God and his ways with man, informed by framework of the *Second London Confession*. As he indicated in 1785, Hart aimed to explore the full range of theological truths in his pulpit:

> Preaching the gospel will lead to an explanation of what the apostle calls "the form of sound words." Which may include the following sublime and important doctrines, viz. the being of a God—a trinity of persons in the Godhead—the fall of Adam, and the imputation of his sin to his posterity—The corruption of human nature, and impotence of men to that which is spiritually or morally good—the everlasting love of God to his people—the eternal election of a definite number of the human race to grace and glory—The covenant of grace—Particular redemption—Justification by the imputed righteousness of Christ—Pardon and reconciliation by his blood—Regeneration and sanctification by the influences and operations of the Holy Spirit—the final perseverance of the saints in grace—the resurrection of the dead, and eternal judgment. This is an epitome of *the faith once for all delivered to the saints,* which ministers are to preach, and for which they should *earnestly contend.*[19]

For all its doctrinal breadth, Hart's preaching consistently centered on the preeminent subject of the evangelical revival, the person and work of Jesus Christ. "Let

Ct and his Gospel be your delightful Theme," he advised young preachers. "Yes Ct is to be the Sum, and Substance of all your discourses. A little dry Morality, however refined, will never feed the Minds of your Hearers." Over time, he earned a reputation all over Charleston for his evangelical ministry. When an unconverted Edmund Botsford came under soul-concern in the early 1760s, a friend advised him that "there is but one minister in this place, who can be of service to you, but he, I am told, is a Baptist; all the rest of the ministers deserve not the name. I would advise you to go hear him." The fact that Botsford's friend was not himself a Christian believer makes Hart's reputation all the more impressive.[20]

Like the other revivalists of his day, Hart believed that something more than a mere human exchange of information was taking place in the moment of proclamation. The Holy Spirit, the third person of the Trinity, came down from heaven to make the preaching of the gospel powerful and effective in the hearts of those who heard it. Accordingly, Hart filled his diaries with prayers for the Spirit's supernatural enablement as he preached. His most frequent petitions were that he might "feel his subject" and preach with "power," "warmth," and "freedom." After one frustrating day of preparation on a Saturday in 1754, Hart confessed, "found myself quite empty: and could scarce rise upon any subject for my meditation." Yet this simply threw him back onto God in prayer. "Blessed be God! My hope is in him. Tho' I am empty, he is full, and I hope to be fill'd out of that fullness which filleth all, and in all."[21] Hart's sense of the Spirit's presence on him while preaching lent a certain gravitas to his pulpit ethos. Furman remembered his sermons as "peculiarly serious," accented by the black gown and bands he wore. Edmund Botsford has left behind one firsthand account of the power Hart's preaching could wield. When Botsford took his friend's advice to go hear Hart, he found himself transfixed. "To describe the exercises of my mind under that sermon would be impossible," he remembered. In his spiritual depression, Botsford had considered returning to his native England, but now that Hart had awakened a hope that he could be saved, he "was perfectly satisfied to remain, if I lived on bread and water only." Hart's pulpit manner was graver and more self-consciously confessional than that of his Separate Baptist friends, yet he preached with no less passion for conversions. Furman recalled that "his eloquence, at least in the middle stages of life, was not of the most popular kind, but perspicuous, manly and flowing, such as afforded pleasure to persons of true taste, and edification to the serious hearer." Botsford, who also heard Whitefield on several occasions, commented in 1769 that if one were to "lay aside oratory," then "Mr. Whitefield's discourse will not do to compare with Mr. Hart's."[22]

Under Hart's awakened preaching, the Charleston Baptists experienced revival in the fall of 1754. From August to October, the youth of the church begged Hart to speak to them on an almost nightly basis in private homes. These meetings were marked by unusual solemnity, though sometimes Hart's listeners groaned under the conviction of sin, were "melted down into tears," or testified to the "sweetness" of Jesus Christ breaking into their souls. At the conclusion of the 1754 revival, ten young people were baptized and added to the church. Hart also promoted revival by supporting George Whitefield's Charleston campaigns from 1750 to 1770. Whitefield in turn preached in Hart's pulpit, worshipped with the Charleston congregation, employed Hart to follow up with new converts from his campaigns, and recommended Hart's ministry to others by letter. Though William L. Lumpkin claims that the Baptist awakening "was not in any primary sense the concern or achievement of the 'Regular' Baptist groups already resident in the South prior to 1755," these accounts tell a different story. They place Hart and the Regular Baptists of Charleston in the middle of the action of the evangelical awakening.[23]

Out of the pulpit, Hart also sought to revive the work of the pastor to his people and of the evangelist to his community. He devoted himself to the winning of and caring for souls with the same activist zeal he had witnessed in Jones and Whitefield. "I am still trying to Labour for God as enabled, but find I come Short of that engagedness which I could Desire," Hart wrote to his father in 1755. "Souls are precious Otherwise the Lord would not have done so much for their Salvation as he has done: and can I Trifle with them? God forbid! I would fain be made Instrumental in bringing many Souls home to Jesus Christ." Hart's conscientious pastoral care at times demanded that he confront sin and error in church members. Hart considered these conversations to be a "disagreeable Necessity" in his role as a shepherd of souls, though he tried to reprove his people "as to evince that it is from Love, to the persons you reprove, however you may dislike their Conduct." On other occasions, his pastoral oversight led him to the bedside of a dying man or woman. This called for delicate handling, knowing that eternity hung in the balance. "To flatter a dying man is little better than Soul Murder; and yet such when penitent are by no means to be discouraged. You will endeavor therefore to act a tender, but withal a faithful part," he said. Hart also personally counseled many individuals through a variety of spiritual issues, some of which has been preserved in his letters. When Furman's daughter received baptism in 1793, Hart immediately dashed off a word of encouragement to the young believer. "Tell her from me, if she would wish to enjoy the Comforts of Religion and be useful in Life, she must keep near to God and be humble at Jesus' Feet. While She is enabled to do so, she will have nothing to fear from Earth or Hell, for she shall be more than a Conqueror through Him who hath loved Her." Hart's zeal for souls also inspired him to undertake an extensive itinerant ministry, making numerous evangelistic tours across several colonies.[24]

Hart received some scars from his revival work over the years. One of the most wrenching episodes in Hart's ministry came in 1765, when his assistant, Nicholas Bedgegood (1731–74) attempted a coup in the church. Bedgegood had originally belonged to the Anglican Communion, serving at Whitefield's Bethesda Orphanage in Savannah. Through Hart's influence, Bedgegood embraced the Baptist way and submitted to baptism by Hart in 1757. Two years later, Hart ordained Bedgegood and brought him onto his staff. Soon, however, he found that the younger, better-educated man intended to supplant him as pastor. The ensuing conflict was a source of deep grief. Hart poured out his troubles related to his friend, James Manning, in a 1765 letter. "How long I am to continue here, and for what purpose, God only knows," Hart wrote. "I have the mortification to see our church in a shattered condition. Some of our members have broke off. We sinned greatly in calling Mr. Bedgegood from Pee Dee, to be my assistant. Poor man—he has been vastly imprudent in many things; insomuch that his character is ruined; and I fear his usefulness destroyed. At present he continues in, and about Charles Town, as a thorn in my side, and answers no better purpose. It would be impossible for me to give you all the particulars of our unhappiness: however, the event is bad enough."[25] Despite the pain of this betrayal, Hart remained at his post. Bedgegood eventually passed off the scene and was later disowned as a minister of the gospel when he failed to answer the charges of polygamy brought against him in 1771.When Samuel Jones suggested that Hart remove to either Pennepek or Southampton church shortly after the controversy, Hart declined. He insisted that he "must have an eye to duty, primarily." "God, I trust, has blest my poor Labours to some poor Souls, which supports me under many Tryals, and indicates that I ought to continue where I am."[26]

On an even more personal level, Hart also endured the death of his wife, "my dear Sarah," on October 20, 1772, as a result of childbirth. In their twenty-four years of marriage, Sarah had borne Hart eight children, four of whom survived her. Two years after Sarah's death Hart took another wife, the widow Anne Sealy Grimball (1741–1813). Anne was a Charleston native and member of the church, having been converted under Hart and baptized by him in 1770. Hart wrote that "as a maid, a wife, and a widow, she has sustained an unsullied character, and been a pattern and ornament to her sex. . . . I esteem that as one of the happiest days that put such a prize into my bosom." For her part, Anne esteemed Hart, seventeen years her senior, for his maturity and wisdom. She remembered him as "my counselor—guide—friend—my most affectionate and loving husband." Over their twenty-two years of marriage, she recalled that "his steady temper—his patience—his fortitude—all contributed to make me happy."[27]

Hart forged a deep bond with the Charleston Church. He told his father in 1755 that his people "continue their regard for me, and Love me, sincerely and fervently; which I endeavor in the best manner I can to return." Observing this in a visit to Charleston, Morgan Edwards said of Hart, "He is an excellent man! And well loved by all who know him." An incident from 1771 illustrates Hart's great esteem in the city of Charleston. When Hart was robbed of 30 pounds, "the gentlemen of other societies made him a present of 730 pounds, which they raised among themselves, without the help of his own people." A similar story appears on January 1, 1779, when Hart reported a "kind and generous friend" calling at his house to present him with "a New Year's gift consisting of 300 dollars." Precise records of the church's membership during Hart's tenure are unavailable, but the congregation clearly prospered under his leadership. Morgan Edwards reported over two hundred communicants in the 1770s.[28]

The influence of Hart's revived ministry extended far beyond his own congregation. His activist spirituality, a hallmark of the evangelical awakening, was the major catalyst for the transformation of Baptist life in the South. In the mid-eighteenth century, Baptist churches in the South were generally small, weak, and poorly organized compared to those in the middle colonies. This picture began to change after Hart arrived in Charleston. Within months, he was helping match faithful pastors with area churches, and by 1751, he had organized four Regular Baptist churches into the Charleston Association, the first organized body of Baptist churches in the South. In the years that followed, Hart led the Charleston Association to promote Baptist doctrine and church order, missionary outreach, and ministerial education in the region. Hart also contributed to the unification of the Regular and Separate Baptist movements. Though some Regular Baptists were suspicious of the frontier preachers, their eccentricities did not repel Hart, because he saw in them a common revival heritage. He wrote to Samuel Jones in 1766, "Through the Goodness of God, there is a happy Revival of Religion in the interior Parts of this Province, among the separate Baptists. I have visited them twice, much to my Satisfaction." Hart made several efforts to include the Separates in the Charleston Association, but his greatest success came through his friendship with the Separate Baptist Richard Furman. Furman, who became Hart's most notable protégé, would succeed Hart in the Charleston Baptist Church and complete the union of the Regulars and Separates that came to characterize Southern Baptists."[29]

As Charleston buzzed with talk of independence in the 1770s, Hart shared in the growing excitement. Along with other dissenting ministers, Hart believed obtaining political freedom from Great Britain to be essential for establishing religious liberty in the colonies. In 1775, he received the opportunity to make a unique contribution toward this goal. Because of his influence among Baptists, the South Carolina Provincial Congress appointed Hart, along with Congregational minister William Tennant III and statesman William Henry Drayton, to a special commission. They were tasked to travel the Loyalist backcountry, informing them of recent political developments and persuading them to sign a plan of union to with the colonial patriots against Great Britain. Hart accepted the mission, departing Charleston on July 31, 1775. He encountered significant resistance at several stops, and even began keeping his journal in code for fear of British interception. By the time he returned on September 6, his party had garnered many pledges of loyalty to the South Carolina Council of Safety. Yet his service came at a steep price. When British troops laid siege to Charleston in March 1780, Hart's friends feared his capture and urged him to flee the city. His backcountry commission had been construed in at least one English newspaper as arming local Indian tribes and inciting them against the British armies and Loyalists. Leaving his wife and children behind, Hart travelled north, preaching and meeting with other Baptist ministers along the way. While still on the road, he learned that Charleston had fallen in the greatest American defeat of the war. Most of his personal possessions were now in British possession, and the Baptist meetinghouse had been seized. Hart arrived in Philadelphia on October 10, 1780, uncertain if he would ever see Charleston again.[30]

Hart wasted no time in making himself useful in his home region. On December 16, 1780, he accepted a unanimous call to the Baptist church in Hopewell, New Jersey. With over two hundred members, Hopewell was more than twice as large as any other church in the Philadelphia Association. Hart wrote in his diary on that day, "O Lord, I beseech thee to direct me by thy Providence and Grace, how to act; and as I am now to have the charge of a numerous people, heretofore divided, grant me wisdom, and every needed grace that I may be made a blessing to them. Amen." With a living secured at Hopewell, Hart attended to the separation from his wife Anne (or "Nancy," as he called her), still in Charleston. His personal writings show him to be utterly miserable without Nancy. For eighteen months, he urged her by letter to join him at Hopewell. He painted an idyllic picture of their life together. "I am settled at Hopewell, New Jersey, and live on a pretty little Farm; capable with proper management, of producing many good Things. One Thing only is lacking; you only can supply that," he wrote. No matter how Hart pined, Nancy resisted her husband's every overture, excusing her delayed departure for every reason from fragile health to anxiety over sea travel. Still, Hart persisted, wooing her northward with the romance of a courtier. "I am free to stake the Whole of my Reputation, with the best Connoisseurs, on the prudence I manifested in the Choice of a Wife. Doth this savour of Pride? Pardon it, my Love, you are the Object; and none other can like this, excite the passion of laudable Pride in my Breast. The moment I had the Happiness of calling you my own, I thought myself one of the happiest of Men, and truly you have rendered me so, to the utmost of my Wishes. With regard to conjugal Felicity, few have enjoyed a greater Share of it than we have been favored with, until the fatal Period which obtruded this painful Separation," he purred. Finally, on September 2, 1781, Nancy arrived in Philadelphia, a month before George Washington's victory at Yorktown effectively ended the American Revolution. Three years later, Nancy gave Oliver, at the age of sixty, a final son: William Rogers Hart.[31]

Meanwhile, the work at Hopewell progressed slowly. Hart continued to exercise his ministry with the same vigor as in the revival years at Charleston, but the visible fruit he had enjoyed there was not forthcoming. "My Soul longed earnestly to see Sinners coming unto Jesus weary and heavy-laden with Sin. But alas, Conversion Work is a strange Work in this Place," he wrote in 1782. Despite their spiritual indifference, Hart's diaries demonstrate that he loved the people sincerely. He sometimes considered returning to Charleston but ultimately remained at Hopewell until his death in 1795. He directed much of his energy to healing old divisions and praying for the Spirit's reviving work. "O Lord pity Hopewell Church," he prayed, "make me an Instrument of uniting, and building them up in the most holy Faith." Hart also maintained an itinerant ministry well into his late sixties.[32]

Hart resumed an active role in the Philadelphia Association in his latter years. He had arrived from Charleston just in time for the 1780 annual meeting, where he was admitted to full membership and unanimously requested to preach. Hart would address the association again in the following years, twice on the purpose and mission of the local church: in *An Humble Attempt to Repair the Christian Temple* (1785) and *A Gospel Church Portrayed* (1791), both printed later by request of the association. Hart based both sermons on the Old Testament figure of rebuilding the Temple and reforming its worship as a picture of the work of reviving the church, a fitting metaphor for his own life's work. Hart also penned a significant doctrinal essay on behalf of the association. Since 1774, the Philadelphia Association had included with its annual circular letter "an improvement of some article of our Confession of Faith." In 1782, Hart produced a careful and profound theological exposition of chapter eight, "Christ the Mediator."[33]

The Philadelphia Association also called on Hart's theological discernment when the doctrine of "universal restoration" swept through Baptist life in the 1780s. Elhanan Winchester (1751–97), the gifted pastor of the Philadelphia Baptist Church, began promoting universalism in late 1780, creating a deep division in the church by the spring of 1781. The association appointed Hart to a committee to investigate the situation and to mediate the dispute. Hart had served alongside Winchester years before in South Carolina, where the younger man had been an instrument of revival. Hart had esteemed Winchester as "a valuable man and . . . very useful." Yet after meeting with both he and the church, Hart determined that Winchester had departed from the bounds of orthodoxy. Winchester left, and the association advised the churches to "beware," and "not admit him, or any who advocate 'universal salvation' to the office of public teaching, or suffer any who avow the same to continue in their communion." In a report to the Warren Association in Rhode Island, Hart wrote, "the minds of but too many are poisoned with the heresy, and the Philadelphia Church is reduced to a deplorable situation. God knows where these things will end. We have thought it our duty, however, to bear an open testimony against this damnable doctrine. Churches, in every capacity, ought to be pillars of truth." Hart viewed the fight against encroaching universalism in the context of an ancient spiritual battle. "This is one of the games at which Satan hath play'd in every age of the Christian Church," he wrote to Backus. "More especially in times of revival, the Enemy will sow such tares among the wheat."[34]

Another theological innovation of the late eighteenth century that concerned Hart was the "New Divinity" teaching, very popular at Rhode Island College. This school of thought, led by the followers of Jonathan Edwards, was also called "New England theology" or "Hopkinsianism" after Samuel Hopkins (1721–1803). It creatively refashioned many standard Reformed doctrines, especially in the areas of free will, original sin, and atonement. Traditional Calvinists like Hart feared that the innovations of the New Divinity men were dangerous. In 1790, the church at Stamford queried the Philadelphia Association about whether or not they should hold fellowship with those who espouse the system of New Divinity. Though the association left the decision to the churches, they warned them, "We apprehend danger, lest by these fine spun theories, and the consequences which are drawn from them by some, the great doctrines of imputation of Adam's sin, and Christ's proper atonement, imputed righteousness, &c., should be totally set aside, or at least, the glory sullied. We therefore advise that great care should be taken to guard against innovations not calculated to edify the body of Christ." As much as Hart loved Rhode Island College, he lamented that it had become "headquarters" for turning out "Hopkinsians" or "New Divinity men" into Baptist pulpits. One example was John Waldo (1762–1826), who preached in view of a call at the Georgetown, South Carolina, Baptist church in 1793. When Hart learned that the church had rejected Waldo over his theology, he told Furman he was "glad the Georgetown people have been better taught than to embrace such sentiments or to approve of such preaching." He applied the words of Scottish divine Ralph Erskine to the New Divinity: "A poor Divinity and jargon loose, such that will never build the house."[35]

During his final years, Hart often lamented his lack of "usefulness." He described himself in his diary as "an unworthy traveller towards New Jerusalem, who desires ever to esteem himself a stranger and sojourner in this dreary wilderness." The revival he had known in his youth and at Charleston seemed a distant memory. His church of thirty years was now thriving under the leadership of Richard Furman, whom the church had called at Hart's recommendation. Hopewell remained apathetic. "I long to see some fruit of my labour in Hopewell," he wrote, "But alas, we are all to carnal and worldly minded. The Things of the World engross our Attention too much."[36] Hart's health was also failing, and he could no longer maintain the strenuous ministry pace of his earlier years. In 1788, Hart attempted a visit to the Charleston Association's annual meeting, but after making it all the way to Winchester, Virginia, Hart's fragile physical condition and other obstacles forced him to turn back. This was a crushing disappointment. Hart confided to his diary, "No one knows how much these Things have affected my Spirits, they rob me of my natural Rest, I feel a Perturbation of Mind which I cannot describe, and what is worse, Satan and unbelief rob me of my spiritual Comforts (if ever I knew any Thing of Religion, which I am tempted to doubt) so that my Burthen is great." The frailties of Hart's old age often turned his mind toward eternity. Meditation on heaven was a staple of the Puritan and Evangelical spiritual tradition, and became more prominent at the end of Hart's life. On occasion, Hart expressed these reflections through poetry:

Foreboding thoughts and gloomy fears
Crowd thick into my breast;
Perplexing doubts and anxious cares
Forbid my soul to rest.
Happy ye Saints, above the skies,
Beyond the reach of woe!
Dear Lord, command my soul to rise
With joyful haste I'll go.
The world in sackcloth and distress,
I'd leave beneath my feet:
And mounting in a heavenly dress,
I would my Saviour meet.[37]

Despite his discouragements, Hart never stopped praying for revival. This, in fact, remained the dominant theme of his correspondence to the end of his life. Hart invariably requested his friends to join him in praying for a spiritual awakening at Hopewell. In 1790, he wrote Furman, "With Grief I inform you that Religion is at a low ebb in this Church. I cannot say there is the least Appearance of a Revival amongst us. Hope we shall share an Interest in your Prayers, that the Spirit of the Lord may breathe on these dry Bones, that they may live." Nothing worse could be said of his church than "religion was nearly a dead calm." He longed for the lively influences of the Spirit he had felt in days gone past. Again, in 1791 Hart groaned, "Vital Piety and practical Godliness among Professors in these Parts, seem to be almost cashier'd. We have had no late Additions to our Church, although we have some new seeking souls among us. O pray for us." Later that year, Hart reported five baptisms at Hopewell. Still, he pleaded: "Will you pray, my Brother, O pray earnestly that these may be the First Fruits of a great Harvest. Who knows but God will hear you for us." As a true "lover of Zion," Hart also celebrated news of awakenings beyond his own field of labor. He wrote to the Warren Association in 1779, "Several of [the churches of South Carolina] have been blest with a happy revival of religion; but at Pee Dee there has been a glorious display of the power, the goodness of God, in the conversion of hundreds. . . . Our earnest desire and prayer to God is, that his work may extend far and wide, until the saving knowledge of God may cover the Earth as the waters do the sea."[38]

By the final week of December 1795, Hart was confined to his bed, struggling to breathe. When a friend asked if he felt comfortable, Hart replied, "God is an all sufficient savior!" On December 29, Hart's son reported that "he called for all around him to help him praise God for what he had done for his soul." The next day, Oliver Hart died at the age of seventy-two. Testimonies of his godly and useful life poured in. A Philadelphia newspaper praised him for "the endowments of his mind; his early and unaffected piety; his abilities as a theologian and minister of the sanctuary; the regularity of his whole life; his domestic virtues, and universal philanthropy." In Charleston, Furman also spoke for Hart. At one poignant moment, Furman addressed the members of the family. "The loss of such a father demands a tear on your part, but on his, you have reason to rejoice. Your venerable parent had lived the full term allotted to man on earth; he had exhibited an example of tried worth; had obtained large experience of mercy and love of God; and, being rich in good works, has come to the end of his days as a shock of corn fully ripe, and ready for the garner above. Dry then your tears, imitate his piety and virtues; aid, by your best endeavours, that sacred cause of God and religion, for which he was so long the public and faithful advocate among us; and prepare to meet him in that happy land, 'where seraphs gather immortality from life's fair tree, fast by the throne of God.'" Perhaps the most significant testimony of Hart's revival spirituality did not come from the polished rhetoric of a public sermon but in the private tribute of his widow. While reviewing Hart's diaries fifteen years after his death, Nancy came across one of his many prayers for revival. At the bottom of the page, she scrawled this note: "My once dear Hart, how did thy soul long for the conversion of sinners. But now thy, thy painful, pleasing work is done. Thou hast entered into the joy of thy Lord—no more tears to shed for hardened sinners. Thou hast received the 'Well done, good and faithful servant.' May I—may your son, follow thy example.—A. Hart, January 15, 1810."[39]

This biographical sketch has merely introduced many important themes that later chapters will explore in greater detail. Yet there is great value in stepping back and viewing Hart's life as a whole, and in its historical context. It allows us already to see how misguided is the common perception that Regular Baptists were resistant to the Great Awakening. On the contrary, Hart's life was shaped at every turn by the evangelical revival that swept across the North Atlantic Protestant world in the eighteenth century.

CHAPTER 2

Revival Piety

At its 1791 meeting, the Philadelphia Association asked Oliver Hart to deliver the annual sermon. At sixty-eight years old, Hart was by then an elder statesman in Baptist life, entering the twilight of a long and fruitful ministry. But as he spoke about the indwelling Holy Spirit, he sounded again like the young man who had preached alongside George Whitefield at the height of the Great Awakening. The Christian life, Hart insisted, "necessarily calls for the continued influence of the Holy Spirit; for without his aid, we can do nothing." In fact, Hart believed that the heart of authentic Christian experience was the spiritual reality of "communion with God, through Christ, by the operations of the Holy Ghost." Hart was well aware that some of his contemporaries viewed any talk of "divine influences" as "enthusiastical," but he paid them no attention. "I look upon it as the quintessence of religion, without which there can be no spiritual—no acceptable worship at all. O, may we experience more of these divine influences!"[1]

The predominant piety of the Great Awakening can be described as Calvinistic in its theology, with special emphasis on the Holy Spirit's dynamic activity in conversion and sanctification. The evangelicals' focus on the Spirit earned them the nickname of "New Lights" from their opponents, though Thomas S. Kidd has demonstrated that colonial reaction to the revival should be charted along a spectrum. At one end, antirevivalists (more commonly called "Old Lights") like Charles Chauncy and Alexander Garden, viewed the awakening as dangerous and disorderly. At the other end of the spectrum, radical revivalists, such as the notorious James Davenport of New London, Connecticut, seemed willing to bless any rapturous experience or bodily manifestation as evidence of God's activity. Between these two extremes, "moderate revivalists" hailed the awakening as a genuine outpouring of the Holy Spirit, while also recognizing much dross mixed in with the movement.

Regular Baptists are commonly perceived today to have been antirevivalists, especially when compared to their Separate Baptist counterparts. This error is, in many ways, understandable. The Great Awakening birthed the Separate Baptists, who then often conducted themselves in "radical revivalist" fashion. The Separates engaged in emotional worship on the frontier, rejected formal creeds and an educated ministry, expanded the role of women in their meetings, and enjoyed spectacular evangelistic success in the second half of the eighteenth century. On the surface, the Regular Baptists appear quite different. They traced their roots to the English Particular Baptist tradition and were established in America before the turn of the eighteenth century. They held tenaciously to a creedal document, the *Second London Confession*, promoted ministerial education, and practiced greater restraint in worship than did the Separates. Yet for all their real distinctions, the two Baptist groups both celebrated the Spirit's work in revival. Popular presentations of the Regulars as suspicious of the Great Awakening, preoccupied with order and fearful of spiritual ardor, are misleading. As one Regular Baptist asked a gathering of Separates during this period, "If we are all Christians, all Baptists—all *New Lights*—why are we divided?" Using Kidd's helpful categories, Regular Baptists should be identified with the "moderate revivalists."[2]

Oliver Hart exemplified Regular Baptist revival piety. With the other evangelicals of the period, he longed to "experience more of these divine influences!" In this, he followed the preceding generation of Regular Baptists like Jenkin Jones, Isaac Chanler, and William Tilly, all of whom appear in Whitefield's letters and journals as trusted supporters of the Great Awakening. His Regular Baptist contemporaries Edmund Botsford, Evan Pugh, and Francis Pelot all joined him in supporting the revival. These Regular Baptists all belonged to what historian Mark A. Noll has described as the "international network of revived Calvinists" that included English Churchmen, Scottish Presbyterians, Welsh Methodists, New England Congregationalists, and more. This chapter will examine the shape of Hart's revival piety.[3]

Hart was not shy about his Calvinistic conviction that God, and not man, was entirely responsible for the work of salvation. His friends remembered him as "an uniform advocate, both in public and in private, for the doctrines of free and sovereign grace." At the root Hart's piety was a humble trust in a transcendent, Trinitarian God—holy, sovereign, glorious—who freely set his love on an elect but undeserving body of sinners before the world began. In eternity past, God "foresaw Adam would fall . . . and that the whole human race would be involved in guilt, and must inevitably perish." In response, the members of the Trinity "formed a council" to "lay the plan" of man's salvation. Each had a part to play in this cosmic drama. The Father, "having predestinated a select number of the fallen race to the adoption of children," proposed the work of salvation to the Son, who agreed to secure the elect through his death and resurrection on their behalf. The Father, in turn, pledged to send the Spirit to the elect at the moment of conversion, making them willing and able to receive the benefits of Christ's saving work. Hart believed that man's salvation stemmed entirely from this mysterious transaction within the Godhead before the dawn of time, known as "the covenant of grace." He compared God's salvation plan to the building of a glorious house in which "GOD, the Father, chose the materials: GOD, the Son, purchased them with his most precious blood:

and GOD, the Holy Ghost, by his powerful and gracious influences, hews, planes, polishes, and fits them for the building." Man contributed nothing to this construction project.[4]

Some evangelicals objected to this strong presentation of God's sovereignty as antithetical to revival and evangelism. After all, if God had already elected those who would be saved, why bother calling men to repent and believe? The awakening's most noteworthy critic of Calvinism was John Wesley, the leader of the Methodist movement. In his 1739 sermon *Free Grace*, Wesley argued in classic Arminian fashion that the doctrines of eternal election and predestination rendered preaching pointless, undermined man's responsibility for holiness and good works, destroyed "the comfort of religion, the happiness of Christianity," charged the scriptures with contradictions, and even blasphemed the character of God. "Here I fix my foot," Wesley roared. "On this I join issue with every asserter of it. You represent God as worse than the devil!" Hart believed such critiques failed to understand what he saw as a clearly biblical teaching. When his friend Samuel Jones questioned the biblical support for the covenant of grace, Hart wrote back, "Blessed be God, that there is such a covenant, justly called the covenant of grace, from its own nature, and in contradistinction from the covenant of works, and this covenant is supported by the clearest (and Scriptural) evidence." Nor did Hart accept that the covenant of grace "destroyed the comforts of religion." To the contrary, Hart preached in a 1759 sermon that "the foundation of our Happiness [is] founded upon an eternal Covenant, Compact, or Agreement, between the Three Persons of the ever adorable Trinity." Hart found that his knowledge of this covenant provided him with tremendous stability in his daily Christian walk, because his salvation rested securely on the faithfulness and mercy of God, not on anything within himself. Trusting in Christ, Hart knew that he belonged to that number that had been "redeemed by his Blood, Justified by his Righteousness, called by the inscrutable Operations of his Spirit; Sanctified by his Grace, and finally glorified." Hart's own sense of smallness before the ocean of God's mighty grace filled his soul with joy, assurance, and gratitude.[5]

Hart's Calvinism did not restrict him from freely offering the gospel to sinners. This was a divisive issue among Particular Baptists of the day, especially in Great Britain. "High Calvinists" among the English Particular Baptists believed it to be disingenuous to offer the gospel to the nonelect. They simply declared the work of Christ as a fact, then entrusted the rest of the work to the Holy Spirit. The most famous proponent of the High Calvinist view was London pastor John Gill (1697–1771). Gill disagreed with the *Second London Confession*'s rejection of eternal justification, writing that justification "does not begin to take place in time or at believing, but antecedent to any act of faith." Gill's position is significant, for through his prolific publications on a wide variety of doctrinal and ecclesial subjects, Gill functioned as the theological doyen among Calvinistic Baptists on both sides of the Atlantic during the eighteenth century. Hart consciously followed Gill in most doctrinal matters, referring to Gill often in his sermons, and leaning heavily on Gill when composing *A Summary of Church Discipline*. Hart also personally corresponded with Gill for several years, though none of these letters survive.[6] Some of Hart's statements suggest he also followed Gill on the matter of the free offer. Consider the following selection from a 1785 sermon:

> Salvation is not of works, but of grace. And these doctrines are to be preached faithfully, without terms and conditions, to be performed by us; and without offers and tenders of grace. Otherwise we blend law and gospel, grace and works, Christ and Moses; and thereby involve the christian doctrine in the greatest inconsistencies and absurdities. It were to be wished that Christian ministers would be consistent with themselves, as also with the gospel; and not at once preach that salvation is of grace; and then, introduce such terms, offers and conditions, as would lead us to believe that it is *not of faith, but as it were by works of the law*. This is not to preach the gospel. Surely such *workmen have need to be ashamed*, for they do not *rightly divide the word of truth*.[7]

In disparaging "offers and tenders of grace," Hart appears at first glance to share Gill's concerns about the free offer. On the other hand, he could have simply been rejecting the rigorous, drawn-out "preparationism" practiced by many Puritan preachers. Judging by Hart's surviving sermons, the latter option is virtually certain, for Hart pleaded with sinners like an evangelical Calvinist. Consider the closing appeal in a 1765 sermon outline on 1 Timothy 1:15, "This is a faithful saying, and worthy of all acceptation, that Christ Jesus came into the world to save sinners, of whom I am chief." Hart closed his message with a fervent appeal: "Let great sinners take encouragement from hence to hope more for mercy and salvation. None need to despair!" Pressing this application, Hart answered a series of imagined objections to the invitation:

> Objection 1: "I have been a Sinner above my fellows, etc."
> Response: "The Blood of J. Ct his Son cleanseth us [from all sin (1 John 1:7)]"
> Objection 2: "I am an old offender—have done nothing but sin, etc."
> Response: "The Blood, etc."
> Objection 3: "I have stifled the Spirit, killed convictions, and murdered my own soul!"
> Response: "The Blood, etc."
> Objection 4: "I have a hard heart!"
> Response: "I will take away the stony heart out of your flesh, and I will give you an heart of flesh (Ezekiel 36:26)."
> Objection 5: "I have 1,000 blasphemous thoughts, etc."
> Response: "The blood of Jesus Christ his Son cleansesth us from all sin (1 John 1:7)."

As this representative selection indicates, Hart never hesitated to call all sinners to repent and believe the gospel. His practice earned him the reputation as the most consistently evangelical preacher in the city of Charleston in the 1760s. Further, his Regular Baptist protégés Edmund Botsford and Samuel Stillman were both "free offer men" who preached hard for conversions. As indebted as Hart was to Gill in developing his systematic theology, he followed Whitefield in his preaching. Whitefield himself, who worshipped at Hart's church, worked with Hart in the revival, and commended Hart's ministry to others, certainly approved of his practice. Hart agreed with his hero that preaching was God's appointed means to save the elect, and, "since we know not who are elect and reprobate, we are to preach promiscuously to all."[8]

Evangelical preachers realized that no one would turn to Christ apart from a deep realization of their sin and need. So they preached sin, and hard. "Tell me then, o man, whosoever thou art, that disputes the doctrine of original sin, if thy conscience be not seared as with a hot iron!" Whitefield thundered, "Tell me, if thou dost not find thyself by nature to be a motly mixture of brute and devil?" Hart too was concerned to reveal man's sinful condition in the starkest of terms, announcing that "it is against this Sovereign Being that we have rebell'd and whose laws we have broke, and to who's wrath we are obnoxious." Following the Augustinian tradition, Hart trumpeted the doctrine of original sin. Adam, acting as humanity's federal representative, plunged his descendants into spiritual ruin through his transgression in the Garden of Eden. Adam's initial relationship with God had been one of "the most cordial amity and friendship." But his disobedience "broke the tender ties of love and esteem," revealed in Adam's immediate fear of and resentment toward God. As a result, Hart observed that fallen man now naturally "dreads the divine presence," and has "contracted a contrariety of soul to the perfections of the Deity, and a horrid enmity against God." Hart compared sinful man to the prodigal son of Luke 15 who "hath left his home, travels into a far country," and now passes through life as "a stranger." Man "hath forsook God and gone after his own heart's lusts;" he has "missed his way," has been "reduced to want," and is now "used with severity . . . deluded by the devil, their hard master." On his part, God was "an injured sovereign, insisting that reparation should be made for the dishonor done him." God now demanded both the "punctual observance" of the law, as well as full satisfaction for his law's violation; yet these were "impossible terms to man in his fallen state." Hart's robust doctrine of sin made for a bleak picture of man's estate.[9]

Hart's private writings show him to be keenly aware of his own sinfulness. As an old man, he bemoaned how he had squandered his early years "in Vanity and a Listlessness to all that was good." Long after his conversion experience, Hart remained sensitive to his ongoing shortcomings in the spiritual life. "I am this Day conscious of my own Weakness and Defects!" he exclaimed in an ordination sermon. "How then shall I impose a charge, in which I have conducted so unworthily my Self?" On a birthday, Hart recorded matter-of-factly, "This day was 66 years old, an old Sinner." Hart grew frustrated by the spiritual inertia sin produced in him. "I have to lament of too much leanness of soul," he regularly admitted. In another place, he remarked, "I do this morning feel myself Opprest under a sense of my Barrenness. . . . I feel the Want of the *Life* and *Power* of religion in my *Own Heart*" On another occasion, the example of a pious widow "made me ashamed when I saw how far Short I come of acting the Christian and Minister. O Lord, revive thy Work in my Heart, remove Deadness from my Soul, teach my Tongue to speak thy Praise." Like other evangelicals for whom the doctrine of sin was so deeply ingrained, humility before God sounded the dominant note of Hart's piety.[10]

Yet Hart's personal humility did not dissuade him from addressing the sins of worldly Charleston. Like many evangelicals, he believed that the ungodliness of his neighbors provoked God's anger, leading to the fires, storms, and wars that ravaged the city throughout the eighteenth century. Hart interpreted these disasters as "so many loud calls to repentance, reformation of life, and prayer, that the wrath of God may be turned from us." Still Charleston continued to be "swallowed up in pleasure and dissipation." As a minister, Hart felt obligated to point this sin out, and pled with the community to repent. He therefore determined, "in faithfulness to my trust, to maintain an open and vigorous war with all the vices and sinful diversions of the age." As one might expect, attacking the lifestyle of the prevailing culture invited anger and ridicule, but Hart viewed this as a prophet's badge of honor. "If I had not been willing to endure the scoff of the world, I should never have made an open profession of the religion of Jesus; much less should I have become a preacher of his much-despised gospel." Hart knew that whoever "ventures to attack vice, in a public manner, ought to be possessed of some degree of fortitude and resolution; for sin is a monster of more than a thousand heads; should he slay some, there will be many yet remaining, and he may expect to be attacked on every side; especially if he should dare to level at some popular darling vice."[11] Though Hart clearly enjoyed his friendships in Charleston society, he was willing to risk alienation to remain faithfully at his post.

With the other early evangelicals, Hart took special aim at "the sin of dancing." To Hart, the Charleston balls represented the epitome of worldliness. Not only did he consider the physical act of dancing to be "extremely immodest, and incentive to uncleanness," but the music was "often very obscene . . . which have a tendency to pollute the imagination, and to raise unchaste thoughts in the mind." Those who lingered at balls also failed to steward their precious time, which was "shamefully misimproved . . . squandered away—it is murdered—it is consumed on our lusts." Dancing schools and gowns represented "an extravagant waste of money" that could otherwise "relieve a virtuous family in distress, or cloath half a dozen orphan children." Further, the conversation at dances was filled with "flattery, lying, ribaldry and nonsense." Hart flatly denounced the ball as "the devil's procession, and whoever entereth there, entereth into his procession. The devil is the leader, the middle, and the end of the dance. So many paces as a man maketh in a ball, so many leaps he maketh towards hell." This was bracing talk in carefree Charleston, but Hart believed it would ultimately serve the gospel.[12]

In addition to open vice, Hart also saw sin manifest in man's confused religious efforts. Following the first two chapters of Paul's letter to the Romans, Hart declared in a 1763 sermon that all men knew that God existed, that he deserved their worship, and that he required appeasement for sin. Yet, "how he is to be worshipped, in an acceptable Manner, by fallen, sinful Men, is a Point beyond the utmost Stretch of human Reason to determine without the Assistance of Divine Revelation." Enveloped in spiritual darkness, fallen man was left to fearfully grope after God as best he knew how. The results were disastrous. "Hence they have been driven to the most extravagant Practices: of macerating their Bodies, cutting them with Lancets; offering human Sacrifices; and causing even their own Children to be rost in the fire, as the most likely victims to appease their angry gods. Awful Indications, these, of the Depravity of human Nature!" Yet, even when the gospel way of salvation was plainly explained, sin drove man to resist God's grace either by trusting in his own morality, or diving headlong into lascivious living. "The proud boasting Pharisee rejects a crucified Saviour with Disdain, and the poor Sensual Sinner, prefers to him the gratification of his beastly Appetites: To those who are being saved, Christ is the Power of God and the Wisdom of God," Hart preached. The saving knowledge of Christ only broke through to the sinner's heart through the Holy Spirit's miraculous work of conversion.[13]

"Should be glad if you could get an Opportunity of conversing with my Daughterin-law, Sally Clark," Hart wrote to Furman in 1790. "I believe her to have experienced a saving Change; and that she is a proper Subject for Baptism." For evangelicals, the doorway to the Christian life was not any form of religious activity or moral resolution but the "saving change," of conversion, wrought in the human soul by the Holy Spirit. This experience, called the "new birth," awakened sinners to repentance and faith in Jesus Christ, and has rightly been identified as "the *raison d'être* of the evangelical movement." Whitefield called the new birth "the very hinge on which the salvation of each of us turns, and a point on which all sincere Christians, of whatever denomination, agree." Hart agreed. He cried out after preaching a sermon on John 3:7, "Oh, that they knew what the New Birth means!" Promoting the miracle of conversion comprised the center of his ministry.[14]

One of his church members, Anne Sealy Grimball, experienced a classic evangelical conversion through Hart's ministry. Grimball described herself as "thoughtless and gay" in Charleston society. Yet at times, she found herself "terrified at the idea of death." Eventually, Grimball began attending the Charleston Baptist Church where she sat under Hart's preaching each week. "Here," she recalled, "I heard the gospel in its purity, but neither the threats of the law nor the sweet gospel sound made any impression on my hard and rocky heart." Yet Grimball was also finding Charleston's "gay scene" increasingly dissatisfying, unable to distract her from concerns about eternity. "I was not happy amidst all my flattering prospects: an amiable and tender husband, the gay circle—diversions—visits—congratulations, etc. Something was missing—and that something I could not find. My mind was not at rest." Over the next few years, Grimball experienced the tragic loss of several children, deepening her sense of life's brevity and her need for peace with God. "My convictions became more powerful—my situation more alarming, I thought no one was exercised as I was—I could not make my case known—I plainly saw that I must perish, dying as I was," she wrote. The services Grimball attended often at this time produced greater disquiet than comfort. "Satan, the grand enemy of souls, beset me with blasphemous thoughts—frightened me from duty—I feared to hear a sermon, lest it should rise up in judgment against me. Tell my unhappy case to anyone, I durst not," she said. She felt torn as she heard stories of others' conversions. On the one hand, she "loved to hear the people of God tell their experience;" on the other hand, she "feared they should ask me any questions" about her own soul. At long last, relief broke through. "After many struggles with my frail and corrupted nature, many conflicts with a hard head of unbelief, our condescending Lord made me willing to follow him into the watery grave. I was baptized by Mr. Hart, May 5, 1770 (in my 29th year)," she wrote. "Thus the Lord in his abundant mercy led me on from step to step as I could bear with afflictions—with comforts and mercies—with crosses and losses—until I was made willing to trust him, alone, for the whole of my salvation."[15]

Anne Sealy Grimball's conversion experience reflects the evangelical belief in the use of means in conversion. The preaching of the law and the gospel, the testimonies of others who had experienced the new birth, and the trials and afflictions of life, all contributed to her conversion. At the same time, the use of means alone was insufficient to effect regeneration. Grimball found herself contending with demonic forces, struggling with her own "frail and corrupted nature" that resisted surrender to Christ, a "rocky heart" and a "hard head of unbelief." It was only the direct operations of the Spirit of God "by which I was made willing to trust him, alone, for the whole of my salvation." Looking back, it was plain that "the Lord in his abundant mercy led me on from step to step." Grimball's conversion was of special significance to Hart's ministry; four years after baptizing her, Hart would take the young widow as his second wife.

Commensurate with Grimball's story, Hart believed the Holy Spirit to be the active agent in conversion, his secret work in the soul serving as the final link in the Trinitarian conspiracy of grace. Hart explained in a 1755 sermon that "the

Grace, Love, or free favour of God is the moving or Impulsive cause" of salvation, and "what Jesus Ct. hath done and Suffered for us is the Meritorious Cause of salvation," while the "Spirit of God is the Communicative and Manifestative cause." The Spirit's initial "communication" or "manifestation" of salvation to man came in an event that Regular Baptists termed the "effectual call." At a divinely appointed moment, the sinner was "called by the inscrutable operations of his Spirit," receiving a sovereign summons to rise and live like Lazarus from within the tomb. The Spirit's call was "inscrutable," or mysterious, because it lay beyond man's control. As the wind blows through the trees, so the Spirit's work in a man's soul could neither be predicted beforehand nor seen with the eye when it arrived, but the effects of the Spirit's visitation were always unmistakable.[16]

Hart elaborated on the effectual call in a 1755 sermon on 2 Timothy 1:9. He first distinguished the effectual, or "internal," call from the "external" call of God. Biblical texts like Matthew 22:14, "many are called, but few chosen," indicated the reality of an external or "general" call that went out to all sinners to repent and believe, through the preaching of the gospel. The external call could be accompanied by the appearance of conversion, but it did not bear the Spirit's power and thus could not prevail upon the sinner's heart. This carried practical implications for Hart's ministry. Hart interpreted the nonresponse of listeners as a spiritual issue, as when he lamented in 1782, "my Soul longed earnestly to see Sinners coming unto Jesus weary and heavy-laden with sin . . . [but] Conversion work is a Strange Work in this Place." The reality of the external call also chastened Hart's enthusiasm over initial signs of conversion. His diaries typically move quickly from celebration over a new Christian to intercession. After hearing a series of professions of faith in 1754, he prayed, "May the Lord carry on his Work in their Hearts; may Conviction end in Conversion, and may none of those awakened turn back again." The external call slammed against man's heart like a wave on a coastal rock, washing away to no effect. This had been Anne Grimball's experience all the years she resisted Christ. But the internal call was a "powerful, efficacious call," in which the omnipotent Holy Spirit overwhelmed the stoutest defiance. The internal call was irresistible, for it wielded the same power that raised Christ from the dead. Hart further described it as "a holy call," which set the sinner apart from his former worldliness to live unto God. It was a call "not according to works," for the sinner had done nothing to make himself fit for the call, but was "according to [God']s purpose," and "according to his grace given to us in Christ before the world began." Hart closed by challenging all who dared to deny the "powerful, inscrutable operations of the Spirit in conversion" to reckon with the biblical case he had presented. He ended by pressing on his listeners the ultimate question in regards to the Spirit's call, that of personal experience: "Have you experienced this inward call?"[17]

The immediate response of those effectually called by the Spirit was evangelical faith, which Hart described simply as "coming unto God by Christ." Converted individuals came to God as "poor sinners stripped bare of their own righteousness . . . pleading for mercy for Christ's sake only . . . believing on Christ for salvation." Hart often illustrated the event of saving faith from Psalm 110:3, "Thy people shall be made willing in the day of thy power," a text he preached more than a dozen times in the years 1773–94. For Hart, this verse perfectly captured the new birth: God's enemies presented themselves as loyal subjects to King Jesus, because God's Spirit had made them willing in the day of his power. At the moment of faith, the converted sinner entered a living relationship with Jesus Christ. It was this dependent relationship of trust in Christ, rather than a self-reliant life of works or religion, that comprised the focus of the born-again Christian. Christ served a multitude of offices on the believer's behalf. Christ was his covenant head, delivering him from Adam's cursed race and securing for him "all the promises and blessings of the covenant." Christ was the Christian's "surety," the substitute who "engaged to do and suffer all that the law and justice of God required, to make satisfaction for their sins." Christ served also as the believer's advocate, who interceded on his behalf before God. Christ became the believer's prophet, who "teaches powerfully and efficaciously, by his word and Spirit." Christ was the priest in whose sacrificial death "a true and proper atonement was made for sin, satisfaction for divine justice was given, the wrath of an offended Deity was appeased, and sinners have free access unto God, as a God in covenant, a Father and Friend." And Christ became the Christian's king, who ruled by "the most wholesome laws," gave the "most glorious charter of privileges," and conquered all the believer's spiritual enemies. On one occasion, Hart used poetry to reflect on the grace-given, Spirit-wrought, Christ-focused nature of saving faith:

Faith! 'tis a precious grace,
Wherein it is bestow'd
It boast of a celestial birth
and is the gift of God!
Jesus it owns a King,
An all-atoning Priest
It claims no merit of its own,
But looks for all in Christ
To him it leads the soul
When fill'd with deep distress,
Flies to the fountain of his blood,
and trusts his righteousness.
Since 'tis thy work alone,
And that divinely free;
Lord, send the Spirit of thy Son
to work this faith in me.[18]

The Spirit's work in conversion also went deeper than the initial burst of saving faith, imparting to the believer an entirely new nature. Upon regeneration, man's disposition toward God was instantly transformed from that of a hostile sinner to that of a humble worshipper. Hart often spoke of the new birth as the Holy Spirit implanting "a divine principle of grace" in man's soul. He preached that saving faith not only rescued man from the negative effects of sin, but "Holiness is Annex'd unto, and is part of the New Nature formed in the Heart." In a 1769 sermon on the new birth, Hart listed seven examples of the renewed nature produced by the Spirit. First, those who have been born again stopped simply using God to get something from him, and instead "loved the Lord for what he is in himself and what he is to us." Second, the Spirit opened the eyes to "attracting views of the Lord Jesus Christ," and moved the individual to make a personal commitment of faith, or coming to "a saving close with him." The Spirit also revealed his activity by lifting the believer's gaze above the plane of this world and giving him or her a "delight" to "converse on spiritual and divine things." Further, the Spirit produced a love for the cause of God in the world, so that "we rejoice when it flourisheth and mourn when it decreaseth." Fifth, the believer's attitude toward obedience underwent a total transformation. God's authoritative directives in scripture were no longer despised as a threat to personal freedom, but "we have a universal regard for all his precepts and commands." Sixth, the Spirit produced a passion for practical godliness, so that "we hate sin, love holiness, and mourn on account of indwelling sin." Finally, the Spirit weaned the believer's soul from its love for this world, giving it "strong desires after heaven." Evangelicals preached an inside-out holiness.[19]

Like other evangelicals, Hart carefully distinguished between holiness that flowed from the new birth and the mere moralism carried out in the power of the flesh. Whitefield had warned, "If we are only mere moralists, if we are not inwardly wrought upon, and changed by the powerful operations of the Holy Spirit, and our moral actions proceed from a principle of a new nature . . . it is to be feared that we shall be found naked at the Great Day." Hart, too, declared that holiness arising from a born-again soul was altogether different from natural man's external religion. "The form of godliness, without the power, is like a body without a soul—a dead carcass. . . . There must be a divine principle implanted in the heart. A carnal, unregenerate man, as such, can never be a spiritual worshipper. None but those, whose hearts are circumcised, can 'worship God in the spirit,'" he said in a 1791 sermon. He insisted that, "Spirituality [the presence of the indwelling Holy Spirit] is of the greatest importance and alone can give life and energy to every branch of divine worship. It is internal, experimental religion only, that will be of any avail—the religion of the heart—to this the Lord looks—this he requires." This was the classic language of a moderate revivalist.[20]

The instrument God used to effect the miracle of conversion was the preaching of the gospel message, which Christ appointed "to call sinners out of darkness into light." Hart believed that when he preached, Jesus himself "sends down his Spirit to make the Preaching of the Gospel Efficacious." Thus, while the Spirit's role in conversion was decisive, Christ invested the gospel preacher with great responsibility in the process. Hart considered preaching "the most important service that ever demanded the attention of man," for as he declared the gospel, the minister "stands between the living and the dead—the living God and dead sinners." Only the Spirit could make them live, but he would use the preacher's words to perform the resurrection. In a striking passage from his 1791 sermon, *A Gospel Church Portrayed*, Hart unfolded his understanding of the mysterious interplay between the preacher and the Spirit in conversion:

> Does success depend on the minister? No. Were he possessed of the wisdom of Solomon, the firmness of Elijah and the zeal of Phineas, united with the sanctity of John, the engagedness of Paul and the eloquence of Apollos, he would be unequal to the task. A divine energy, only, can render his labours successful. Nevertheless, those who are engaged in this arduous service should attend to it "after the due order." They should preach the pure gospel, and not a mere system of morality. Cautious should they be of blending law and gospel, grace and works. They should preach salvation, through Christ, in a way of free, rich and sovereign grace. "Not of works, lest any man should boast." It behooves them to "be instant in season and out of season," and to speak with so much life and energy as to evince that their whole soul is engaged in the work. Their language should be plain, yet masculine; their reasoning clear, yet nervous; their countenance, open and free; their action, easy and graceful.[21]

As heaven's ambassador, Hart believed Christ had commissioned him to not only explain the gospel terms but to warmly entreat sinners to repent and believe. "Ministers of the Gospel were sent to invite poor Sinners, and that is their Delight," he said. In a 1765 sermon on 1 Timothy 1:15, Hart labored to establish "that the greatest, or chiefest of Sinners may obtain salvation through Jesus Christ." He spent the first portion of the sermon proving from scripture that Christ was both abundantly able and willing to save sinners; he spent the latter portion calling for a response. He piled up biblical encouragements for hesitant sinners to fly to Christ. "How often do we hear [God] declare that he Willeth not the death of a Sinner, but if the sinner repent, etc. [Ezekiel 33:11]?'" Hart asked. "And Christ hath declared that he came not to call the Righteous but Sinners to Repentance [Mark 2:17]." Hart then unleashed a string of biblical invitations, as if issued directly from Christ: "Ho! Everyone who thirsteth, come to me [Isaiah 55:1]; . . . Come unto me, all ye that labour and are heavy laden, and I will give you rest [Matthew 11:28]; . . . Look unto me, all ye ends of the earth, and be ye saved [Isaiah 45:22]!" Hart told his listeners that Christ not only invited them to come to him with their sin but he reassured them that they would be welcome when they arrived, quoting John 6:43, "Whosoever cometh to me, I will in no wise cast out!" Hart then shifted to another tactic, recounting the unlikely conversions of scripture's most notorious sinners. "What a miserable Wretch was Mary Magdalene? A Vile Prostitute, possessed of seven Devils, and yet she obtained mercy, and became as remarkable for Piety: she had much forgiven, and therefore she loved much," he preached, alluding to Luke 7:36–8:2. He kept going. King Manasseh, Saul of Tarsus, the three thousand at Pentecost, and the thief on the cross all seemed irredeemable, but were saved when they simply took Christ at his word. "Let great Sinners take Encouragement from hence to hope more for Mercy and salvation—None need to despair!"[22] This was preaching Hart believed the Spirit honored with conversions.

Though conversion often occurred at the end of a long course of convictions, those who "came through" in new birth were only beginning their Christian experience. The principle of holiness "formed in the Heart" at the new birth then had to "extend to the lips and life, or in other words, the words and actions," as Hart said in a 1755 sermon. This required diligent effort from the believer. The new nature had to be "drawn out into action," in "the exercise of grace, in faith, hope, charity, and the whole assemblage of Christian virtues." This lifelong process of weakening old patterns of sin and nourishing new habits of grace was known as sanctification. As in conversion, Hart believed that "this necessarily calls for the continued influence of the Holy Spirit; for without his aid, we can do nothing." Even as they called for man's participation in discipleship, evangelicals preached a supernatural Christian life.[23]

The indwelling of the Holy Spirit was a cardinal doctrine for evangelicals, whose insistence on a direct experience with God clashed with the formalism of their opponents. Hart declared that all true believers "enjoy the renewing, comforting, and sanctifying influences of the Holy Spirit." After all, Christ had promised to send the Spirit to "convince the world of sin, renew the soul, comfort the people of God, sanctify and make them meet for Heaven." Hart realized this was a controversial issue, and that many rejected the doctrine of "divine influences" as "enthusiastical." Enthusiasm was a charge Whitefield had repeatedly received. "We no sooner mention the necessity of receiving the Holy Ghost in these last days, as well as formerly, but we are look'd upon by some as enthusiasts and madmen," he said. Antirevivalists feared the excesses that accompanied the Spirit's "direct operations," including a blind obedience to impulses and impressions, claims to visions and direct revelations, a presumed ability to detect conversion in others, dramatic physical manifestations, and the criticism of established ministries that did not support the revival. Charles Chauncy, one of the revival's chief antagonists, drew a direct line from the revivalists to the Antinomian controversy that rocked New England in days gone by. In Charleston, Anglican commissary Alexander Garden clashed mightily with Whitefield in print and from the pulpit. In his sermon *Take Heed*

How Ye Hear (1740), Garden drew parallels between the revivalists and all types of religious radicals, including the Münster Anabaptists of the 1530s. Many evangelicals acknowledged the abuses of the doctrine of the indwelling Spirit, and Jonathan Edwards's *Treatise on the Religious Affections* (1746) stands as the classic evangelical attempt to discern between true and false marks of the Spirit's work in revival. Still, they refused to abandon their position. As Whitefield preached, "every Christian, in the proper sense of the word, must be an enthusiast. That is, must be inspired of God, or have God in him. For who dare say, he is a Christian, till he can say, God is in me?"[24]

Hart agreed that the Spirit's indwelling represented "the quintessence of religion," and addressed the doctrine in a pair of sermons on July 9, 1769. In the morning, he taught from Romans 8:9: "Now if any man have not the Spirit of Christ, he is none of his." He began by noting that though the doctrine was widely "ridiculed" today, the apostle Paul urged his readers "to make inquiry whether or not we have the Spirit of Christ" as a test of authentic Christianity. Hart then sought to establish what Paul intended by "having the Spirit of Christ." He could have simply intended "the temper of Christ," as the antirevivalists would have interpreted it. In other words, anyone who followed Jesus's moral example was a true Christian. But Hart instead argued that Paul meant for all believers to possess the very person of "the Holy Ghost," the third person of the Trinity, in order to belong to Christ. Whitefield had covered the same ground in his published sermon, *The Indwelling of the Spirit the Common Privilege of All Believers*, which Hart appears to have read. For both men, the indwelling of the Spirit was the ultimate mark of true Christianity. Hart then expounded the role of the indwelling Spirit in greater detail. He was "a Spirit of illumination and conviction," for he alone could open the eyes and pierce the heart in regard to one's true condition before God. The Spirit came as "a Spirit of regeneration and conversion," granting spiritual life in the place of death at the new birth. The Spirit also was "a Spirit of sanctification and holiness," implanting the new principle of grace in the heart, and gradually conforming the believer to the character of Jesus. The Holy Ghost came also as "a Spirit of prayer and supplication," moving the saint to humbly call on God as Father. The Spirit worked in the believer as "a Spirit of self-denial and mortification," who energized the Christian to make holy war on the indwelling sin and impulses of self that remained after conversion. Finally, the Holy Ghost was "a Spirit of comfort and consolation," resigning the believer to all the losses and crosses of this life as part of God's personal sanctification program, and reassuring him of the Father's unfailing love. Hart's vision of the Spirit's role in the daily life did not include a focus on ecstatic speech or enraptured visions, as the antirevivalists may have assumed. The Spirit's work had much more to do with producing holiness of character, deepening the believer's relationship with God, and producing a life of love toward others.[25]

In the afternoon, Hart took up Romans 8:14: "For as many as are led by the Spirit of God, they are the sons of God." He noted that the idea of "being led by the Spirit" contained two complimentary truths. First, it pointed to an ongoing "impotence and weakness" in the believer, who remained dependent on the Spirit's drive and direction to persevere in holiness. At the same time, it highlighted that all of the believer's "good habits and actions" were not of themselves, but of the Spirit's agency. The doctrine of the indwelling Spirit thus enabled evangelicals at their best to guard against spiritual pride or false notions of self-improvement as they advanced along the path of holiness. Hart then explained a number of specific ways in which the Spirit led the individual Christian. The Spirit leads the believer "from sin," empowering him to "mortify the deeds of the body." The Spirit also leads the believer "from all dependence of ourselves and brings us to Christ's righteousness" and "leads us to ask for pardon." The Spirit served as the ultimate teacher in the Christian life, leading the believer "to a true sense of the doctrine of the Gospel and into the path of duty." Further, as the believer met with hardship on the Christian way, the Spirit "leads them through the difficulties and afflictions of this world from one degree of grace to another." Ultimately, those who had the Spirit could be confident that he would lead them all the way to heaven, for "those who are led by the Spirit can't fall away." Hart closed the sermon by urging the congregation to examine their hearts and "inquire if we are the sons of God" by discerning the Spirit's indwelling presence. No question could be more urgent.[26]

As these sermons indicate, Hart viewed sanctification as a synergistic endeavor between God and man. The indwelling Spirit enabled the believer to strive for holiness, but the believer was indeed commanded to strive. "Take heed to yourselves likewise, with regard to your growth in Grace; labor to be continually making advances in the divine life. That you may abound in Spiritual Things," Hart counseled. Christian growth only came through conflict, for sanctification plunged the believer into "a continual and irreconcilable war" between the Spirit and the flesh, as the *Second London Confession* asserted. In the course of this war, the saints often suffered defeat, for "remaining corruption for a time may much prevail." Yet, strengthened by the Word and the Spirit, motivated by the glory of Christ, and directed toward a heavenly calling, the believer pressed forward toward godliness, knowing that ultimate victory was already secured through Christ. This gritty approach to sanctification comprised the message Hart lived and preached. One example comes from an undated sermon from 2 Timothy 2:3, "Share in suffering as a good soldier of Christ Jesus." Hart drew attention to the variety of New Testament metaphors for the Christian life, "all tending to show that a Christian's work is a great work, and what he is concerned about, matters of the greatest importance, and consequently can be properly attended unto any otherwise than with all our heart with all our might and with all our strength." Hart then guided his listeners on a tour of those New Testament images, showing that the Christian was compared to a wrestler, to one who runs in a race, to a fighter, and to a soldier.[27]

Hart also commonly applied images of health and fitness to the spiritual life. He often included in his letters such sentiments as, "I enjoy a great share of Bodily health; O that my Soul may be in health, and prospered even as my Body!" For optimal spiritual condition, Hart urged Christians to "labor to maintain grace in its vigorous exercise." The daily workout he prescribed could be summed up in classic evangelical language as "vivification and mortification," which comprised what Whitefield called "the whole of the divine work in the new-born soul." The twin disciplines of vivification and mortification comprised the saint's pursuit of holiness from both positive and negative perspectives. Vivification described the act of stirring up the Spirit's work in the soul through intentional action. The Christian's soul atrophied if neglected, but vivification strengthened and expanded the graces. Hart exhorted every believer to take up this duty: "Be careful to maintain the life and power of godliness in your souls," he wrote to the churches of the Charleston Association in 1775. Hart envisioned no Christian "drifting" into godliness; rather, the staccato exhortations at the close of the New Testament epistles provided the model for his spiritual advice. "We recommend to you all to pray fervently; believe firmly; wait patiently; work abundantly; live holily; die daily; watch your hearts; guide your senses; redeem your time; love Christ; long for glory," he wrote in 1778. In a 1759 charge to young pastors, he urged them to "labor to maintain that grace in its vigorous exercise. Be lively, and active for God in the constant exercise of every Christian grace and virtue. Let your faith be strong, your hope firm, your love fervent, your repentance sincere. In a word, imitate your Divine Exemplar in patience, meekness, humility, self-denial, and the like."[28]

Mortification served as the negative counterpart to vivification. Two generations earlier, the Puritan John Owen captured the essence of mortification when he wrote, "To kill a man, or any other living thing, is to take away the principle of all his strength, vigour, and power, so that he cannot act or exert, or put forth any proper actings of his own; so it is in this case." John Gill had defined mortification simply as "the weakening of the power of sin." Following these divines, Hart envisioned the mortification of sin as basic to all Christian discipleship. "We exhort you, brethren, to be diligent in every good word and work, dying daily to sin, and living unto God; that so you may be prepared for every dispensation of Providence, and at last received up into glory," he wrote in 1778 to South Carolina Baptists. Though "killing sin" could be grim work, evangelicals viewed mortification as essential for a vibrant, Spirit-filled Christian experience. The saint's consistent war against his own sinful inclinations signaled the presence and activity of the Spirit, who indwelt the believer as "a Spirit of self-denial and mortification." Thus, though many unregenerate men attempted to mortify their sins in their own strength, in an effort to earn salvation, only Spirit-indwelt believers were equipped for true mortification.[29]

Related closely to mortification, Hart urged Christians to keep their souls in fighting trim through the practice of ongoing repentance. Following the *Second London Confession*, Hart preached that as the Spirit brought the Christian under conviction of sin, he granted the believer the "grace of repentance" as the pathway to ongoing spiritual renewal. Repentance was therefore not a one-time event at the hour of conversion but designed to be "continued through the whole course of our lives." In a 1769 sermon, Hart suggested four aspects to evangelical repentance. First, the believer must obtain "a sense of the evil committed." Beyond a surface-level acknowledgment of sin, the serious Christian must labor to grasp "the sinfulness of his sin" before God, if he is ever to turn from it. Yet this sober self-evaluation did not resign him to perpetual condemnation. The second step of repentance moved directly to the cross, and "an application of the blood of Christ." Here, the believer personally received the gospel promise of forgiveness through Christ's atoning death by faith. Third, having received the assurance of Christ's pardon, true repentance always involved getting decisive about change, producing "a final resolution to forsake evil." Finally, repentance had done its full work when the believer moved past the negative work of confession and "yielded obedience" in place of the former rebellion. Among key areas of obedience, Hart suggested that repentant believers focus on loving God, Christ, and fellow Christians; attending to prayer and religious conversation; and practicing watchfulness and self-denial.[30]

The evangelicals' thorough-going doctrine of sin made them keenly aware of their propensity for spiritual deception. They thus viewed the discipline of self-examination as imperative for growing in grace. Hart pressed this issue in a 1759 ordination sermon from 1 Timothy 4:16. "Take heed unto thyself, and unto the doctrine; continue in them: for in doing this thou shalt save both thyself, and thy hearers," he preached. Though intended for ministers, his words applied more broadly to all believers. "Turn into your own Hearts, and labour after the most intimate and extensive acquaintance with your own Souls. Look well unto your own State; give all Diligence to make your Calling and Election sure." Hart's admonition spoke to the Puritan's preeminent concern of self-examination: the determination of whether or not one had truly experienced conversion. "Nothing can be more awful than to preach an unknown Ch't," Hart cautioned. "Be frequent in Self-examination, which attend to, with all that holy Severity, which the Nature, and Importance of the Thing calls for. Never content your Selves without the most Substantial Evidences of your Interest in Christ, and a work of grace begun and carried on in your own souls," he said. "You cannot be qualified to deal with wounded Spirits, unless you have been sensible of your own Wounds. It is not possible you should, in a suitable manner, direct Sinners to Christ, without an actual Closure with him yourselves."[31]

Self-examination also helped Christians identify patterns of spiritual decline in their lives. Hart warned his congregation in 1769 that "Christians are subject to an awful declension which is displeasing to Christ," alluding to the church in Ephesus that had "lost its first love (Revelation 2:4)." Common symptoms of spiritual declension that Hart noted included "indifference and coldness in the worship of God," "coldness to the ministers and people of God," "fretful or peevishness of spirit," "a desire after and delight in vain diversions," as well as "murmurings under afflictions." But these were merely the presenting problems for which Christians must search in their examination. Hart also urged his listeners to probe deeper to identify the root causes of spiritual decline. "The want of watchfulness," for instance, left the believer vulnerable to the sifting of Satan. Likewise, the allowance of "spiritual pride" in even small measures was a classic precursor to a serious fall. "The omission of secret prayer" drew the heart away from intimacy with God and exposed it to the world's allurements, as did "the keeping of bad company." Failure to mortify less conspicuous sins of the heart, such as "giving into passion, anger, and wrath," led to an overall decay of spiritual vitality. Finally, "eagerness after the world" posed a constant threat to the growing saint. Hart often used heart-searching questions in the application of his sermons to stimulate his hearers to self-examination, as at the close of *Dancing Exploded*: "For what was I made?" "Do I answer the end of my being?" "Is God glorified by all my actions?" "Must I not shortly die, and give an account of my actions to God?" "Have I any time to spare from transacting business for eternity?"[32]

Hart's diaries reveal an introspective tendency that caused him to be rather severe in his own self-examination. So stringently did he inspect his soul that he sometimes entertained doubts about the reality of his conversion. "Satan and unbelief robs me of my spiritual comforts (if ever I knew anything of religion, which I am tempted to doubt), so that my Burden is great," he moaned in 1788. In a 1791 letter he lamented his dismal spiritual performance. "With Pain I reflect upon my Leanness and Unprofitableness through the whole of my past Life. . . . Ever since I profess'd to know the Lord I have been too—too languid in his Service. I sometimes wonder how any People can prefer me as their Teacher." This kind of spiritual brooding over his shortcomings was probably not productive. Yet in its healthiest form, self-examination guarded evangelicals against spiritual presumption and slothfulness. When accompanied by repentance and a renewed faith in Christ, the practice could even become a pathway to peace and joy. Hart's diaries often strike this note. Despite his spiritual failures, Hart was ultimately comforted by the unchanging reality of the gospel. As he wrote to Furman in 1792, he was "under the care of the most kind, and most skillful of all Physicians. The Medicine he uses is indeed of an extraordinary Nature; it is his own Blood. A sovereign Remedy this! None ever made use of it, but obtain'd a Cure."[33]

Essential to evangelical piety was the role of certain spiritual practices, or "means of grace." Simply going through the motions of practices like prayer and Bible reading carried no value, but when practiced by faith, these disciplines served as "so many conduit-pipes, whereby the infinitely condescending Jehovah conveys his grace to their souls," to use Whitefield's image. Through the means of grace—especially scripture, prayer, worship on the Lord's Day, and Christian friendship—Hart made it his ambition to "begin, and end, every day with Thee."[34]

It is impossible to overstate the primacy of the Bible in Hart's spirituality. With the *Second London Confession*, he believed the scriptures to be "the only sufficient, certain, and infallible rule of all saving knowledge, faith, and obedience." An open Bible was to him nothing less than the "mouth of the Lord," and in an effort to listen, Hart read, meditated, memorized, sang, trusted, and obeyed scripture. Hart studied the Bible front to back, familiarizing himself with the full sweep of its contents. As a young man, he was convinced that he needed "a Larger, & better acquaintance with; and a more copious knowledge of, the Word of God." So he resolved, "with the Permission, and Assistance of God, to Read ten Chapters every Day, (at least for a time, or till I see an inconveniency arising from it) allowing for times to Travel, and unforeseen events." All the while, he relied on "the Spirit of illumination" as he read, praying, "may the Lord grant that I may Read to Advantage." Hart also meditated on scripture, lingering slowly and prayerfully over individual verses. John 10:11 inspired him to pray, "Oh that Jesus may be my Shepherd, and that I may by him be led to Green Pastures. Blessed Jesus! Wilt thou take me into the Number of thy Sheep, and lead me in and out; and may I be Enabled to follow thee Withersoever thou goest." Specific promises held a special place in his meditation, particularly in days of doubt and fear: "These indeed are precious Words—*Cast thy Burthens upon the Lord, and He will sustain thee* [Psalm 55:22]," Hart wrote. "I see many gracious Promises and Declarations, and have been attempting to plead the Blood and Righteousness of Christ, and to lay hold on the Skirts of his Robe, but the Arm of Faith seems to be withered. I try to say, Lord, I believe, help thou mine Unbelief—O Lord give me Faith." According to William Rogers, Hart's devotion to the Bible was evident in his daily conduct. "He read and believed his Bible, and comformably to its precepts, he was full of charity and good works! If not rich in earthly things, he was rich in faith."[35]

If the Bible was how Hart heard from God, prayer represented his believing response to what he heard. Furman remembered Hart for his "affectionate, fervent addresses to God in prayer." Hart believed that "keeping close to God in prayer" was essential for maintaining "the life and power of godliness in your souls." He often warned his listeners that neglecting this holy conversation would "tend to coldness in religion, and renders the soul more unfit for communion with God." His diaries indicate that Hart kept a set time for private prayers, first thing each morning. The entries from his 1769 missionary travelogue begin with a familiar rhythm of, "Rose early, prayed, breakfasted, and were on our way." His diary served as important outlet for his private prayers. He filled its pages with supplications for his own growth in grace, his pastoral and preaching ministries, and revival in the churches. In an undated entry, Hart penned a poetic description of the act of prayer: "O Thou, Most wise and gracious God, Who rules all nature with a nod, Look down, I pray, and pity me, In my distress, I fly to thee." Outside of his prayer closet, Hart led his household in regular family prayers. His approving description of the sacrificial practices of his close personal friend, Francis Pelot, minister of the Baptist church at Euhaw, South Carolina, is suggestive of his own. "The morning and evening sacrifices of prayer and praise were constantly offered up to the God of our lives and mercies. He not only endeavoured to train up his children in the paths of virtue and religion, but he also took much pains with his servants to teach them the fear of the Lord and the way to eternal happiness," he wrote. He encouraged the churches of the Charleston Association in 1775 to "maintain the worship of God in your families; pray with and for them, instruct them in the principles of religion, and enforce your precepts by the best examples." Hart also enjoyed praying with friends, often closing out an evening of "religious conversation" in someone's home with singing and prayer.[36]

Some of the most vital means of grace in Hart's life could only be accessed in fellowship with his community of faith. Christians who neglected the gathering with a local church courted spiritual disaster; "their own souls become lean, their brethren are grieved, their ministers discouraged, seekers retarded, and sinners hardened." To establish the priority of corporate worship, most evangelicals consecrated each Sunday as "the Christian Sabbath," a day when all other activity ceased in order to seek God's face. Hart argued that God had appointed the Sabbath as a creation ordinance, binding to the end of time. God had sanctified the Sabbath as "a good and happy day, which then was, and thenceforth should be appropriated to the most blessed purposes of praising and adoring Jehovah; and should prove a blessed day to all true worshippers." Upon the resurrection of Jesus, God reinstituted the Sabbath as the Lord's Day for his New Covenant people.[37] Accordingly, Hart's diaries show him spending his Sundays conducting public services as a minister and sharing spiritual fellowship in the homes of Christian friends. For Hart, the Sabbath functioned as "a miniature weekly Protestant 'retreat,'" akin to the Jesuit practice, as historian of Christian spirituality Richard F. Lovelace has observed.

Among the means of grace available through the local church were the observance of baptism and the Lord's Supper. Hart compared these two "gospel ordinances" to the "windows of the church," wherein Christ shone the light of his presence and grace to his people. For Baptists, the public immersion of a believer at the beginning of Christian discipleship dramatically displayed the gospel to both the covenant community and the unbelieving world. It symbolized the believer's spiritual union with Christ in his death, burial, and resurrection, the washing away of the Christian's sins, the consecration of the whole person to walk in newness of life, and the inclusion into the fellowship of God's people. One vignette from Hart's 1789 diary indicates how important this ordinance was to the church. A woman named Mrs. Patience Blackwell unexpectedly presented herself as a candidate for baptism at a scheduled meeting of the Hopewell Baptist Church. She related "her experience" of conversion to the congregation, which all found to be "satisfactory." Overjoyed, the church immediately elected to forego the scheduled sermon and travelled to the creek at Deacon Nathaniel Stout's property "in order to attend to the business." There was just one problem: it was the month of January in Hopewell, New Jersey, and the creek was frozen solid. Yet this did not deter the church leaders from carrying out what they deemed an urgent matter of Christian obedience. Hart reported some men "casting away the Ice (which was of considerable Thickness)." The sixty-six-year-old Hart then led the candidate down into the water "according to the ancient Practice," and he baptized her "in the Name of the sacred Trinity." Hart reported that when they came up out of the water, "neither of us received any Damage, altho' there was Snow on the Ground as well as Ice in the Brook." The entire company then returned to the meetinghouse, where they completed the day's exciting events by receiving Mrs. Blackwell as a full member of the church "in the usual way, by cov'[enant], then pray'd, sang, and dismiss'd." Baptism was a vital means of grace for the entire Baptist community.[38]

Hart also cherished the Lord's Supper, which, like baptism, visibly displayed the gospel to Christ's believing people. Hart's goal when serving the Lord's Supper was to "raise the faith and affections of the communicants to a crucified Savior." Hart set aside six Sundays each year to observe the ordinance. He viewed these occasions with such reverence that he also gathered the church the day before for a "preparation day," when he preached a sermon on Christ's atonement to prepare them for Communion. By the end of the eighteenth century, many Baptists spoke of the Lord's Supper in terms of a bare memorial of the death of Christ, but Hart preferred the richer language of the Reformed tradition. He believed that Christ met with his believing people in a unique and powerful way during the Communion hour, nourishing them spiritually as they looked to him in faith. After one service, Hart reflected, "the Lord stood by me and encourag'd me in his Work, and particularly in breaking Bread, the Lord broke in with much Sweetness upon my Soul. Others also met the Lord at his Table." He approvingly quoted Dutch Reformed theologian Herman Witsius (1636–1708) as he described the Christian's experience at the Table, where, "the promises of the New Testament and enlivening communion with Christ, made perfect by sufferings, both in grace and glory, are signified and sealed" to the hearts of believers. The Lord's Supper was another act of evangelical piety that drew Baptists like Hart out of an individualistic spirituality and into the company of the redeemed.[39]

Protestant evangelicals in the early modern Atlantic world commonly recognized fellowship with other believers as an important means of grace, and the cultivation of Christian friendships played an especially prominent role in Hart's life. Furman recalled that he "possessed in large measure the moral and social virtues, and had a mind formed for friendship." The high value Hart placed on friendship shines in a poignant diary entry upon the death of his fellow South Carolina Baptist minister Francis Pelot, in 1774. "I have lost the best friend . . . I ever was blest with in the world," Hart wrote. "The most intimate friendship had subsisted betwixt us for about four and twenty years. In all which time I ever found him a faithful friend and gratified to give advice in the most critical cases." The two had experienced much over those twenty-four years. Hart had convinced Pelot to surrender to gospel ministry when Hart first arrived in Charleston. After Hart ordained Pelot in 1752, the two worked together to strengthen the Baptist cause in the South, taking leading roles in the Charleston Association and coauthoring *A Summary of Church Discipline* in 1773. When Hart remarried after the death of his first wife, he asked Pelot to perform the ceremony. "He was the sincere, open, constant, and hearty friend, could keep a secret, and in short, few men were ever better qualified for friendship than he."[40]

Eighteenth century evangelicals like Hart developed their friendships through the popular practice of letter writing. Written correspondence allowed members of the evangelical community to share their personal experiences with God and exchange news of the revival throughout the American colonies and across the waters of the Atlantic. As much as any other factor, the prolific letter writing of the eighteenth century added to the sense that evangelical Protestants were participating in a historic, worldwide movement of God. This is evident in the life of Oliver Hart, who loved nothing more than sending and receiving letters from a wide range of correspondents. When Samuel Jones expressed serious doubts about the veracity of scripture as a young man, Hart took up his pen to assure him that "whatsoever is revealed therein [scripture] comes handed down to us with the greatest certainty, and upon the clearest evidence." Edmund Botsford desperately reached out to Hart through the mail after the unexpected death of his wife. "O my father! My father! No one, that has not been exercised in the same way, can have any conception of what I feel. . . . O my father! Pray for me, write to me," he pleaded. Hart passed along stories of revival to Isaac Backus, collaborated on how to advance the Baptist interest with Richard Furman, and even maintained a wide transoceanic correspondence on a variety of matters, mentioning in 1763 that "I have corresponded with Dr. Gill and several more of our London ministers, for many years past." Hart also used his letters to share light moments with his friend. On hearing of the birth of mutual friend Evan Pugh's second son, he joked with Jones that Pugh was "successful in his generation work if not in that of regeneration."[41]

True to his disciplined nature, Hart often kept up with his correspondence more faithfully than did his friends. In a letter to Jones, Hart noted that he had not heard from his friend since his recent marriage. "Sure you have not suffered a Wife to lay an Embargo on your Pen," he teased. He carried his banter further with Manning. "Altho' you are already in my Debt, I am about to give you fresh Credit; hoping thereby to induce you to an immediate Discharge of the Whole you owe," he wrote. "I have Sometimes thought that the Habit, or Disposition of People, is somewhat similar to the Climate in which they live: if so, no Wonder if you Gentlemen, who live so contiguous to the frozen Zone, have cold Hearts. It should seem as if their Hands are cramped with the cold too, and rendered incapable of Holding a Pen. Otherwise, why is it that I hear from them so seldom? Perhaps you are all better employ'd. Convince me of that, and you will atone for every past Neglect. Well, my dear friend, how is it with you? Does the Lord cut out much work for you to do? How does your Soul—how does Religion—how does your Church, and how does the College prosper? I hope the Kingdom and interests of Jesus Christ flourishes in your Parts."[42] Hart's commitment to letter writing supplies one further example of his participation in the evangelical spirituality of the Great Awakening.

Hart and the Regular Baptists are commonly perceived to have stood aloof from the spiritual "ardor" of the Great Awakening, clinging instead to the "order" of their rigid confessionalism. As this chapter has demonstrated, such an understanding is deeply flawed. A careful survey of Hart's experiential Christian theology, which focused on regeneration and spiritual rebirth, demonstrates that Regular Baptists were far more evangelical and revivalistic than historians have traditionally understood. Along with a host of his Regular Baptist brethren, Hart championed the same "revival piety" as did Edwards, Whitefield, and the other "revival Calvinists" in America's early evangelical movement. At the heart of this piety was a desire to experience "more of these divine influences," through the dynamic activity of the Holy Spirit.

CHAPTER 3

Revival Narrative

In his later years, Oliver Hart assembled a special diary summarizing the major events of his life. These included his conversion, his call to ministry, his marriages, and the births of his children. In the fall of 1754, he recorded simply, "Revival of religion." As the previous chapters have shown, the evangelical awakening of the eighteenth century shaped Hart's entire life. Yet the fall of 1754 represented a unique episode in Hart's biography, one he later described to his father as "the remarkable revival in our church." From August to October 1754, Hart found himself at the center of a spiritual awakening in the Charleston Baptist Church that resulted in the baptism of ten new converts. Though a modest ingathering of souls when compared to other revivals of the period, it proved to be a major milestone in the church's history. Happily, Hart kept a detailed record of this awakening in his diary, which today can be classified as part of that significant genre of evangelical literature birthed by the Great Awakening, the revival narrative.[1]

Jonathan Edwards wrote in 1737, "There is no one thing that I know of, that God has made such a means of promoting his work amongst us, as the news of others' conversion." Edwards scarcely could have imagined then how the news he shared in *A Faithful Narrative of the Surprising Work of God in the Conversion of Many Souls* would promote the work of revival around the world.[2] A little-known Congregational minister at the time, Edwards had participated in an unprecedented awakening in Northampton, Massachusetts, during the years 1734–35. At the request of Boston minister Benjamin Colman (1673–1747), Edwards detailed his experience in an eight-page letter in 1735, which he later expanded into *A Faithful Narrative*.

Edwards began his report with an account of Northampton's low spiritual condition leading up to the winter of 1734. "It seemed to be a time of extraordinary dullness in religion," Edwards recalled. He noted particularly the licentious behavior of the young people, "a spirit of contention" in the town, and the spread of Arminian doctrine. But through the sobering deaths of two young people, and a timely Edwards sermon on justification by faith, circumstances began to change rapidly. "The Spirit of God began extraordinarily to set in, and wonderfully to work amongst us," Edwards wrote. Day by day, "a great and earnest concern about the great things of religion and the eternal world became universal in all parts of the town." These initial concerns soon gave way to widespread, thorough conversions. "The work of conversion was carried on in a most astonishing manner, and increased more and more; souls did as it were come by flocks to Jesus Christ." By the spring of 1735, Northampton had been transformed. "This work of God, as it was carried on, and the number of true saints multiplied, soon made a glorious alteration in the town. . . . The town seemed to be full of the presence of God: it never was so full of love, nor so full of joy; and yet so full of distress, as it was then." Edwards guessed that, in the span of six months, about three hundred people were converted. Nor was this all. The revival broke out of Northampton and spread to some thirty-two surrounding communities in the Connecticut River Valley. "This seems to have been a very extraordinary dispensation of Providence: God has in many respects gone out of, and much beyond his usual and ordinary way," Edwards marveled. Edwards submitted his narrative to Colman "to dispose of it as you think most for God's glory, and the interest of religion."[3]

A Faithful Narrative was an overnight sensation. In the preface, English Dissenters John Guyse (1680–1761) and Isaac Watts (1674–1748) exclaimed, "Never did we hear or read, since the first ages of Christianity, any event of this kind so surprising, as the present narrative." After decades of slow progress they rejoiced that true revival had finally come. "Our ascended Savior now and then takes a special occasion to manifest the divinity of the Gospel by a plentiful effusion of his Spirit where it is preached: then sinners are turned into saints in numbers, and there is a new face of things spread over a town or a country." They expressed hopes that Edwards's story foretold a further-reaching revival that would convert the nations.[4]

In fact, *A Faithful Narrative* did become the literary catalyst of the transatlantic, evangelical revival. Upon its publication in London, the recently converted John Wesley read it while walking from London to Oxford. He was awed. "Surely 'This is the Lord's doing, and it is marvelous in our eyes,'" he wrote in his diary. Wesley would later republish *A Faithful Narrative* for the Methodist people in 1744 and 1755, though he was careful to remove all references to Edwards's Calvinistic theology. In Scotland, William McCulloch (1691–1771) and James Robe (1688–1753) devoured the story; it would shape their account of the Cambuslang revival in 1742. Howell Harris (1714–73) of Wales read it also. When revival reached his homeland in the ensuing years, he remarked, "Sure the time here now is like New England." In 1738, *A Faithful Narrative* was printed in German, and in 1740, a Dutch translation appeared. Edwards's pioneer work in revival narrative had an incalculable influence in shaping the burgeoning transatlantic evangelical community. One leading scholar of eighteenth-century revival narratives, D. Bruce Hindmarsh, has observed, "As his narrative of revival was read aloud to congregations, as it was serialized in revival magazines in London and Glasgow, it inspired ministers to expect that such an experience could be replicated among their own people."[5]

Edwards's work also inspired a host of other revival narratives. Between the years 1741–43, evangelicals founded four major periodicals in Great Britain and America: the Calvinistic Methodist *Christian's Amusement* in London (later *The Weekly History* under the leadership of George Whitefield), William McCulloch's *The Glasgow Weekly History*, Thomas Prince's (1687–1758) *The Christian History* in Boston, and James Robe's *The Christian Monthly History* in Edinburgh. Each was devoted to relating stories of "the progress of the gospel at home and abroad." The *Christian History* was described by one contemporary as "containing accounts of the revival and propagation of religion (of late) in Great Britain and America: which exhibits to us a large number of very satisfactory and joyful accounts." Many of these stories explicitly followed Edwards's narrative structure: an appraisal of the town before the revival, a description of the beginnings and effects of the revival, detailed accounts of individual converts' experiences, and a report on the continuing or declining state of the revival.[6]

One spin-off narrative came from the pen of Samuel Blair (1714–51) in 1744. Born in Ireland, Blair trained at William Tennent's Log College before settling at a Presbyterian church in Fagg's Manor, or New London–Derry, Pennsylvania, in 1739. Blair also began a school modeled after Tennent's, where Samuel Davies (1723–61) received his training. In 1740, Blair's Fagg's Manor congregation experienced "a very comfortable enlivening time to God's people, and great numbers of secure careless professors, and many loose irreligious persons thro' the land were deeply convinced of their miserable perishing estate, and . . . many of them were in the issue, savingly converted to God." Thomas Prince asked Blair to contribute to *The Christian History*. Blair was happy to tell his story, "convinced that it is our duty, in the most open manner to declare and bear testimony unto the work of God's grace among us at this day, for the honor of his name, and the good of his church, both in the present and future generations." Yet Blair did not think the *Christian History* would be widely read in the middle colonies, so he published his letter separately.[7]

Blair self-consciously followed Edwards's template as he told his story. Before the revival, Fagg's Manor knew an outward form of religion, but precious little experimental piety. The people were devoted to such worldly practices as parties, horse racing, and dancing. "Thus religion lay as it were a dying, and ready to expire its last breath of life in this party of the visible church," Blair commented. All this began to change in the spring of 1740, "when the God of salvation was pleased to visit us with the blessed effusions of his Holy Spirit in an eminent manner." An anonymous guest preacher first awakened "deep soul-concern" among Blair's people, and Blair quickly followed up with his own intense gospel preaching. The results were remarkable. "I think there was scarcely a sermon or lecture preached here thro that whole summer, but there were manifest evidences of impressions on the hearers, and many times the impressions were very great and general." The manifestations at Fagg's Manor matched those at Northampton in their intensity and diversity.

"Several would be overcome and fainting; others deeply sobbing, hardly able to contain, others being in a most dolorous manner, many others more silently weeping, and a solemn concern appearing in the countenance of many others."[8]

Like Edwards, Blair carefully noted that he did not aim to create these physical manifestations, nor did he view them as certain signs of God's work. He was more interested in the inner transformation Edwards had witnessed in Northampton. "The general carriage and behaviour of the people was soon very visibly alter'd," he wrote. This included a new delight in the Bible, sound Christian literature, religious conversation, and public worship. Blair also followed Edwards by including accounts of the town since the revival had faded, as well as conversion stories of a young woman, an older man, and two little girls. In closing, Blair assured his readers that he had "endeavored all along to be conscientiously exact in relating things according to the naked truth." Though tempted to embellish the story, Blair understood "that I must not speak wickedly even for God, nor talk deceitfully for him, and upon the whole I must say it is beyond dispute with me, and I think it is beyond all reasonable contradiction that God has carry'd on a great and glorious work of his special grace among us."[9]

Living about seventy miles north of Fagg's Manor in Warminster Township, Hart likely read the narratives of both Edwards and Blair, along with many others, during the 1740s. Hart's later correspondence reveals an insatiable appetite for revival reports. It should therefore come as no surprise that when he recorded the events of the 1754 Charleston revival in his diary, his account was shaped by the revival narrative genre. Some significant differences between Hart's diary and Edwards's narrative do exist. Hart's account takes the form of a private diary, not a letter. It is not known if Hart ever intended anyone to read his story, though Richard Furman would quote from it at length in a memorial sermon for Hart. Hart also did not attempt to place the revival in the context of the city's spiritual condition, but focused entirely on his own congregation. Yet the influence of revival narrative on these pages remains unmistakable. At least six key revival themes from Edwards's *Faithful Narrative* appear in Hart's diary: pastoral consecration, conversion-oriented preaching, private meetings for seekers, the use of personal testimonies, the presence of powerful affections, and an awareness of spiritual deception.[10]

The morning of August 5, 1754, found Oliver Hart in low spirits. He lamented, "I do this morning feel myself Opprest under a sense of my Barrenness. Alas, what do I do for God? I am indeed employed in his Vineyard, but I feel to little purpose; I feel the Want of the Life and Power of religion in my Own Heart; this Causes such a Languor, and faintness in all my duties to God. This makes me such a poor [manager?] of time. Alas! I am frequently upon my Bed, when I Ought to be upon my knees. To my Shame, sometimes the Sun appears in the Horizon; and begins his

Daily Course; before I have paid my tribute of Praise to God; and perhaps while I am Indulging myself in Inactive Slumbers upon my Bed. Oh Wretched Stupidity! Oh that for time to come I may be more active for God." The passage illustrates several concerns central to the spirituality of the Great Awakening. First is Hart's desire to feel the "life and power of religion in my own heart." Evangelicals on both sides of the Atlantic longed to move beyond formal participation in the institutional church, to experience "the life of God in the soul of man." This intense desire for a personal relationship is most closely associated with Continental Pietism. In a preceding generation, German pastor Philip Jacob Spener (1635–1705) had sounded a call for spiritual renewal in the Protestant church in the small book *Pia Desideria* (1675). Spener lamented how few church members "really understand and practice true Christianity (which consists of more than avoiding manifest vices and living an outwardly moral life)." Despite possessing religious knowledge, many were "altogether unacquainted with the true, heavenly, light and life of faith." Spener responded by offering "several simple Christian proposals" for promoting vital godliness in the church, including personal Bible reading and the formation of Christian societies outside the church's regular services. Spener's "pious desires" and the movement of Pietism he launched "helped condition the faith and practices of early American evangelicalism," contributing "an intense focus on the heart, often in conflict with the decayed state of formal, established religion."[11] These concerns permeate Hart's writings. He often quoted Proverbs 23:26 in his sermons, "My son, give me thine heart," finishing the verse with a drawing of a heart on his sermon manuscript.

The diary also reflects another standard feature of evangelical piety, the commitment to devotional practices. When Hart confessed "a Languor and faintness in all my duties to God," he alludes to the personal disciplines of early morning prayer and praise. These were among the primary means of grace whereby individual Christians could draw near to God. Hart's angst in his diary reflects the perennial evangelical preoccupation with the "quiet time." The faithful performance of these duties required the close management of one's time, another enduring evangelical concern. James Gordon, a student of Protestant evangelical spirituality, has pointed out that "the regular hour, usually early in the morning, careful watching of the clock to make sure time was carefully used, [and] anxiety to make sure all opportunities were 'improved,'" are classic features of evangelical devotion. One's consistency in this hour of private worship often served as a measuring stick of evangelical spirituality. Any perceived shortcoming in these duties left a sincere believer like Hart lamenting his "wretched stupidity" and feeling "shame" for sleeping in.[12]

On this occasion, Hart concluded his self-examination with firm resolution:

> Ever I have heretofore done: I would Resolve to be a better manager of my Time than I have hitherto been, to Rise Earlier in the Mornings; to be sooner with thee in Secret Devotion; and oh, that I may be more Devout therein! I would be more Engag'd in my Studies; grant, O Lord that may Improve more thereby! And when I

> go out, Enable me better to Improve my Visits; that I always may leave a Savour of divine things behind me. When I go to thy House in order to Speak for thee, may I always go fraught full with Divine things and be Enabled faithfully and feelingly to dispense the Word of Life. In a word, I would begin, and End, every Day with thee; Teach me to Study thy Glory in all I do, and will thou also be with me in the Night Watches; teach me to Meditate on thee, upon my bed, and may I Sleep for thee; and Desire no more than Nature Requires, fit me for thy Service. Thus, Teach me to Number my Days that I may Apply my Heart unto Wisdom.[13]

The passage exemplifies the evangelical ideal of an active spirituality. Hart's vision of the godly life was lively, energetic, strenuous. It did include strategic periods of holy seclusion—the "secret devotion" of morning prayer and engagement in "my studies"—yet these respites largely served the end of "fitting me for thy service," or public ministry. Hart aspired not only to the bare performance of spiritual duties but for greater intensity and fruitfulness in them. He resolved to "rise earlier" and "be more devout" in prayer; to be "more engaged" in study; to "improve" his visits; to preach "faithfully and feelingly." He closed with a prayer for nothing short of total consecration to God: "in a word, I would begin, and end every day with thee," aspiring to even improve the hours he spent on his bed.

Hart was not finished making resolutions. Two weeks later, he added another new initiative, specifically related to the study of scripture. Convinced of his need for "a Larger, & better acquaintance with; and a more copious knowledge of, the Word of God," Hart decided to take action. "I came to a Resolution this Morning, with the Permission, and Assistance of God, to Read ten Chapters every Day, (at least for a time, or till I see an inconveniency arising from it) allowing for times to Travel, and unforeseen events." Again, Hart expressed a hallmark of the evangelical awakening, a renewed commitment to seeking God in the Bible. Unlike many previous generations of Christians, evangelicals had ready access to copies of the scriptures in their own language, and promoted personal Bible reading as the primary means of privately drawing near to God. During the Northampton revival, Edwards had reported that "while God was so remarkably present among us by his Spirit, there was no book so delighted in as the Bible. . . . Some by reason of their esteem and love to God's Word, have at some times been greatly and wonderfully delighted and affected at the sight of a Bible." So with Hart, because both Old and New Testaments were nothing less than "the Word of God," to obtain "a more copious knowledge" of the Bible was to grow nearer to God himself.[14]

One can hardly read Hart's resolutions without thinking of Edwards's more famous *Resolutions*. Like Hart, Edwards was driven by a desire to redeem the time for God's glory, as in his Resolution 5: "Resolved, never to lose one moment of time; but improve it in the most profitable way I possibly can." Within his spiritual commitments, Edwards also focused on Bible knowledge: "28. Resolved, to study the Scriptures so steadily, constantly, and frequently, as that I may find, and plainly perceive myself to grow in the knowledge of the same." Both Edwards's youthful *Resolutions* and his more mature reflections on personal spirituality in *A Personal Narrative* exhibit the same evangelical desire for consecration to God as in Hart's diary.[15]

Hart soon put feet to his new commitments. He filled the ensuing pages of his diary with reports of praying, studying, preaching, counseling, traveling, and generally "laying himself out for God." It seems Hart was never happier than when the pace was most demanding. By September 2, he had pulled out of the doldrums and was exulting again, "Blessed be God, I can say, altho' I am at times weary in my Lord's work, yet I am not weary of it: and I hope I never shall. The more I am engag'd in it, the better I like it; the sweeter I find it!" Hart's personal renewal in August of 1754 is pertinent to the story of the 1754 revival. Historians of the Charleston Baptist church point out that the events of the awakening followed directly on the heels of Hart's own private consecration. As in Edwards's case, the congregation in Charleston would follow the lead of its impassioned minister. Scholar George M. Marsden has drawn attention to the impact of Edwards's personal piety on the Northampton Awakening. "The town seemed to be made over in his image . . . . People identified with this demanding young preacher who set before them an exalted spiritual vision." Marsden observed.[16] So in 1754, Hart's personal renewal served as a model in the Baptist revival at Charleston.

Hart was well acquainted with revival preaching, having sat under the electrifying addresses of George Whitefield, Gilbert Tennent, John Rowland, and Jenkin Jones. In 1754, Hart's own preaching was a primary agent of the Charleston revival. He preached often, with two formal services each Sunday, a doctrinal lecture every Wednesday, impromptu meetings in church members' homes, and itinerant work over the Ashley River. One of his earliest entries from the period captures the essence of his pulpit ministry. "Blessed be God, had a Good Day to Day. Preached twice with some degree of warmth: in the Afternoon from Jn 3:7 Ye must be born again; felt my Soul drawn out after the Conversion of Sinners; Oh, that they knew what the New Birth Means!"[17] This quote suggests a brand of revival preaching that was biblical, conversion-oriented, and passionate.

Preaching for Hart always meant the proclamation of scripture. As Hart preached from John 3:7 on August 4, so he centered all his sermons on a biblical text, often a single verse. He then developed the message according to the Puritan method: after introductory remarks on the context and relevance of the selected verse, he provided an exposition of the text's doctrine, then moved to personal application. Other preaching texts Hart mentioned in the diary include Revelation 1:5: "Unto him that loved us"; Galatians 4:19: "My little children"; 1 John 2:1: "But if anyone does sin, we have an advocate with the Father, Jesus Christ the Righteous";

and Malachi 4:2: "But unto you that fear my name shall the Sun of righteousness arise with healing in his wings; and ye shall go forth, and grow up as calves of the stall." The terms Hart used to describe the act of preaching also point to his Bible-centeredness. He typically spoke of "expounding": explaining the biblical message and pressing it onto his listeners. "I have for sometime Past felt a love for Expounding, and have had frequent Opportunities so to do." For example: "I Expounded some part of the last chapter of Luke"; "I Expounded part of the 21st chapter of St. John"; "Expounded Matthew 15 from 21st to 23rd." Hart also uses the metaphor of "opening" the biblical passage, as one might raise the lid of a treasure chest to reveal the riches it contained: "I opened the first part of Isaiah 42"; "opening up the first five verses of the 2nd chapter of Isaiah"; "opened & spiritualized the first chapter of Jonah." "Spiritualizing" was another method of applying scripture, drawing spiritual principles from biblical narratives. In the preceding example, Hart compared his listeners to Jonah slumbering in the storm and prayed, "Lord, wilt thou Awake Sleeping Sinners, that they may Call upon thee for Mercy: and wilt thou think upon them that they perish not." Hart also spoke of "spiritualizing blind Bartimaeous," and "spiritualiz[ing] Namaan's case." Whitefield often employed this method in his own preaching, and Hart perhaps used his published sermon on "Blind Bartimaeus" as a model. Hart's Bible-driven preaching practice was grounded in his theological convictions about the Bible. He believed that scripture, being the Word of God, had the power to awaken and to convert: "I hope some felt the Word," he often remarked after preaching. He longed for his listeners to be "affected under the Word" and prayed, "Oh that their hearts were opened to hear the Word, and that they might receive it!"[18]

Hart deliberately aimed at spiritually awakening his listeners and moving them toward conversion. While salvation was a supernatural work, the instrument God used to effect the new birth was earnest, Spirit-empowered preaching. Hart yearned to see God work this miracle through his sermons, as when he felt his "soul drawn out" for his listeners' conversion. Similar statements abound in his diary. "Found my heart much drawn out in the Afternoon after the Conversion of Young People. Lord take thine own Work, into thine Own Hands," he wrote. After addressing a gathering of young people: "I believe that some of them are under some Awakening: Oh! May the Lord Carry on his Work in their Hearts; may Conviction End in Conversion, and may none of those Awakened turn back again." In another example, he related that a young man named "W. R." was "struck with Convictions" as he preached. "Lord may they never wear off, till they End in a Saving Conversion to thee." Speaking about a sermon from Isaiah 55:6–7, he wrote, "Towards the latter End of my Discourse, my Heart was much drawn out after the Conversion of sinners, and the Increase of Grace in the Hearts of these Young persons lately converted."[19]

Hart's revival preaching was also notable for its passion, and in ways very similar to other evangelical ministers of the eighteenth century. When critics of the Great

Awakening accused Jonathan Edwards of playing too heavily to the emotions, he replied, "Our people don't so much need to have their heads stored as to have their hearts touched; and they stand in greatest need of that sort of preaching that has the greatest tendency to do this." Hart followed the same philosophy. After a sermon from Galatians 4:19, he wrote, "I am sure I spoke from the heart, and firmly believe I felt what the Apostle did when he said, 'I travail in birth till Christ be formed in you.' Some, Blessed be God, seemed affected under the Word." One gets a sense of Hart's passion from the vocabulary he uses to describe both his delivery and the hearer's reception of the message. "Warmth" was a favorite image, as in, "preached twice with some degree of warmth." Affectionate preachers before him, from the Puritan Richard Sibbes (1577–1635) to Edwards, had also insisted that a sermon contain both light and heat.[20]

Other dominant preaching images in Hart's writings include "power" and "freedom": "Blessed be God this was a good Day throughout. I had great freedom in Dispensing the Word, and I hope, and believe many felt the power of it." Hart prayed for God's converting power to visit his hearers while preaching: "Lord, smite their Hearts powerfully, and may they not Rest, till they find rest in thee"; "work powerfully upon their young hearts!" He could also use gentler imagery, describing the Word as coming with "sweetness": "I Expounded to many of my People, with great freedom and sweetness, I trust to myself and others." After preaching Song of Solomon 1:2, "For thy love is better than wine," he wrote, "I hope some felt the sweetness of Christ's Love and Could say from experience that Christ's Love was better than Wine." Warmth, power, freedom, sweetness—this was the vocabulary of a passionate revival preacher. It is not uncommon to read in his diary that "several were much Affected. . . . Some could scarce forbear Crying out," or when he saw many "melted down into tears." Hart labored to inform the mind by clearly explaining the text, yet also maintained that revival would come only if God himself "broke in with Light, Power, and Sweetness upon the Heart."[21]

In preaching for conversion, Hart often found a ready field for action in low-country South Carolina, as the case of Samuel Stillman makes clear. Stillman would one day become the pastor of the First Baptist Church of Boston, Massachusetts, where he occasionally counted John Hancock, John Adams, and Henry Knox among his listeners. But in 1754, he was simply the unconverted teenage son in a Charleston Baptist family. Stillman has left behind an eyewitness testimony of the power of Hart's preaching during the 1754 revival. He described himself in these days as a spiritually indecisive young man, until his "mind was again solemnly impressed with a sense of my awful condition as a sinner" after hearing a weighty message from Hart. This time, his sense of urgency did not wear off as before. "This conviction grew stronger and stronger. My condition alarmed me. I saw myself without Christ and without hope. I found that I deserved the wrath to come, and that God would be just to send me to hell. I was now frequently on my knees, pleading for mercy. As a beggar I went, having nothing but guilt, and no plea but mercy," he remembered. Evangelicals in both the Old World and the New World described this as a sinner's experiencing the power of God's Law. Before one could value Christ's salvation, one first must be brought to understand God's holiness, and the perfect standard to which he held his creatures in the Law. The Law exposed the sinner's desperate need for grace, shattered all former self-righteousness, and drove him to despair of saving himself. Evangelicals like Hart deemed this process essential for bringing careless sinners like Stillman to the alarming realization that he was a "beggar," "having nothing but guilt, and no plea but mercy."[22]

Stillman transitioned from despair to hope on August 27, when Hart declared the gospel from Matthew 1:21, "And she shall bring forth a son, and thou shalt call his name Jesus; for he shall save his people from their sins." Through this sermon, Stillman finally "received consolation." He recalled that "Christ then became precious to me, yea, all in all. Then I could say of wisdom, 'Her ways are ways of pleasantness, and all her paths are peace.' That I still think was the day of my espousal. Glory be to God, for the riches of his grace to me. Why me, Lord?" Stillman's transformation was immediately evident. He became a leader among the other awakened youths, often leading in prayer and hosting meetings in his family's home.[23]

Hart's revival preaching is important in understanding his revival spirituality as well as the spiritual ardor of the Regular Baptists of the lower South. Separate Baptist preachers like Shubal Stearns are rightly remembered for their passionate, evangelistic, revival-oriented preaching ministries. Morgan Edwards recalled Stearns' preaching voice as "musical and strong, which he managed in such a manner as, one while, to make soft impressions on the heart, and fetch tears from the eyes in a mechanical way; and anon, to shake the nerves and throw the animal system into tumults and perturbations." Hart's diary indicates that Regular Baptists also knew what it meant to preach in the great revival tradition of George Whitefield. Without question, the different backgrounds, personalities, and ministry contexts of the Regular and Separate Baptists contributed to distinctive preaching styles. Hart appears to have been more serious in his manner, more precise in his sermon construction, more polished in his delivery, and more constrained by his confessionalism than Stearns. Yet by no means was Hart dispassionate, unconcerned about the conversion of sinners, or suspicious of the Spirit's operations while in the pulpit; he was a thorough-going revivalist.[24]

Among the most recognizable features of the evangelical awakening in the eighteenth-century Atlantic Protestant world was the renewed emphasis on private religious meetings among laypeople. The idea of an *ecclesiolae in ecclesia* is another evangelical practice that stemmed directly from Continental Pietism. The early Pietists were earnest Christian individuals, hungry for "something more" than the regular meetings of the institutional church could provide. Addressing this need, Philip Jacob Spener recommended the adoption of *collegia pietatis*, or private gatherings for piety. Spener called Christians to meet in small groups outside the regular church services for prayer, the devotional reading and discussion of scripture, and mutual spiritual encouragement. He envisioned the minister remaining present to encourage lay participation, providing the people an opportunity to ask questions and receive counsel. The formation of *collegia pietatis* was a vital piece of Spener's blueprint for restoring vitality to the church, and the early evangelicals seized on it. Various manifestations of the small group principle appeared among the Moravians at Herrnhut, the early Methodists, and in Edwards's Northampton revivals. In *A Faithful Narrative*, Edwards indicated that an important catalyst for the awakening had been the organization of the young people into small groups for "social religion," including biblical instruction, prayer, singing, and spiritual conference. These meetings grew especially popular among the awakened young people. Previously given to "frolicking" and generally careless living, they now voluntarily met in groups for spiritual improvement. Edwards observed that "the place of resort was now altered; it was no longer the tavern, but the minister's house, that was thronged for more than ever the tavern had been wont to be." Following this pattern, Hart promoted private religious meetings in the Charleston revival. Reports of small-group gatherings outside formal church hours and off church premises appear on every page of his diary. Hart organized many of these meetings himself, as when he lectured to a "society" on Wednesday afternoons on a doctrinal subject, or when he instructed baptismal candidates in his home. More commonly, the young people planned the meetings. They simply showed up in groups at Hart's doorstep, or requested that he address them at the house of a church member. On other occasions, the youth gathered with no pastoral oversight.[25]

Hart's entries during the week of Tuesday, August 20, to Monday, August 26, indicate something of the frequency and character of these private meetings. On Tuesday night, Hart sat at his desk at ten o'clock, still exhilarated by the events of the day. "Blessed be God who hath now brought me through another Day, and supplied all my Wants therein: and gave me an Opportunity this Evening of Expounding to several Young people, Who came to my House."[26] Hart took great pains to accurately diagnose the spiritual condition of each of his people, and on this Tuesday evening, he believed many of his young charges had entered the earliest stages of the conversion process. "I believe that some of them are under some Awakening: Oh! May the Lord Carry on his Work in their Hearts; may Conviction End in Conversion, and may none of those Awakened turn back again."[27]

On Wednesday, Hart delivered his regular Bible lecture. Alluding to Revelation 3:18, he prayed, "Lord give us all that white Raiment, that our Souls may be Cloathed therewith!" Afterward, a large number of people assembled at a Mrs. Baker's house to listen to Hart expound another portion of scripture. "May the Lord Bless these our Weak Endeavors to serve him! And may something be done in these Societies, to his Glory," Hart prayed. While Hart reveled in the pace of the revival ministry, it also took a physical toll on him. "I feel myself a little indispos'd in Body," he confessed. Yet in the heat of revival, Hart even turned sickness and fatigue to spiritual profit: "Oh may I be prepared for my Dissolution; and may I live in a habitual preparation for Death!" The next night, Hart reported another private meeting before retiring for the night. "Blessed be God who hath brought me to the Winding up of Another Day; and for all his Mercies Conferr'd upon me therein; and particularly for an Opportunity of Expounding this evening," he wrote. Friday was also eventful. "I find when God gives me a Heart to Work for him, he also finds me Work to do," he wrote. Hart was leading the kind of spiritual awakening he had previously read and dreamed about. "Lord give me the Wisdom which is from above! That I may teach my people thy fear. Blessed be God! I have more Reason to believe that some of our Young people are Concerned for their Souls, and it may be that the Revival may prove to be more Extensive than first Expected. Lord grant that many may be Awakened to a sense of their Misery, and Enabled to fly to the Rock of Ages for Refuge."[28]

On Saturday, Hart secluded himself in his study to prepare Sunday's messages. The constant preaching from the previous week had totally depleted him. "Spent this Day in my Study; with a View to make some preparations for the Sabbath; but found myself quite Empty: and Could scarce rise upon any Subject for my meditation." Hart took this occasion of weakness to turn to God. "Blessed be God! My Hope is in him. Tho' I am empty, he is full, and I hope to be fill'd out of that fullness which filleth all, and in all." On Sunday, after preaching two sermons to the church, Hart recorded, "In the Evening had my House Crowded, mostly with Young People, who came to hear me Expound, which the Lord Enabled me to do with a good degree of Freedom; many were Affected: Blessed be God the work among our young people seems to go on gloriously!" Monday found Hart again following up with awakened individuals, conversing with "several under Soul Trouble" and concluding that they were "in a fine way."[29] Hart's record of these private meetings provide further evidence of his enthusiastic participation in the Great Awakening. The conferences Hart arranged show his industry in promoting revival as well as his awareness of the practice in other places throughout America, England, and beyond.

The sharing of personal conversion stories played a prominent role in the Northampton revival. Early on, a notorious young woman, "one of the greatest company-keepers in town," experienced the new birth. Edwards wrote that "God made it, I suppose, the greatest occasion of awakening to others, of anything that ever came to pass in the town. . . . The news of it seemed to be almost like a flash of lightning, upon the hearts of young people all over the town, and upon many others." As the revival gathered momentum, it became common for the people of Northampton to share their spiritual experiences with one another. Critics of the revival lampooned this practice. Timothy Cutler (1684–1765) sneered in a 1735 letter, "The Calvinistic scheme is in perfection about 100 miles from this place. Conversions are talked of, *ad nauseum usque*. Sixty in a place undergo the work at once. Sadness and horror seize them, and hold them for some days; then they feel an inward joy, and it first shows itself in laughing at meeting. Others are sad for want of experiencing this work; and this takes up for the present the thoughts and talk of that country; and the canting question trumped about it, 'Are you gone through?' i.e. conversion." These charges of enthusiasm did not deter Edwards, who maintained that "it has been a practice which, in the general, has been attended with many good effects, and what God has greatly blessed among us." Indeed, the sharing of one's conversion story became a staple of the evangelical movement.[30]

Hart also promoted the use of personal testimonies in the Charleston revival. On one night when a group of young people had gathered at his home, he recalled that "it pleased God to manifest his love to Miss 'S. R.'" Hart compared the young lady's immediate expression of her experience to a fountain overflowing. "She was so full [of God's love] she could not help discovering of it to all present." Vocalizing one's testimony became an important mark of an authentic, inner work of salvation. Early evangelicals identified the young woman's experience with Paul's description in Romans 5:6 of "the love of God . . . shed abroad in our hearts by the Holy Ghost which is given unto us." This experience was epitomized in John Wesley's famous Aldersgate experience, when he reported, "I felt my heart strangely warmed," and moments later "testified openly to all there what I now first felt in my heart." Like Wesley and countless other evangelicals during the Great Awakening, Miss S. R. "could not help discovering" the saving change in her heart to the people around her.[31]

The most detailed example of testimony in Hart's diary comes on September 5, 1754. On this night, Hart conversed with several young people, "some of whom now have their Mouths open to Speak for God, and can freely tell what he hath done for them." One of these was Margaret Mageay, a young woman who had lived with the Harts, apparently as a servant, for almost two years. After laboring "under some considerable concern of soul," Margaret informed Hart she had finally "got comfortable last night." As Hart interviewed Margaret, he found "her able to give a Clear Account how the Lord Manifested himself to her Last Night." Critical in her experience was the remembrance of a scripture verse: "She had these Words, I have Loved Thee with an Everlasting Love, [Jeremiah 31:3] set home with so much Light, and Evidence, that she could not avoid taking Comfort from them." Margaret thus derived the assurance of her salvation from both objective and subjective sources. Objectively, she trusted not in inner voices supplying "new revelations" but in the unchanging promises of God recorded in the Bible. At the same time, the Holy

Spirit personally "set home" these promises to her heart "with so much Light, and Evidence" that she "could not avoid taking Comfort from them." No longer did she merely assent that the promises were true in a general sense; she now leaned on these promises as true for her. This was the personal element Wesley had famously emphasized in his testimony: "I felt I did trust Christ, Christ alone for salvation; and an assurance was given me that he had taken away *my* sins, even *mine*, and saved *me* from the law of sin and death." Margaret's conversion testimony followed the same pattern that Edwards had frequently observed within his congregation at Northampton, where "there is often in the mind some particular text of Scripture, holding forth some evangelical ground of consolation; sometimes in a multitude of texts, gracious invitations and promises flooding in one after another, filling the soul more and more with comfort and satisfaction." As Margaret personally believed God's promises, she became "Serene and Comfortable," and "in a Humble and Holy frame of Soul."[32]

David Bebbington has identified this immediate sense of assurance upon conversion as a new feature of the evangelical movement, the decisive point of discontinuity with all previous manifestations of Protestant spirituality. When evangelical pastors like Edwards and Hart interviewed hopeful converts, they did not follow their Puritan forbears and "encourage them to wrestle through their own doubts and fears over a protracted period," in Bebbington's words. Instead, "if [they] were satisfied that they had been truly converted, [they] assured them that they were real Christians." Bebbington attributes this shift to the influence of Enlightenment epistemology, which gave Christians such as Edwards, Wesley, and Hart a heretofore unknown confidence in the powers of human knowledge. The new believer need not slog through an agonizing season of spiritual insecurity as John Bunyan (1628–88) had in a previous generation; they could know they had been saved.[33] Whether or not one accepts all of Bebbington's claims regarding evangelicals and the Enlightenment, it is clear enough that the doctrine of assurance underwent some transformation in the shift from the Puritan or scholastic era to the era of Pietism or Evangelicalism. Hart's diary demonstrates his participation in this important transition.

While Hart conferenced with Margaret, five more young women entered the room, also "under some Awakenings." Like a spiritual midwife, Hart acted to assist in the new birth process he believed to be taking place in them. But rather than exhort them with the gospel himself, Hart instead relied upon the personal testimony of their peer, Margaret. He asked Margaret "if she could not now tell what God had done for her." She eagerly complied. "Oh yes sir said she, I could now speak for God if the world was to hear; for I now have felt his Love and know that he hath Loved me with an Everlasting Love; Oh! What a night had I last night! What a sweet night! And then Turning herself to one of the Young Women, Oh Miss Betsy! Said she, Jesus Christ is Sweet, he is precious, had I known his Sweetness, said she,

I would not have liv'd so long without him; and then turning herself to another, said, Oh, Oh! Miss Nancy, Christ is Sweet! And since he hath had Mercy on such a vile Wretched Sinner as me, I am sure none need ever to Despair, Oh! Come to Christ! Come to Christ!'" After Margaret's testimony, the other young women were "much Affected," and "Could no Longer Contain but Crying out, got up and went out of the house to Vent their grief."[34] As at Northampton, the personal testimonies in Charleston not only served as valuable evidence of personal conversion but also as an effective means of evangelism. Moreover, this selection of Hart's diaries shows how something of the egalitarian impulse of the evangelical revival broke through to the Charleston Baptists in 1754. Hart was happy to hold up Margaret, a young lady who seems also to have been a slave in his home, as a model of piety and a spokesperson for the new birth. Of course, it was an egalitarianism within limits: Margaret's exhortations were confined to other females, in the privacy of the Hart home, and under the supervision of her white male pastor. Nevertheless, Margaret discovered that night what so many women did over the course of the eighteenth-century awakenings, that the experience of evangelical religion offered her a voice in her community otherwise unthinkable.

At the center of the Great Awakening was a renewed emphasis on "experiential religion." Some of the emotional displays in the revival, such as weeping and groaning, drew derision from antirevivalist detractors who viewed these displays as antinomian "enthusiasm." While recognizing the danger of excesses, Edwards perceived that blanket denunciations of the revival were rooted in a cold, formal view of Christianity. Contesting this perspective, Edwards contended that God had made the affections "the spring of men's actions." Therefore, when God renewed a man in the new birth, he began here, so that "true religion must consist very much in its affections."[35] Hart's 1754 diary provides an extended account of the awakened affections of the Charleston Baptist Church. This began with Hart himself, who is anything but stoic in the pages of his diary. Characteristic of the narrative are selections like the following: "Oh! may the Mercies of this Evening be Writ for a memorial upon my very Heart! I had such a sence of God's Goodness, Love, and Mercy to me in every respect, that I had almost said, Lord it is Enough; hold thy Hand. And is all this possible! Is it Really so! Lord, why me! Why me! Not unto us, not unto us O Lord, but unto thy name be all the Praise!" Rather than sounding like the stereotypical Regular Baptist who stood aloof from the revival, Hart's diary entries could have been lifted directly from George Whitefield's *Journals*.[36]

The youth of the Charleston congregation also exhibited deep emotion on either side of the conversion experience. One night, a group of young men arrived at Hart's house "deeply Concerned to Discourse with [him] about their Souls' Affairs." As Hart drew the boys into conversation, the impromptu visit developed into a full-scale revival meeting. "But oh, what an Evening we had!" Hart wrote, "Some Complained, and Cry'd out under a Sence of the Desperate Wickedness & Corruption of their own Hearts: of which they had such a Deep sense, that they seemed to Study to find out such words to express themselves Concerning it, as might set it forth in the strongest Terms.—Some were Crying out under a sense of sin; never were such a Company of great Sinners met together in the world, if they themselves might be Judges; but the most of them were Crying out for Jesus Christ; Oh give me Christ! Give me Christ! Oh if I had but Christ!" Desperate for relief, the young men turned to those who had already "come through" in conversion to "help them to Christ." They were in pitiful condition, but Hart hoped it indicated their sincerity. Soon, they could only express themselves in the kinds of inarticulate moans toward God that Edwards had witnessed in Northampton. Hart interpreted this as the birth pains of a new creation. "Oh! the Groans and Sighs of these poor creatures; which coming from the Heart, penetrated Heaven's Gates, and I doubt not, Entred into the Ears of the Lord God of Sabbaoth: Lord hear their Cries! And give them a sence of their Interest in thy Love; for thy Son's sake Amen!"[37]

On the other side of the new birth, converts demonstrated genuine faith by their affectionate sense of God's love for them in Christ. Margaret described her conversion as having finally "got comfortable." "Sweetness" had been a favorite descriptor of religious experience for both Edwards and Whitefield; Abigail Hutcheson declared in *A Faithful Narrative*, "I am brimful of a sweet feeling within!" Similar statements appear frequently on the lips of new converts in Hart's diary. After his spiritual travail, Samuel Stillman informed Hart that "he had now got Christ and felt the sweetness of his Love." A young man named "K B" cried out, "Oh . . . Jesus Christ is sweet!" Hart also wrote that God "broke in with Light, Power, and Sweetness, upon the Heart of a poor Young Creature (Miss Nancy K) who had been for some time past under Deep Convictions. But now she is Triumphing in Almighty Grace!" These Regular Baptists were no strangers to the powerful affections of the evangelical revival.[38]

The "moderate revivalists" of Hart's day hailed the evangelical awakening as a genuine outpouring of the Holy Spirit, while also recognizing much dross mixed in with the movement. Jonathan Dickinson (1688–1747) offered one voice of cautious enthusiasm in his *Display of God's Special Grace* (1742). But the moderate revivalist par excellence was surely Edwards, who applied his unsurpassed intellect to analyzing the difference between true and false works of the Spirit of God. At the height of the Great Awakening, Edwards penned three works designed to shepherd the revival movement: *The Distinguishing Marks of a Work of the Spirit of God* (1741), *Thoughts on the Revival of Religion in New England* (1742), and his magisterial *Treatise Concerning Religious Affections* (1746). Edwards believed pastoral discernment between true and false signs of revival to be of the utmost importance in what he called "this extraordinary day, when that which is so remarkable appears; such an uncommon operation on the minds of people, that is so extensive; and there is such a variety of opinions concerning it, and so much talk about the work of the Spirit." For all his excitement over the Spirit's work in his congregation, Hart's diary indicates that he shared the concerns of the moderate revivalists. Throughout the fall of 1754, Hart remained cognizant of the possibility of spiritual deception during days of heightened religious excitement. Consider the caution in a diary entry from September 1, the very beginning of the movement. "Many seem now to be under Soul Concern. there are some appearances of new ones Touch'd almost Every Evening. Lord grant that Abortions may be prevented! May all these under Concern, be Really Born again! Amen!" Like Edwards, Hart bore the responsibility to interpret the otherworldly events that were turning his community upside down.[39]

Hart's first step in guarding against counterfeit revival was to carefully interview each individual who professed conversion. On September 17, at a full society meeting of attentive young people, Hart "examined Each one of them in particular, and most of them Wept much." Afterward he prayed, "Oh that they may have true Repentance, even a Repentance which need not be Repented of." Again, on September 22, Hart reported conversing with two young girls about twelve years old, and receiving "much Comfort and Satisfaction" from the conversation. "Believe God hath begun a Work of Grace in their Hearts: and hope he will give them to Evidence it by their Lives," he wrote. It was earlier noted that Hart was more open to granting immediate assurance to his converts than previous generations of Puritan pastors had been. Here, it is equally evident that the assurance Hart offered to new believers was not glib or unqualified. He still took a "wait-and-see" attitude with those who professed faith. Hart rejoiced over any indications of new spiritual life, but he always spoke guardedly about his "hope" that his interviewees had been truly "brought clear." He was pleased after hearing some of them pray in public, but he was still concerned about the authenticity of their devotion. He prayed, "Lord grant they may be Influenced by a principle of Love to thee!"[40]

Secret prayer was another essential means of guarding his people from deception. In the privacy of his study, Hart prayed for the preservation and perseverance of the new believers. After noting that some of the young people had met without him, he added, "Oh, may they continue in the Good ways of the Lord, to their Lives' End; I dread the thoughts of their going back, or giving up. Lord! Forbid that this Should be the Case of any of them." As the revival gathered momentum, he soberly prayed that convictions might "never wear off, till they End in a Saving Conversion to thee." On August 30, he recorded the reported conversions of two more young people. This meant he had "hope now that six persons are brought clear" and several others were still wrestling with God. Hart immediately committed these individuals to God in prayer. "God Grant that not one of these your Creatures may be Deceived;

if one Soul of them should Miscarry, it would be bad; but if it should all prove a Delusion, the Lord pity us! for it would be an Awful Case Indeed," he prayed. Hart believed he was witnessing a genuine work of God's Spirit, but he also confessed that he was "afraid of Spiritual Pride." So he continued, "I cannot preswade myself as Yet to think so, but if it should I hope the Lord will prevent its progress; but if it is his Work as I hope and believe it is, Lord Carry it on and Increase it for Thy Name's sake; & for Jesus' sake Amen & Amen. And may the Good Lord keep me truly humble under such Honours Conferr'd upon me."[41]

Even when he was diligent to interview and pray for new converts, Hart still could not shake the fear that there could be "too much of delusion in this Work going on. If this should be the case, that Satan Should have a Hand in it, it would be Dreadful." Hart decided to consult with an outside source. He took his concerns to one "Mr. Moody, a good Old Disciple of Jesus Christ." Hart gave Moody "as particular an account of the Manner how so the Work was begun; and Carried on, as I was Able; and Desired his Opinion Concerning it." Moody told Hart "not to be Discourag'd; but to Wait, and time would Discover how it was; but he thought, he had seen nothing in it but what might be look'd upon with a favourable Aspect, and as proceeding from the Motions of the Spirit of God. Only says he, when God Works, the Devil will Work too, and you need not wonder if all don't turn out Right." The two were then joined by Swiss-born Reformed minister John J. Zubly (1724–81), who supported Moody's counsel. This eased Hart's mind. Having "Receiv'd some Necessary Cautions, and Directions from this precious Old Disciple of Jesus Ct.," Hart returned home "with [his] Hopes somewhat Strengthened."[42]

The converts received a final inspection from Hart upon their baptisms. Before making his or her faith public, each candidate met with Hart to give an updated account of his or her soul. Thus, in a meeting with Samuel Stillman and the girl Margaret, Hart concluded that both "gave Indubuitable Evidences of a Work of Grace begun, and carrying on in their hearts," though they were still deficient in "Doctrinal Knowledge." Hart scheduled a baptism for October 10, when he and the majority of the church crossed over the Ashley River to the home of Mr. Screven. There, Hart publicly examined ten young people who all "gave very good satisfaction: and most of them Spoke Surprisingly of what God had done for their Souls." Hart then "baptized them according to the primitive Mode" and the work was done.[43]

Hart may never have intended for his 1754 diary to be read, but its preservation is a great boon for historians. First, it clarifies our understanding of Hart's own spirituality, demonstrating how deeply his religious values were shaped by the Great Awakening and especially by revival narratives. More broadly, Hart's diary also helps us appreciate the pervasive influence of the Great Awakening, showing how the evangelical revival reached into the lower South in the 1750s. The Charleston

Baptists' small-scale revival should be considered one of the many "important, widespread revivals" that occurred during the "long great awakening" through the eighteenth century. Finally, Hart's diary sheds further light on the spirituality of the Regular Baptists of the colonial South, providing further evidence that Regular Baptists participated in the Great Awakening to a greater degree than is usually acknowledged. The significance of this finding is further seen when one considers that the Separate Baptists, typically credited as those "who brought revival to the South and laid the foundations for the Baptist denomination in that region," did not arrive in Sandy Creek, North Carolina, until the year 1755.[44]

CHAPTER 4

Revival Activism

Two clipped sentences from Oliver Hart's diary in 1754 perfectly capture the ethos of his spirituality: "Find my Self in a good State of Bodily Health. Lord may I lay out my Strength for thee!" As this brief memorandum indicates, Hart's piety was on the move. As he saw it, God had given him physical health and strength in order to spend it, to "lay it out" in a life of service. Hart even employed the discipline of diary keeping, generally associated with calm self-reflection, to describe the work he had done and hoped to do. Hart's personal writings reveal his unrelenting drive to be ever more "active" and "useful" for God. While earlier Christian traditions obviously contained activist elements, early Protestant evangelicals gave activism a unique place of prominence in their spirituality. This impulse is exemplified in Hart's hero, George Whitefield. Whitefield was a force of nature, preaching an estimated eighteen thousand sermons over his lifetime, crisscrossing the Atlantic Ocean thirteen times, raising support for his Bethesda Orphanage in the colony of Georgia, maintaining a massive correspondence with the great and the small, and generally holding together a transcontinental, transdenominational revival movement comprise just a sampling of his historic activism. "Keep me travelling, keep me working, or at least beginning to begin to work for thee, till I die," he prayed. This pattern of strenuous Christian service left an indelible mark on Hart's own ministry. While Regular Baptists are today portrayed as lagging behind their energetic Separate Baptist counterparts during the eighteenth century, Hart's story demonstrates that many Regulars also labored to advance the gospel with great zeal.[1]

Hart reflected on the active Christian life in *An Humble Attempt to Repair the Christian Temple*, a sermon preached before the Philadelphia Baptist Association on October 21, 1783. He selected Haggai 2:4 for his text, "Yet now be strong, O Zerubbabel, saith the Lord, and be strong, O Joshua, son of Josedech the high priest, and be strong all the people of the land, saith the Lord, and work; for I am with you, saith the Lord of hosts." Hart opened the sermon by lambasting the widespread problem of "lukewarmness and indifferency in religion." He viewed spiritual apathy as the church's great enemy, "injurious to the best cause in the world, contrary to the spirit of Christianity, and highly provoking to the King of saints." Hart cited Christ's rebuke of the church at Ephesus for "losing its first love" and to the church at

Laodicea for being "lukewarm, and neither cold nor hot." He then turned sharply on the messengers of the association. "And are not some of our churches equally reprehensible? Have not most of them lost their first love? Are not ministers and people become too remiss? Alas! Where is our flaming love, burning zeal and assiduity in religion?" And yet there was hope of recovery, which led him to the heart of his message. "The gospel means of revival are still in our hands. Let us then rouse from our lethargy: gird on our strength, and work vigorously in repairing the Christian Temple, which through sloth and negligence is too much gone to decay." Hart identified vigorous activism as the answer to the church's woes and as the key to revival. Just as all the Jews in Haggai's day helped build the Temple, Hart believed "even so should Christians of all ranks and characters, labor in building up the church of Jesus Christ. Every one has a work to do; none should be idle."Hart drew upon military imagery that must have carried special force in Revolutionary Philadelphia:

> The Lord will have no three months, nor three years men employed in his service. All these artificers should enlist for life, and constantly persevere in the work till disabled by death. Some who have engaged in this service, have grown weary of it, and given up. Others, on account of some difficulties, have slunk away, like cowards, and deserted the cause. Many, upon finding that building the Christian temple might interfere with their ease, health, interest, or reputation, have given over, and left the work to other hands. Blessed be God, all are not of this stamp. Christ hath still some faithful servants left, who adhere firmly to the work assigned them. Should we say unto such, as Jesus said unto the twelve, "Will ye also go away?" each one would answer, "God forbid! Lord, to whom should we go. I love my Master—I love his work. Let him bore mine ear through with an awl, for I will serve him forever."[2]

Hart's message in *An Humble Attempt* matches the spirit in which he lived his own Christian life. This chapter will explore five arenas in which Hart applied his spiritual activism: evangelism, gospel partnerships, education, politics, and slavery.

Writing to Samuel Jones on December 1, 1763, Hart prayed what he considered the ultimate blessing on his friend's ministry: "May you be made wise to win Souls, and may you have many to be your Joy and Crown!" Communicating the gospel to unbelievers with the aim of seeing them converted lay at the center of Hart's ministry. Early in his time at Charleston, he expressed his passion for evangelism in a letter home to his father. "I am still trying to Labour for God as enabled, but find I come Short of that engagedness which I could Desire," he confessed. "Souls are precious Otherwise the Lord would not have done so much for their Salvation as he has done: and can I trifle with them? God forbid! I would fain be made Instrumental in bringing many Souls home to Jesus Christ." As we have already seen, the conversion of sinners was Hart's paramount concern in his weekly preaching ministry. Hart believed that the "grand design" of preaching was "to save sinners, of Adam's race, from eternal misery, in a way consistent with the claims of the violated law, and the honor of the divine perfections and government." The story of Edmund Botsford's conversion supplies a window into the gravity with which Hart proclaimed the gospel from his Charleston pulpit.[3]

Hart also promoted the gospel outside formal church gatherings. He preached to local military personnel, as on July 17, 1757, when he addressed "Col. Boquet's regiment of soldiers in Nightengales Pasture." On other occasions, Hart carried the gospel to condemned prisoners. On July 22, 1777, a young soldier called Malcolm had been sentenced to die for deserting the American troops. Hart, dressed in his gown and bands, went to the military barracks to visit Malcolm and two other soldiers, where he "conversed and prayed with them" for some time. Afterward, Hart walked with them to the scaffold. He "conversed with them all the way," speaking to Malcolm over the noise of fife and drums. Despite his best efforts, Hart "discovered but little signs of penitence in either of them." Still, Hart accompanied Malcolm to the place of execution, where he prayed with him again and said farewell. When one of Malcolm's commanding officers addressed him a final time, the young soldier called for Hart. Though Hart suspected that "all he wanted was to protract time," he prayed with him once more, and then watched in sorrow as Malcolm was shot before the firing squad.[4]

Hart also strove to commend the gospel in the course of ordinary life, a theme he explored in a 1759 ordination charge. He urged ministers to "walk Sircumspectly, not as Fools, but as Wise," in the community, recognizing that they lived "in the midst of a censorious world." Hart knew that unbelievers scrutinized his conduct, searching for a reason to condemn him and the message he preached. To promote the gospel in such an environment required "the Wisdom of the Serpent, tempered with the Innocense of the Dove," so as to give "no just occasion for offense." Hart called the young men to pursue a "Uniformity of Conduct" at home, in the church, and before the world. Yet they must also be discrete enough to suit their behavior to "Time, Place, and Sircumstances." He recommended that they be "grave, but not sullen, or morose; you may be cheerful, but not light or vain. You will be happy if you can so conduct as to be respected, and yet rever'd." Secular business dealings represented a potential snare for the minister, and Hart advised them to "act a just and upright Part, doing to all, as you would they should do to you." Even casual conversation should serve the gospel. "Let your Speech at all times be seasoned, as that it may minister Grace to the Hearers. Be neither too open, nor too reserved in Conversation, but labour to find out the happy Medium. A loquacious Disposition is attended with many disadvantages; therefore be more ready to hear than to give the Sacrifice of Fools," he warned. "And yet, when you can speak to advantage, especially if an opportunity offers to speak for God; by no Means be Silent."[5]

Hart's evangelistic passion regularly drove him beyond his own community. He maintained a steady itinerant preaching schedule, sometimes travelling far from home for extended periods of time. On January 19, 1756, Hart left Charleston to seek a missionary for the association and did not return home until November 4, 1756. Hart preached throughout the middle colonies on this journey, apparently to good success. He told his father, "I believe the Lord hath Owned my poor Labours while in Pennsylvania, and the Jerseys: I have received several Letters, giving me some encouraging accounts of Something being done by such an unworthy instrument while there; may all the Praise be to him to whom alone it is Due." Reports of shorter missionary excursions pepper his diaries. Hezekiah Smith mentioned Hart accompanying him on a tour of some of the communities near Charleston in the spring of 1763. From November 1769 through February 1770, Hart and Evan Pugh preached through North Carolina and Virginia. Hart even used his flight from Charleston in the spring of 1780 to spread the gospel, stopping to preach in places like Stone River in North Carolina; in Fauquier Country and Leesburg, Virginia; and in Frederick Town and Baltimore, Maryland. Still, he wrote on his fifty-seventh birthday, "through Mercy am in good Health, but am ashamed that I have lived so long to so little Purpose, and sorry that I am now in no way of Usefulness."[6]

One of the clearest proofs of Hart's evangelistic priorities is his ongoing partnership with George Whitefield during the years 1750–70. Three separate sources link the two ministers during this period. The first is John Gano, who came to Charleston on a missionary tour in the spring of 1755. As was typical of his practice with visiting preachers, Hart offered Gano his pulpit. It proved to be an unforgettable invitation for the young missionary. Hart spread word among the people that Gano was to preach, and a crowd soon assembled at the Baptist meetinghouse. Gano remembered that he "went, with my tattered garb on; and when I rose to speak, the sight of so numerous and brilliant an audience (among whom were twelve ministers, and one of whom was Mr. Whitefield), for a moment, brought the fear of man on me." Gano eventually summoned his courage and delivered the kind of stirring message that came to characterize his long ministry. The incident not only supplies a fascinating anecdote from Baptist lore but also shows Whitefield worshiping at Hart's Regular Baptist meetinghouse in Charleston in 1755, further identifying Hart and the Charleston Baptists with the eighteenth-century colonial revival at a much earlier date than historians have been prepared to acknowledge.[7]

The second source linking Hart and Whitefield is a letter from Whitefield's hand, from the same period as the Gano incident. A female correspondent, "Mrs. C.," had solicited Whitefield for spiritual counsel after hearing him preach. On March 3, 1755, Whitefield responded by commending her to Hart's pastoral care: "I would have you write to Mr. [Hart] by the bearer, who is an experimental Baptist preacher from the northward. O that he may say something, that may do my dear family some good."

Whitefield's recommendation of Hart stands as a strong proof of the evangelical character of Hart's ministry in Charleston and the lowcountry South.[8]

Whitefield likely maintained regular contact with Hart whenever he passed through Charleston in the years that followed. A collaboration in ministry near the end of Whitefield's life proved to be their most fruitful. On March 4, 1770, Whitefield preached in Charleston for the last time. On this occasion, a former slave named John Marrant wandered up, planning with a friend to disrupt the meeting by blowing a French horn. Instead, the scoffer experienced deep conviction under Whitefield's message. Marrant fell to the ground, unable to move. He was carried to the vestry where Whitefield later visited him, saying, "Jesus Christ has got thee at last." Marrant was then transported home and committed to a sickbed. Before Whitefield left Charleston, he first asked Hart to call on Marrant. Marrant recalled that Hart walked upstairs and entered his room, increasing his sense of distress. Hart tried to take hold of Marrant's hand for prayer, but Marrant escaped to the other side of the bed. Yet in his weakened state, Marrant collapsed from the effort. Hart immediately moved in, taking Marrant by the hand, raising him to his feet, and addressing him warmly about his soul. When Hart was ready to pray for Marrant's conversion, he fell on his knees, pulling Marrant down with him. After several minutes of fervent prayer, Hart stood up and asked Marrant "how he now did." Marrant's reply that he felt "much worse" did not deter Hart in the slightest. "Come, we will have the old thing over again," Hart said, and he again pulled Marrant down to kneel with him. After several more minutes of earnest prayer, Hart again asked Marrant, "How do you do now?" Marrant feebly cried, "Worse and worse" and he asked Hart "if he intended to kill [him]." Still, Hart was not discouraged. "No, no," he replied, "you are worth a thousand dead men, let us try the old thing over again." For a third time, Hart and Marrant fell on their knees to pray but this time with a different result. "Near the close of his prayer," Marrant remembered, "the Lord was pleased to set my soul at perfect liberty, and being filled with joy I began to praise the Lord immediately; my sorrows were turned into peace, and joy, and love." Hart asked a final time, "How is it now?" and Marrant answered, "All is well, all happy." Hart visited Marrant every day for the next several days, exhorting him on their last visit to "hold fast what thou has already obtained, 'till Jesus Christ come." Whitefield died six months later in Newburyport, Massachusetts, but his life's work lived on in Marrant. He travelled to England where, in 1785, he received ordination at the Countess of Huntingdon's Bath Chapel, and then he carried the gospel to a black Loyalist community in Nova Scotia. His published narrative of his life saw some fifteen editions.[9]

Regular Baptists are sometimes caricatured as lacking evangelistic zeal in comparison to the Separate Baptists. Certainly, Regular Baptists cannot claim the dramatic results that the Separates enjoyed on the rapidly expanding southern frontier in the late colonial period. After the American Revolution, Hart marveled at their success. "It should seem as if the Trees had become Men and them Men Baptists. This is the Lord's doing, and it is marvelous in our Eyes!" he exclaimed to Furman in 1793. "Little did I think when Brother [Pugh] and I travelled through that Wilderness in so solitary a Manner, that so great a Change would have taken place in so short a space of time, if ever." Yet Hart's ministry demonstrates that the charge of insularity cannot be substantiated against the Regulars as a whole, particularly not in the lower South. Along with dedicated Regular Baptist evangelists like Jenkin Jones, Isaac Chanler, John Gano, Hezekiah Smith, and Edmund Botsford, Hart was one of many Regulars who celebrated and participated in the fervor to spread the gospel created by the Great Awakening.[10]

Hart's activist legacy cannot be measured by his own individual achievements; Hart's greatest contribution was his unsurpassed skill at forming gospel partnerships, the fruit of which endured far beyond his lifetime. It is Hart's legacy of relentlessly promoting cooperative ministry among Baptists in the colonial South that qualifies him as "Southern Baptists' most important pioneer." When Hart moved to Charleston in December 1749, he found that very little organization existed among the Baptist churches in the region. Of the four Regular Baptist congregations then in South Carolina, three were in fragile condition. The Charleston Church had just weathered a tumultuous decade without a minister and with dwindling numbers. The Ashley Ferry congregation had suddenly found itself without its capable pastor upon the death of Isaac Chanler. The Euhaw Baptist Church had existed with no regular minister since 1744, relying solely on Chanler's occasional services, and the ministry of a "probationer," a lay preacher named Francis Pelot. Further inland, the Welsh Neck Baptist Church had two ministers, Phillip James, assisted by John Brown (1714–90?). Yet on the banks of the Pee Dee River, this congregation of Welsh immigrants remained disconnected from the other Regular Baptist churches in the region.[11]

Hart worked quickly to strengthen these churches. Within months of landing in Charleston, he helped Ashley Ferry to secure the services of John Stephens from the Philadelphia Association. Hart recorded Stephens's arrival in his personal diary, preached Stephens's installation sermon on June 1, 1750, and immediately began to work with him in the regional Baptist cause. Hart was also responsible for the acquisition of Euhaw Church's pastor. Their lay preacher, Pelot, had shrunk from ordination for several years, but Hart convinced him to commit. Hart remembered that Pelot "continued as a candidate (resisting, through modesty and self diffidence many solicitations to ordination)," until Hart's own arguments finally won him over. On Monday, January 13, 1752, Hart preached Pelot's ordination service assisted by Stephens. He exhorted Pelot with Christ's sober words in Matthew 10:16, "Behold, I send you forth as sheep in the midst of wolves. Be ye therefore wise as serpents and harmless as doves," and reported that "many attended the solemnity and in general they were much affected."[12]

As Hart connected these individual churches with able ministers, he was also working toward a bigger vision. Baptists insisted on the autonomy of the local congregation: no pope, bishop, or any ecclesial structure could supplant the authority of Jesus Christ ruling over an individual congregation through his Word. At the same time, the churches in the Philadelphia Association in which Hart grew up also recognized the value of those autonomous congregations voluntarily uniting for cooperative ministry. By 1749, Hart's last year in Pennsylvania, the Philadelphia Association had developed a detailed philosophy of associational life, outlined in Benjamin Griffith's essay, "the Powers and Duties of an Association." When the messengers voted to adopt Griffith's essay, Hart was there to affix his signature in approval. He was eager to replicate this associational model from the moment he arrived in Charleston. Soon after Stephens settled at Ashley Ferry, and while Pelot still considered the call at Euhaw, Hart acted to unite the Regular Baptist churches of the eighteenth century colonial South. He invited the churches at Ashley River, Euhaw, and Welsh Neck to send messengers to Charleston on October 21, 1751. Delegates from Ashley River, Welsh Neck, and Charleston met as scheduled, but Euhaw's messengers were hindered by flooding. Baptist historian Loulie L. Owens has correctly identified this gathering as "the most historic single event in Hart's ministry." No detailed report of the meeting remains, but among Hart's papers exists a written address outlining the benefits of an association. Church historian Robert A. Baker has plausibly argued that this must have been Hart's inaugural address at the Charleston Association. Whenever Hart may have delivered this message, its contents reveal Hart's vision for the association. He focused on six main responsibilities.[13]

First, the association must endeavor to mediate disagreements. Divisions inevitably arise among the most sincere Christian believers, and some disputes will require outside mediators. The association should view the opportunity to heal breaches between a pastor and people, between feuding church members, or even between sister congregations, as both a duty and a privilege. "While there is a Woe denounced against those by whom [the divisions] do come; so on the other Hand there is a Blessing exhibited for all the Peace-Makers. And it is certainly the business of an Association to study, and prosecute, the things which make for Peace," Hart preached. The association should also oppose false doctrine. Hart noted this to be the main purpose of the Jerusalem Council of Acts chapter 15. The first-century church had there confronted the "Judaizing heresy," a divisive teaching that non-Jewish Christians must also keep Jewish ceremonial law in order to be saved. Early church leaders like the apostle Paul had recognized that the Judaizing doctrine was "like to spread to the detriment of the Churches, and the wounding of the cause of

Ct." Thus, the Antioch church sent Paul and another early leader named Barnabas to meet with the apostles and elders at Jerusalem to address the issue. Through these messengers, the church officially ruled against the Judaizers and afterward alerted the churches of their decision by letter. Hart believed that the Jerusalem Council established a biblical precedent for the South Carolina churches to form an association. "If such Care and Pains were taken in the purest Age of Christianity, to prevent the progress of false Doctrine," Hart reasoned, "ought not we also to exert ourselves in the same as being the most likely way to answer so good a Design? If we act wisely, no doubt we Shall."[14]

The association was also obligated to identify false preachers in the area. In this day of limited communication, it was not uncommon for a stranger to appear claiming to be a minister while concealing an immoral lifestyle or heretical beliefs. An infamous example of the time is that of Desolate Baker (1694–1778). Baker immigrated to the American colonies from England under the assumed name of "Henry Loveall." Baker had adopted the alias to hide his checkered past: he had run away from his master, committed bigamy, and engaged in sexual relations with black and Indian women, ultimately contracting syphilis. Nathaniel Jenkins, minister of the Cohansey Baptist Church, commented that the "Loveall" moniker was "a very suitable name agreeable to his properties who loves so well the black, the swarthy, and the white so as to lie with them." Thinking of this and other examples, Hart warned that "there are too many, who run unsent; and who either by their irregular Conduct, corrupt Principles, or licentious Practices bring the holy Religion of Jesus into Contempt." He again appealed to the New Testament to substantiate his call to stand against false teachers, quoting Paul's adamant statement of Galatians 2:5 that "we gave place by subjection, no not for an hour, that the truth of the gospel might continue with you." Reflecting on the Bible's serious stance against false doctrine, Hart asked, "And ought not the truth of the gospel to be equally precious to us? No doubt! Therefore ought we with equal Zeal & Spirit to use our Endeavours to suppress all such unruly Pretenders." With its collective theological understanding and its network of communication, the association stood in a unique position to serve as a gatekeeper against impostor preachers.[15]

Next, the association should help churches solve "difficult Cases of Conscience." Problems often surfaced in congregations that had no clear-cut biblical solutions, ranging from technical matters regarding ministerial ordination to ethical questions about the marriage and divorce of members. When these complex questions arose, Hart asked, "What better Method can they then take than to apply to the association, who, there is Reason to believe, will be instructed by the Spirit of God, when thus particularly concerned in things relative to his Interests." Whenever called upon, the association should act to "relieve a distressed brother" and "ease a Wounded Conscience." Hart also called the association to look beyond the issues of their individual churches and to collectively "consider Affairs in general which relate to the Welfare of Zion." This concern for God's broader work in the world could, on occasion, lead the association to set apart days for humiliation or for thanksgiving. The association should also be concerned with the next generation of ministers, and should "conclude upon some Methods for educating, and trying the gifts, and honorably calling out Persons to the great Work of the Ministry." As the association became aware of needy churches, it should connect them with capable pastors, as the Philadelphia Association had done with Hart and the Charleston Baptist Church. The association might even find it necessary to appeal to the pastor of an established church to itinerate in a destitute area "when there is a greater Prospect of Usefulness in that way than in their own Charge." The association could also serve the broader church by sending out "Sircular Letters" informing churches "of their proceedings, and determinations, and to give such advice with regard to their Moral and Religious Conduct as is necessary."[16]

Finally, Hart urged the association to conduct its business with godly decorum. Hart foresaw the potential for disagreement within the assembly, and cautioned them "to be instant & fervent in Prayer, and to conduct with a gravity becoming those who are working for God and transacting Business for Eternity. To guard against a clamorous, contentious disposition; and by no Means to give Way to a Sprit of Anger or Revenge; but to adhere to their contrary Virtues, of Meekness, Patience, Humility and the like." Again, Hart looked to the Jerusalem Council of Acts 15 as his model. "While Peter is speaking all is hush'd. When he had finished speaking, the same attention is paid to the Speech of James," Hart said. "After this, tho' these seem to have been the chief speakers, what they had offered was weigh'd, and judiciously considered by the whole body, and the conclusion drawn accordingly.—A Pattern well worthy of imitation!"

The messengers embraced Hart's proposal. They committed to meet annually, convening on the Saturday before the second Sunday in November. The first two days of the meeting would be devoted to public worship, and the business of the association would commence with an introductory sermon on Monday morning at ten o'clock. These decisions were ratified at the next year's meeting, signed by Hart, Stephens, Pelot, John Brown, and Joshua Edwards (1703?–84), along with eight lay messengers. After meeting in Charleston for its first several years, the association eventually adopted that city's name. Hart served as its moderator in the years 1759, 1764, 1769, 1773, 1775, and 1778, and as clerk from 1752–57 and 1777. Uniting Baptist churches in the South through the establishment of the Charleston Association endures as Hart's most significant contribution to Baptist history. As Baptist historian Robert A. Baker observes, "There were other Baptists in this era who glimpsed the larger denominational fellowship involving the communion of the saints, but it was Hart who first initiated the movement in the South to put this grand design into structured form." Hart stands at the headwaters of southern Baptist denominational life. Today, the Southern Baptist Convention is the world's largest Protestant denomination, comprised of more than forty-six thousand churches and over fifteen million members.[17]

The Charleston Association provided Baptist churches in the colonial South with an important platform for cooperative missionary endeavors. By the early 1750s, the interior colonial territories of Virginia, North Carolina, and South Carolina had attracted an influx of many new settlers, creating an urgent need for gospel ministers in the area. The Philadelphia Association had already begun addressing this as early as 1752, when it sent Benjamin Miller and John Thomas on a short term mission to Virginia. They planned to visit a church Thomas had established on an earlier mission and administer the ordinances to them. The party also intended to bring reformation to a General Baptist church in the area that was left destitute after the moral failure of its pastor. They were to instruct the people in sound doctrine through Calvinistic preaching and also examine individuals for personal experiences of grace. They brought with them a young Baptist layman named John Gano. Gano had never been licensed to preach, but the trip afforded him several unplanned opportunities to exhort, instruct, and counsel, and Gano performed brilliantly at every turn. Yet when Gano returned to his home church in Hopewell, New Jersey, they called him to account for "irregular preaching." Gano related his story, insisting that "my own conscience acquitted me" and that he would do the same if placed in the same position again. Rather than discipline Gano, the church invited him to "exercise his gifts" before them. Gano again preached to such effect that the church immediately licensed him. Soon, Gano was supplying the pulpit at a Baptist church in Morristown, New Jersey. A significant event in Gano's brief ministry here was the conversion of Hezekiah Smith, who later became a friend of Hart and pastored the Haverhill, Massachusetts, Baptist Church for forty years.[18]

In the spring of 1754, the Philadelphia Association approached Gano about returning to Virginia for itinerate missionary work. On his first stop, Gano visited a group of General Baptist congregations in North Carolina and persuaded them to embrace the Calvinistic views of the Regular Baptists. These churches were eventually incorporated into the Philadelphia Association.[19] Gano then went further south to Ashley Ferry, where he preached for John Stephens. The congregation, comprised mostly of African American slaves, received Gano warmly. The slaves formed two lines outside the meetinghouse to thank Gano after the service, prompting Stephens to remark to Gano that he made "a very good Negro preacher." Gano later made it to Charleston, where Hart also opened his pulpit to him. This was the same occasion on which Gano preached to George Whitefield at the Charleston Baptist meetinghouse. Gano returned home in the fall of 1755, at which time he married Sarah Stites and resumed his ministry at Morristown.

Hart observed Gano's effective missionary service on the southern frontier with keen interest. He saw in the young itinerate a powerful evangelist who could help the churches of the Charleston Association evangelize the lower South. Accordingly, Hart urged the association's messengers at their 1755 meeting to "take into consideration the destitute condition of many places in the interior settlements of this and the neighboring provinces." He recommended that their churches pool resources to fund an itinerate missionary to this area. The association approved, authorizing Hart to secure an evangelist for the mission upon collection of sufficient funds. By January of 1756, the money had come in, and Hart boarded the sloop *Fancy* to sail for Philadelphia. He spent the next nine months preaching constantly, visiting family, and strengthening ties with Philadelphia Association church leaders. Hart also met with Gano, prevailing upon him to come to Charleston on temporary loan from the Morristown Church. At their 1756 meeting, the Charleston Association charged Gano "to visit the Yadkin first and afterwards to bestow his labours wherever Providence should appear to direct." Over the next year, Gano exerted tremendous energy to fulfill his charge, and his labors in North Carolina were "crowned with remarkable success." Many individuals professed the gospel and churches grew stronger through his efforts. After Gano returned to Morristown, New Jersey, the Charleston Association issued him a letter of thanks "for his faithfulness and industry in the mission."Hart's request for an association-sponsored missionary set a precedent for cooperative missions among Baptist churches in the South.[20]

Hart's passion for gospel partnerships extended beyond his own Regular Baptist community to a new group of Baptists who entered the South in the mid-1750s, the Separate Baptists. The Regulars traced their origins in South Carolina to William Screven's transplanting of the Kittery, Maine, congregation in Charleston in 1682. The Separate Baptists had broken away from established congregational churches in New England during the Great Awakening and made their way down to Virginia and North Carolina around the year 1755. Historians have generally overplayed the theological differences of the two Baptist groups, particularly their stances on Calvinism and revival. Their essential theological unity was revealed when Regular Baptist John Gano visited a Separate Baptist Association meeting in 1759. The unlettered Separates first eyed the Princeton-educated Gano with suspicion, but his warm gospel preaching to their gathering won them over. On his part, Gano reported back to the Philadelphia Association, "Doubtless the power of God was among them; that although they were rather immethodical, they certainly had the root of the matter at heart." After hearing Hart's Regular Baptist protégé Edmund Botsford preach in person, Separate Baptist patriarch Daniel Marshall exclaimed, "I can call thee brother, and give thee the right hand of fellowship, for some how I never heard *convarsion* better explained in my life; but I would not have thee think thou preaches as well as Jo Reese and Philip Mulkey. However, I hope you will go home with me." The kinship of the two movements was formalized in a 1787 statement published by a general committee of Separate and Regular Baptists in Virginia. The committee emphasized their doctrinal agreement, asserting that "the doctrine of salvation by Christ and free, unmerited grace alone ought to be believed by every Christian and maintained by every ministers of the gospel. Upon these terms we are united; and desire hereafter that the names *Regular* and *Separate* be buried in oblivion." Despite their different histories, both Regular and Separate Baptists worked from the same, basic theological framework of evangelical Calvinism.[21]

At the same time, significant cultural differences between the Regulars and Separates must be acknowledged. Their primary disagreement revolved around the use of written creeds in the church. In Separate Baptist leader John Leland's (1754–1841) words, "The Regulars adhered to a confession of faith, first published in London, 1689, and afterwards adopted by the Baptist Association of Philadelphia, in 1742; but the Separates had none but the Bible." The Separates were anxious to prevent any manmade document from displacing the scriptures in the life of the Christian and "usurping a tyrannical power over the conscience." When the Regulars proposed to unite with the Separates around the *Second London Confession*, the Separates "expressed fears, that the confession of faith might in time bind them too much, as there were some objectionable parts."[22] From the Regular Baptist perspective, a confession of faith was not intended to usurp the Bible's authority but to guard its essential truths from heretical interpretation.

The Regulars and Separates also differed in worship practice. While affirming that the Separates had "the root of the matter at heart," Gano did admit that their meetings were "rather immethodical." By this, he probably referred to the Separates' openness to nonordained church members, including women, speaking openly in their gatherings when they believed themselves to be led by the Spirit. John Leland observed from Virginia, "The Regulars were orthodox Calvinists, and the work under them was solemn and rational; but the Separates were the most zealous, and the work among them was very noisy. The people would cry out, 'fall down,' and, for a time, lose the use of their limbs; which exercise made the bystanders marvel; some thought they were deceitful, others, that they were bewitched, and many being convinced of all, would report that God was with them of a truth." Leland's description has often been lifted from its broader context of Baptist history and held up as the classic expression of the supposed order-ardor dichotomy that existed between the Regulars and Separates. Yet it should be remembered that Leland spoke of the Baptist scene in Virginia rather than in the lower South. Further, while Leland's general impression of the two groups does point to real distinctions in style and personality, one should not extrapolate from this statement a whole-scale rejection of revivalism by the Regulars or of orthodox Calvinism by the Separates.[23]

Style of dress represented another matter of disagreement between the two Baptist groups. Wood Furman identified among "the peculiarities of the Separates" a certain "preciseness in dress and language, somewhat similar to the Quakers." Separate Baptists believed that maintaining a strict dress code served as an important expression of Christian holiness in the midst of a worldly society. Separate Baptist men "cut off" their hair and repudiated "superfluous forms and modes of dressing . . . [such as] cock't hats." The austere appearance of the Separates made them the object of ridicule among the Anglican gentlemen of Virginia. It also caused them to stand out from the Regular Baptists, who did not share their convictions about dress. The Separates considered the Regulars to have compromised "not sufficiently particular in small matters, such as dress, etc." For their part, the Regulars maintained that the Separates' scruples over clothing to be extra-biblical requirements and unnecessarily restrictive.[24]

In the first several years of their coexistence in the South, leaders on both sides explored the possibilities of uniting the two Baptist groups. Every effort ended in frustration. In 1762, Separate Baptist Philip Mulkey (1732–1801) sent several inquiries to the Charleston Association about establishing a union. The Charleston Association responded by sending Hart and Evan Pugh to a Separate Baptist general meeting in North Carolina, but nothing came of their visit. In 1769, the Regular Baptists of the Ketocton Association in Virginia commissioned messengers to present an official letter of reconciliation at a Separate Baptist meeting in North Carolina: "If we are all Christians, all Baptists—all *New Lights*—why are we divided? Must these little appellative names, *Regular* and *Separate*, break the golden bond of charity?" Yet they, too, failed to persuade. In 1772, the Separates of Congaree Association in South Carolina began corresponding with the Philadelphia Association at the urging of Regular Baptist Morgan Edwards, and the next year sent messengers to the Charleston Association meeting. Again, negotiations for union broke down when the Separates "would be satisfied with nothing short of the Regulars coming fully into their own views." Bridging the divide between these Baptist movements seemed to be a lost cause.[25]

In the end, when formal action could not reconcile the South's Baptists, friendship did. Here, no Baptist played a more vital role than Oliver Hart. Hart made several journeys into the Carolina frontier to preach at Separate Baptist congregations over the years. He celebrated the "happy Revival of Religion in the interior Parts of this Province, among the separate Baptists." Hart mentioned two visits to the Separates, once with Evan Pugh to assist in ordaining two ministers. On another occasion, Hart witnessed ten new believers receive baptism. One of the converts, a little girl, impressed Hart by giving "an amazing account of the Lords Work on her Heart." Hart remembered both visits with the Separates "much to my Satisfaction." In a 1775 tour of the Carolina backcountry, Hart lodged with Separate minister Philip Mulkey of Fairforest Church. Hart even submitted, at Mulkey's insistence, to the Separate Baptist rite of footwashing. "This evening before we lay down to rest, Brother Mulkey requested that he might wash my feet," Hart said. "With some reluctance I consented," Hart recalled, and "after declaring that I did not believe it to be an ordinance of Christ, he then, being girded with a towel, and having water in a basin with great humility and affection, proceeded to wash my feet, talking religiously and affectionately all the time." The incident, in which awkwardness and hesitation between the Regular and Separate Baptist leaders gave way to tender, mutual acceptance, seems parabolic of the uniting effort Hart was quietly leading in the 1770s. He struck up a correspondence with New England Separate Baptist Isaac Backus in 1777, whose written works Hart read and highly esteemed. In his flight from Charleston in 1780, Hart stayed and preached with Separate Baptist leaders John Leland and John Waller (1741–1802) in Orange County, Virginia. Yet the most significant friendship Hart formed among the Separate Baptists was undoubtedly with Richard Furman.[26]

Hart first met Furman at the Separate Baptist High Hills of Santee Church on January 2, 1774, where the eighteen-year-old delivered the evening sermon. Hart commented afterward that "it was a time of refreshing to the people of God." The relationship between the seasoned Regular statesman and the young Separate preacher grew from there. It would prove pivotal in uniting the Baptists of the South. After Furman accepted the pastoral call at High Hills, Hart urged him to lead his Separate Baptist brethren to join the Charleston Association. "I hope we shall have your Voice, and Influence, for the Junction there proposed," Hart wrote. "If You, and the Congaree, will come into the Plan, it will be strengthening of us all. I am much of the Opinion, it would be much to the Advantage of the Baptist Interests of this State." In addition to the more obvious religious benefits, Hart believed a united Baptist front was necessary for establishing religious liberty under the new constitution. The union of all Baptists "will necessarily render us more conspicuous to the State."[27]

When Hart fled South Carolina after thirty years at the Charleston Baptist Church, he recommended Furman as his replacement. "I have wrote to them to give you a Call, which hope you will accept, if you can see your way clear, as I know not of anyone that I should chuse in Preference, to fill up that Place," Hart told Furman. "I hope God will direct you in this great Affair, for his own Glory, and the Good of his Church." The comparatively urbane Charleston Baptist Church was the flagship congregation of southern Regular Baptists. Furman was a Separate preacher from the frontier of the Santee River. In 1769, Baptist Jeremiah Dargan visited the High Hills region and called it "this wicked, wicked neighborhood," and "this wild place," where he preached "to no purpose except provoking them to outrage." When Furman accepted the call to Charleston, the long-desired union between Regular and Separate Baptists was solidified. For the rest of his life, Hart carried on an affectionate correspondence with Furman, who preached a moving memorial sermon from the Charleston pulpit upon Hart's death. Furman, often recognized as "the father of the Southern Baptist Convention," would carry forward many of Hart's plans for Baptist denominational life. In addition to expanding the influence of the Charleston Association and carrying the torch for Baptist missions through the Triennial Convention, Furman would also asrise as a champion for Baptist education. In each of these endeavors, Furman stood on the shoulders of Oliver Hart.[28]

A plaque in the First Baptist Church of Charleston, South Carolina, lauds Oliver Hart as "Father of the education movement among South Carolina Baptists, 1755." Though Hart himself had received only "a plain English education" in his youth, the former carpenter devoted himself to study after entering the ministry, laboring to grasp "the Bible-system in all its parts." Furman recalled that "the powers of his mind were strong and capacious, and enriched by a fund of useful knowledge," gained by "an intimate acquaintance with the sacred Scriptures, and an extensive reading of the most valuable, both ancient and modern authors." At various points in his writings, Hart mentions reading the works of Augustine, Herman Witsius, Matthew Poole, Matthew Henry, Joseph Caryl, Richard Baxter, and John Gill. As Baptist historian Thomas J. Nettles has observed, Hart had also memorized large portions of the *Baptist Catechism*. Hart frequently identified himself as "a friend of learning," and spent his life advocating education among Baptist ministers. "Learning is an excellent handmaid to grace. None slight it but such as know not its value," Hart insisted. "Without some assistance therefrom, it will be difficult, if not impossible, to expound some passages of Scripture. Ministers' knowledge cannot be too extensive."[29]

When Hart arrived in Charleston in 1749, almost no new ministers were arising from the Baptist churches in the South. The pastors of southern churches generally hailed from the northern colonies or from other regions in the early modern Atlantic. Moreover, the Baptists of America as yet had established no theological school for ministers. Pastoral candidates received their training through personal study and guided apprenticeships with experienced ministers. As early as 1751, Hart envisioned a solution to both issues. At the inaugural address of the Charleston Association, he argued for the promotion of ministerial education as a primary way that an association contributed to "the welfare of Zion." He urged the churches to "conclude upon some methods for educating, and trying the gifts, and honorably calling out persons to the great work of the ministry."Hart acted on this conviction in 1755. The year before, Samuel Stillman had been converted in Hart's church. Hart considered Stillman "an extraordinary Youth" whom he believed "would come to be publickly Useful to the Church of Jesus Christ." Stillman's great promise as a minister likely prompted Hart to launch a formal program of pastoral and theological training that was later called "the Baptist Religious Society." The Society's stated goal was "to assist pious young men in obtaining education for the public services of the church." Two years later, Hart strengthened the society by involving the other churches of the Charleston Association. In 1757, he inquired of the association's messengers, "whether there could not be some method concluded upon, to furnish, with suitable degree of learning, those among us who appear to have promising gifts for ministry?" The churches of the association each pledged to contribute to the purchase of a library for the society, collecting a total of 133 pounds (the Charleston Church contributing almost half). These funds the association entrusted to a committee comprised of Hart, Francis Pelot, and John Stephens, with Hart serving as the humble "education fund's" first treasurer. It was another historic achievement for Hart. His society is considered "the first religious partnership among Baptists in America in the interest of religious education."[30]

No sooner had Hart begun to actively involve himself in the education of these and other young men than there was a striking increase in the number of Baptist ministers in the American South. In the years that followed, numerous young men benefitted from the society. No formal enrollment records exist, but Hart's personal writings are filled with references to the novice ministers he trained, among them Stillman, Edmund Botsford, Edmund Matthews, Nicholas Bedgegood, David Williams, and Evan Pugh. Hart enjoyed a warm relationship with his students, who viewed him as their father in the ministry. "I'm now studying with dear Mr. Hart," Pugh wrote to a friend in 1762, "and he seems to signify of their trying to settle me in Town which would be very agreeable to me for I like the Place & People much." Outside his formal role as a teacher in the society, Hart personally invested in many other younger men, like Hezekiah Smith and Richard Furman. Through Hart's deliberate efforts, the picture of Baptist ministers in the South began to change. On February 26, 1759, Hart ordained Stillman, who served a church at James Island before leaving for the First Baptist Church of Boston, and Bedgegood, who went on to serve the Welsh Neck Church. Hart ordained Pugh in 1763, who pastored the Cashaway Church (later Mount Pleasant) and preached at large in the area for the rest of his life. It must have been especially rewarding for Hart and Pugh to share in the ordination ceremony of another new minister six years later, when they set apart Joseph Reese in 1769. Reese served the Congaree Church for decades and also planted the High Hills Church in 1770. On March 14, 1773, Hart oversaw the ordination of Edmund Botsford, who had been both converted and called to ministry under Hart. Eight months later, Hart and Pelot travelled to Savannah, Georgia, to constitute a new Baptist church gathered there under Botsford's revival preaching. The list of ministers who Hart directly influenced, and who then replicated Hart's mentoring pattern in the lives of other young pastors, could be multiplied many fold. To Hart, these relationships were vital for the health of "the Baptist interest" in the lower South for generations to come. On a personal level, each of these young preachers was precious to him. Hart viewed them as "the Fruit of my Labours, the Seals of my Ministry, my Joy and Crown."[31]

Hart's passion for ministerial education never waned. Over the years, many Baptists objected to the formal education of ministers as nonessential at best and at worst a dangerous substitute for a divine calling. Hart lamented the anti-intellectual bent of the Baptist people, expressing his desire "for the Interest of the Religion we profess, [that] we may all grow in Grace, Knowledge, and Understanding, that the Baptists may be distinguished by Something superior to Folly and Meanness." He sought to answer the opponents of education patiently, but directly. One of his most eloquent responses came in 1791, almost forty years after launching the Religious Society in Charleston. Hart described ministers as the "pillars" of the church, which must be "hewn by the axe of the law, smoothed by the plane of the gospel, painted by the gifts and graces of the Spirit, and varnished by human erudition." It was the final step in the process, receiving the "varnish" of theological education, to which so many of his brethren objected. Hart agreed that an education could not replace a divine calling to preach, yet he insisted that it was "a qualification of great importance, and ought never to be dispensed with, when it can be obtained." He then gave voice to a long-held dream, the establishment of a Baptist theological seminary. "In ancient times, there were schools of the prophets; and they are not less needed now. May such institutions be encouraged. We can do little or nothing else towards preparing these pillars. It is a pity that we are so reluctant in this. I am sorry to say, that several young ministers, of bright natural parts, and gracious endowments, are groaning for want of this advantage." More than sixty years later, another South Carolina Baptist sounded these same notes, as James Petigru Boyce convinced the South Carolina Baptist State Convention to adopt a plan for founding of a theological seminary for the Baptists of the South. Whether he realized it that night or not, Boyce, who came to faith as a boy in the pews of the First Baptist Church of Charleston, was following in the footsteps of Oliver Hart. Not only was Boyce building on Hart's vision but the books originally purchased with the money from Hart's fund "became the nucleus of the library at Furman University," and subsequently of the library at The Southern Baptist Theological Seminary.[32]

Hart's efforts in Baptist education also extended beyond the southern colonies. He warmly supported Rhode Island College, the first educational institution founded by Baptists in America. The institution known today as Brown University originated in the desire of the Philadelphia Association to "secure for the Baptist churches an educated ministry without the restrictions of denominational or sectarian tests." At their October 12, 1762, meeting, the Philadelphia Association made a motion to establish such a college. Founding the school would require tireless labor from Baptists throughout the British North American colonies over the next decade, and Hart was eager to do his part. "It gives me great Pleasure that we are like to have a College in those Parts," he told Samuel Jones, "and should be glad to have it in my Power to serve so valuable an Institution." In early conversations, Hart even offered to travel to London on behalf of the college, though he eventually laid aside these plans to promote the school from Charleston. In 1769, Hart opened the Charleston Baptist Church to the college as a base for raising funds in the South. The college had enlisted Hezekiah Smith, a trustee, to lead the fundraising effort. Hart had ordained Smith to gospel ministry in 1763 and had remained in friendly contact with the Princeton-educated preacher. Throughout the winter of 1769 and the spring of 1770, Smith's journals contain numerous references to staying in Hart's home and preaching from Hart's pulpit when he wasn't scouring about South Carolina raising funds for the school. Hart often accompanied Smith as he travelled into the South Carolina backcountry. After Smith returned home, Hart praised Smith to James Manning, president of Rhode Island College. "No Man could have done more, and few would have done so much as He has, to serve the Institution. He has met with much Opposition, and bore many Reflections, but none of these Things have discouraged him. I heartily wish the Benefactions of this Province may greatly promote the Welfare of the College," he wrote.[33]

The college later asked Hart to help raise funds himself. They commissioned him, along with Pelot and Gano, to "address the Baptist Associations throughout America, and urge their cooperation in these efforts to raise funds for the college." Hart subsequently led the Charleston Association in 1774 to adopt a motion, "recommending to every member to pay sixpence sterling, annually, for three years consecutively, to their Elder, or some suitable person; this money to be paid to the Treasurer of the College." Though not a large sum, this financial pledge during a time of approaching war indicated a serious commitment to establishing the institution. Both the Philadelphia and the Warren, Rhode Island, associations later adopted the Charleston plan. Rhode Island College acknowledged Hart's contributions in 1769, bestowing on him at its first commencement ceremony the honorary master of arts degree. Hart's friend William Rogers, himself a well-educated university professor, insisted that Hart's degree was well-deserved. "Such were the improvements of his mind by self-application, close reading, and habitual reflection," Rogers remembered, "that few men more richly deserved those honours, which, by our first seminaries of learning, have been in many instances too incautiously bestowed!" Hart later remarked on this event when Furman, another self-educated minister, hesitated to receive the same gift. "It is an honorary Title," said Hart, "frequently bestowed on Persons who have not had the advantage of a liberal Education. I know one, at least, on whom it was bestowed, who was every Way more undeserving of it than Mr. Furman."[34]

Hart also sent his oldest son, John, to Rhode Island College as a student. This turned out to be a mixed blessing for the school. Upon John's conversion and baptism in 1786, Botsford remarked to Hart, "Whatever *you* may have known, *we* all knew J. to have been the wildest of Mr. Hart's children." While at school, John's misbehavior earned him the rod of Manning's discipline. John's name appears in an official statement from the school as having been reprimanded "for habitually neglecting your studies, being out of College in the evening in town beyond the time specified in the laws and absent from his room in study hours and making disturbance by noise or otherwise, and suffering others to spend their time idly in his room at entertainments or otherwise." Manning relayed these developments to his old friend Hart, who was mortified. He responded promptly. "I am sorry John has conducted so as to give you so much Trouble, and to forfeit the Place he had under the Management of Mrs. Manning," Hart apologized. "Had I been apprised of his unworthy Conduct sooner, perhaps I should have remanded him back to Carolina; for I am not in such affluent Circumstances as to throw away Money in the education of one who has no View to his own Advantage.—I thank you however for all the Pains you have taken with Him, and that you have made Trial of the Discipline of the Rod. Let me entreat you unweariedly to exert your best Endeavors for his Advantage. Who knows but God may give Him a Turn? I should be sorry he should return a thoughtless Blockhead." At the close of the same letter, Hart would again plead with Manning for assistance with John: "Could you not prevail on John to write to me? I have received but one Letter from Him for the Space of twelve Months past, altho' I have sharply reproved Him for the space of twelve months past, although I have sharply reproved him for this Neglect, over and over again." This vignette reveals that Hart not only battled uphill to promote Baptist education in the public square but in his own home.[35]

Hart displayed his activist spirituality more broadly by participating in the tumultuous political events at the end of the eighteenth century. The plaque honoring Hart in Charleston's First Baptist Church also identifies him as "Patriot, American Revolution, 1775–1780." In his lifetime, Hart's service to his country during the Revolutionary days was well known. Richard Furman praised Hart for "his usefulness as a citizen of America," for being "prompt in his judgment, ardent in his love of liberty, and rationally jealous for the rights of his country." For Hart, who saw the American cause as bound up with the Baptist interest of religious liberty, patriotic service was simply another manifestation of his desire to "do something useful for God."[36]

After the war, Hart preached a sermon entitled *America's Remembrancer* (1791), in which he traced God's providence in forming the new nation. As he reflected on the events that led to the war, Hart did not hesitate to identify Great Britain as "the aggressor" in the conflict. He viewed England throughout the 1760s and 1770s as growing in jealousy over the "rising glory" of America, which had grown from a dependent child to "a man's estate." Parliament had "framed oppressive acts" that "not only embarrassed our commerce, but taxed us without our consent, and proceeded so far as to declare that of right they might bind us in all cases whatsoever." Hart referred to the Stamp Act of 1765 and the Townshend Acts of 1767, which the colonists viewed as illegitimate "taxation without representation." As Hart and his fellow Patriots saw it, accepting Parliament's repressive measures was unconscionable. "What could we, the devoted sons of America, now do? To tamely put on the shackles fabricated for us, we apprehended, would argue a meanness of soul, unworthy the offspring of Freemen—a baseness, derogatory of human nature," Hart said. Yet America still "retained an affection for Great Britain, although strangely metamorphosed from a tender mother into a tyrannical step-dame." The colonists submitted a series of protests against these acts. When these cries went unheard, and after Britain's issue of the Intolerable Acts, delegates from the thirteen colonies assembled in Philadelphia as the first Continental Congress in the fall of 1774. With one voice, the colonies petitioned the Crown to ease its repressive measures. They found "the haughty monarch was deaf to our supplications." On April 19, 1775, the King's troops "commenced hostilities," opening fire on American militia at Lexington and Concord. Hart received the news on May 8; he knew war would soon come to Charleston.[37]

The colony of South Carolina had formed the First Provincial Congress at the beginning of 1775, after her five delegates returned from the first Continental Congress. In June of 1775, they reassembled to make serious preparations for war: calling for fifteen thousand troops, creating a "Council of Safety" vested with extensive executive powers in the province, and composing an oath of allegiance to the colonial cause called "the Association." As the Council scrambled to enlist support for the Association, they knew their greatest challenge lay in South Carolina's Back Country. The western Carolina frontier was a different world from Charleston. The poor settlers who populated the backcountry had been far removed from the daily clamor for independence the city had known since the 1760s. The backcountry men were also loyal to the King and generally averse to helping the aristocrats of Charleston. The Council of Safety recognized that winning the backcountry over would be vital to their success. They proposed to send a team of three men "to make progress into the Back Country, to explain the causes of the present disputes between Great Britain and the American colonies," and to persuade them to sign the Association. The first member of the team was William Henry Drayton, a wealthy planter, lawyer, and statesman of Charleston, an aggressive patriot, and a future president of the South Carolina Provincial Congress. The second man was William Tennent III, pastor of the Congregational church in Charleston and grandson of Log College founder William Tennent I. A riveting orator, Tennant held master's degrees from both Princeton and Harvard. Oliver Hart, the self-taught Baptist preacher, was the third member. The Council of Safety recruited Hart to this eclectic coalition for his ability to communicate with Baptists, who formed a large percentage of the backcountry's population. The letter Hart received, signed by Henry Laurens, assured him, "Your compliance will be esteemed by the Council of Safety as an instance of your zeal in public service, when the aid of every freeman and lover of constitutional liberty is loudly called for."[38]

Hart eagerly accepted the charge. His cousin, John Hart, would sign his name to the Declaration of Independence on behalf of New Jersey. His brother, Joseph, served as an officer in the Continental Army of Pennsylvania. His son John, home from college, would fight under South Carolina war hero General William Moultrie. At fifty-two, Hart was not in fighting trim, but he could preach the message of liberty to ordinary Baptist folk. He wrote in his diary, "On Monday, July 3, 1775, I set off for the frontiers of the province, being appointed by the Council of Safety to accompany the Honorable William Henry Drayton and the Rev. Wm. Tennent to try to reconcile a number of the inhabitants, who are disaffected to the government." It would be a costly service. As Hart rode away, his new wife, Nancy, was pregnant with their first child. Silas Hart would be born August 30, while Hart was still gone. Tragically, the boy would die less than a month later, when Hart was again missing, at the bedside of his deathly ill daughter, Nelly. In the end, he was "absent at the birth and death of the child, a heavy trial to my dear Nancy." Along with a host of other members of the daring Revolutionary generation, Hart was willing to make tremendous personal sacrifice in service to the cause of liberty.[39]

Yet these events still lay in the future as Hart rode off to fulfill his commission. Though he would rendezvous with Drayton and Tennent at various points on the journey, they each followed different routes. Hart rode first to the familiar Congaree Baptist Church, led by his friend Joseph Reese. There, on August 2, he preached from John 8:36, "If the Son therefore shall make you free, ye shall be free indeed." In his sermon, Hart deftly shifted from extolling spiritual freedom in Christ to political freedom, addressing his listeners with "the subject of the times." The congregation received his message positively, and he afterward prevailed upon Reese to join him for the rest of the journey. As the two travelled together, they talked with anyone who would listen about "the state of the times." At one stop, Hart delivered another creative twist on a classic gospel text, Galatians 5:1: "Stand fast therefore in the liberty wherewith Christ hath made us free, and be not entangled again with the yoke of bondage." Hart "took occasion to speak on the state of national affairs," while the people "heard with attention." He learned afterward that "one opposer was convinced, and sharply reproved one who quarreled with the sermon." Along with many Revolutionary clergy, Hart did not hesitate to use the Bible or his position as an ordained minister to promote his political stance.[40]

The trio's most pleasant event in the journey came on August 21, at William Wofford's home on the Tyger River. There, Drayton, Tennent, and Hart hosted a picnic for the locals, drawing a large crowd. "A beef was barbecued, on which we dined," Hart recorded. After the meal, Reese, a good singer, opened with a song. Drayton then spoke for over an hour on the recent developments between the colonies and the Crown. It was an evangelical revival meeting for American Liberty, complete with an invitation to make a decision at the end of the night. Hart recorded that the people listened attentively, and at the end of the meeting, more than seventy men came forward to sign the Association Agreement. In fact, the people were "so active and spirited" they insisted on forming a provincial regiment on the spot.[41]

Not every stop was so encouraging. On August 10, Hart and Reese arrived at the home of Separate Baptist Phillip Mulkey at Fairforest Creek. Mulkey, whose name has appeared before in these pages, was serving under a moral cloud at this point in his ministry. Back in 1767, Hart had written to Manning that Mulkey had been greatly used as an instrument of revival in the region, yet "he, poor man, has sadly fallen, having become the father of a spurious child by a widow woman, a member of his own church. On account of which religion has suffered much, especially in those parts, and among those people." Baptist historian Morgan Edwards also alluded to the Mulkey scandal in 1772 when he noted that "a thorn was put into [Mulkey's] flesh about 4 years ago which will . . . teach his votaries that he is but a man."Despite his checkered past, Mulkey maintained a significant following for many years. But by 1790, the Charleston Association had disfellowshipped Mulkey entirely, warning churches of his "enormous crimes; such as adultery, perfidy and falsehood, which have been attended with very aggravating circumstances, often repeated and continued in for years; and part of the time, united with his highest pretensions of zeal and piety." Whatever Mulkey's personal difficulties may have been at the time, he welcomed Hart and Reese with gracious hospitality on the night they arrived on his doorstep. But to Hart's dismay, Mulkey revealed himself to be a staunch Loyalist.[42]

Mulkey and his neighbors had fallen under the sway of a prominent Tory leader in the area, Colonel Thomas Fletchall. Hart remarked that "Col. Fletchall has all those people at his beck, and reigns amongst them like a little king." Fletchall had even composed an "Association" of his own, pledging loyalty to the crown. Hart called it "a jejune incoherent piece, but serves to delude the people." As Hart engaged Mulkey's neighbors in conversation, he saw that "no argument on the contrary side seemed to have any weight with them." The next day, Hart was addressing a few dozen men when a crowd of angry Loyalists interrupted, shouting that they "wished 1,000 Bostonians might be kill'd in battle," and one "wish'd there was not a grain of salt in any of the coast towns on the continent." Hart dryly noted on that night that, "On the whole, they appear to be irritated in the extreme." Fearing British interception, Hart began writing his diary in code. He had reason to be nervous; Tory resentment ran deep against the patriots in many portions of the backcountry. Drayton and Tory leaders nearly touched off a civil war. Adding to these anxieties, the group chose an unseasonably rainy August to travel across the frontier. Muddy roads and swollen creeks made progress difficult. Hart reports crossing "several deep creeks" as well as rivers that were "very high and ran rapidly." He must have been relieved to arrive safely in Charleston in September 6.[43]

One can only speculate as to what Hart's "Back Country Commission" accomplished in the American Revolution. Loulie L. Owens wondered publically in her 1966 biography of Hart whether some of the backcountry sharpshooters at the pivotal Battle of King's Mountain in 1780 may have "listened to Tennent in log meetinghouses or sat with Hart into the night." This, of course, cannot be confirmed. Yet some facts are clear: after covering over three hundred miles in a month's time, speaking an average of once a day, and holding hundreds of personal conversations about "the state of the times" with backcountry neighbors, Hart and his party garnered numerous pledges of loyalty to the South Carolina Council of Safety, for which the Provincial Congress formally thanked them on November 29, 1775. Hart's participation in the backcountry commission has been called the most significant contribution to the American Revolution by any individual South Carolina Baptist.[44]

Hart's military service had ended, but he still took an active part in the political events of the day, underscoring his activist spirituality. On March 30, 1776, Hart and other area ministers from across the denominational spectrum met at the High Hills of Santee Church, to adopt a resolution to send to the Provincial Congress of South Carolina. "We hope yet to see hunted Liberty sit Regent on the Throne, and flourish more than ever," they wrote. "We bless God that he hath begun our deliverance, and that he will complete it shall be our constant prayer." One prominent reason for Hart's devotion to the American cause was the prospect of obtaining religious liberty. At this time, Baptists and other dissenting ministers were still fined and jailed in those regions where the Church of England was established. Hart viewed state-established religion as "the sole cause of all those horrid persecutions which have so much disgraced Christianity and set the world on fire." Securing the freedom to worship according to one's own conscience represented "a capital blessing," and "the natural and inalienable right of all men." Upon William Tennent III's untimely death in 1777, Hart took the occasion to preach about the principle he and his friend shared. "I am clear in my opinion, that the peace, welfare and happiness of this state, depends much upon our having our religious, as well as our civil liberty constitutionally fixed. All who have just notions of freedom, and have embarked in the glorious cause, will certainly expect this. It is so just and equitable, that the meanest citizen may demand it, as his right. It is our inalienable property, as much so as limb or life; and we cannot dispose of it, without being guilty of great injustice to ourselves, and impiety toward God. We hope therefore, that our representatives will do justice to their constituents, by fixing religious liberty on the broadest bottom, and the most permanent foundation." Hart rallied his fellow ministers to this cause. "We now have a hopeful prospect that we shall obtain religious liberty, in its full extent, in this state; it cannot fail if the Dissenters will be careful to attend the next Session of Assembly," he told Furman. He labored to unify Regular and Separate Baptists for religious liberty. "I am the more for this junction, because I fear that some of the Baptists on the Frontiers will be deemed unfriendly to Government," he wrote. "Therefore let all of us who are in Support of our happy Constitution unite together in one band; we shall thereby appear the more respectable in the Eyes of Government." Hart was unconcerned with charges of pragmatism or of politicizing the church. "Let not these thoughts be rejected as Human Policy," he wrote. "While in the World, we must be concerned with it, and I am sure the Religion of Jesus forbids us not our making ourselves as comfortable in it as possible."[45]

Hart's friends feared that the British military would punish him for his conspicuous service to America if they ever seized Charleston. These anxieties were well grounded. In 1781, his wife Ann reported reading an article in a British political magazine that mischaracterized Hart's Back Country Commission as an attempt to incite an Indian uprising. The article identified Hart as one of "two rebel clergy" who went on "the pious mission to the Cherokee Nation to endeavor to draw over those people to the interest of America, to bribe them to take the [British] superintendent, if they failed to do this, way lay him and assassinate him." The British would arrest sixty-five known patriots after taking Charleston, imprisoning them for a time in St. Augustine, Florida. They were later paroled but deported with their families from the state. Accordingly, when the British threatened Charleston in October of 1775, Hart moved his family and their possessions by schooner to Euhaw, where they stayed with the widow of Francis Pelot. In the process, Hart contracted a fever that kept him from preaching for more than a month. It was August 3 of the following year before the Hart family felt safe to return to Charleston.[46]

In February of 1780, Sir Henry Clinton again brought the British army against Charleston. In light of this imminent attack, doctors advised Hart, once again weakened by a fever, "to leave town for a change of air." Hart and Nancy vacated the city for the house of his son-in-law, Thomas Screven, in St. Thomas Parish, South Carolina. There, Hart convalesced for two months, where he received reports of Clinton's impending arrival. Hart shared in the anxiety of all Charleston citizens in these tense days. "Often did I petition God with prayers and tears that poor Charles Town might be spared, and not suffered to fall into the enemy's hands. Never could I give it up until I heard of its surrender," he later wrote. News of the city's fall reached Hart on May 21, 1780. He acted quickly. "To escape being made prisoner, I left my family, and travelled northward." He elaborated in another place: "I packed a few clothes in haste and took leave of my dear wife and the family (the most affecting parting I ever experienced), and mounting my horse, set off. But whither was going or when I should return I did not know." Hart could only "endeavor to leave my connections and place myself in the hands of the great and wise Disposer of all events." Accompanied by Botsford, Hart travelled and preached his way northward, supported by financial contributions from his listeners. Along the way, Hart learned that his personal possessions, including a large volume of his own poems, had been lost, and the Baptist meetinghouse had been seized for the storage of salt beef. Hart arrived in Philadelphia on October 10, 1780. One year later, Hart was again in Philadelphia, attending the annual meeting of the Philadelphia Association. On October 24, 1781, he heard the Liberty Bell tolling out news of a great victory. He wrote, "This day arrived, from General Washington, the account of the surrender of Lord Cornwallis and the whole army under his command to General Washington on the 19th inst. A glorious event!" Far from subscribing to a spirituality that withdrew from the political events of his day, Hart's activism led him into the center of the political tumult of the Revolution.[47]

A profile of Hart's activism would be incomplete without a brief glance at his stance on slavery. Historian Catherine A. Brekus has noted the tension in the life of an early evangelical like Sarah Osborn (1714–96), who "could spend hours writing about the theater as an abomination while turning a blind eye to a real evil," namely the African slave trade. This same tension is found in Hart. Like Sarah Osborn, Hart was content to own slaves for much of his life, all while expending considerable energy opposing the comparatively trivial vices of dancing and stage plays.[48]

Slavery was an everyday reality in colonial Charleston. By 1740, twice as many slaves as free whites inhabited South Carolina. So predominant was the black population in the colony that one of Hart's contemporaries described it as "more like a negro country." As historian Robert Olwell describes the racial scene of eighteenth century Charleston, Hart would have encountered many Africans every single day. "Slaves always formed the larger part of the people who walked or rode down the city's streets, who mingled and traded in the market, who were punished upon the pillory, and who stood in the aisle or gallery, or merely on the porch, of the church each Sunday." White visitors to Charleston in Hart's day were struck by the sight of "blacks, . . . playing paw-paw, huzzle cap, pitch penny, and quarreling round the doors of the churches in service-time."[49]

Charleston's enormous slave population was necessitated by the exploding rice and indigo industries of the Carolina lowcountry, which had made Charleston the wealthiest city in the colonies. Yet, even as white Charlestonians enjoyed the economic benefits of the slave force, the vast numbers of slaves also created an atmosphere of tension and fear. South Carolina lieutenant governor William Bull (1683–1755), South Carolina's lieutenant governor from 1738 to 1755, wrote that slave owners worried lest "their Negroes, which were their chief support may in little time become their Enemies, if not their Masters, and that th[eir] Government [would be] unable to withstand or prevent it." There was some substance to these fears. The bloodiest slave revolt in American history took place twenty miles outside of Charleston on September 9, 1739, at the Stono River Bridge. In Bull's words, "a great number of Negroes arose in rebellion, broke upon a Store where they got Arms[,] killed twenty one White Persons, and were marching the next morning in a Daring manner out of the province, killing all they met." The grisly memory of the Stono Rebellion haunted the white citizens of Charleston for generations. As with many other European settlers, Hart was sometimes caught up in the generalized panic of a potential slave uprising. On March 4, 1779, he reported that "the town was alarmed" at ten o'clock when St. Michael's Church bells rang out. When several Charleston citizens rushed to the steeple, they found "a negro man, pretending to be fast asleep, and apparently drunk." When they roused the man, he claimed "he knew nothing about ringing the bells." Hart worried that this had been more than an isolated prank but "a signal for the perpetration of some diabolical plot. It may be for burning the town, or perhaps something worse. Thro' mercy, no harm came of it."[50]

The Great Awakening made significant inroads into colonial slave cultures, as many Africans, slave and free, were swept up into the revival. Thomas S. Kidd has noted that the white revival promoters in the 1740s "routinely expressed happiness to see African Americans and Native Americans in the attentive crowds," as the newfound success among these groups "helped validate the revivals." Both Jonathan Edwards and George Whitefield celebrated the African American response to the gospel. Edwards rejoiced in his *Faithful Narrative* that "several Negroes . . . appear to have been truly born again" during the Northampton revival. The conversion of these blacks drew Edwards's mind to the dawning of the millennial glory, when "many Negroes and Indians will be divines, and that excellent books will be published in Africa, in Ethiopia, [and] Turkey." From a strictly spiritual perspective, Edwards believed that black believers enjoyed the same value before God as any white. He admitted nine blacks and two Indians into full communicant membership while serving as pastor at Northampton. Whitefield likewise encouraged the African American embrace of evangelical religion. For instance, after a sermon in Philadelphia on the woman healed by touching the hem of Jesus's garment, Whitefield "invited the poor Negroes to touch Jesus Christ by faith." He promised that they "would gain freedom from the slavery of sin and Satan" if they did. Furthermore, Whitefield warned southern slave owners that "God has a quarrel with you, for your abuse of and cruelty to the poor negroes." He was especially concerned about the spiritual abuse of slaves, and excoriated slave owners for "keep[ing] your negroes ignorant of Christianity, or otherwise, why are they permitted through your provinces openly to profane the Lord's day, by their dancing, piping, and such like?"[51]

Yet for the most part, early evangelical slave advocacy was limited to spiritual matters. As historian Catherine A. Brekus writes, many evangelicals "preached the gospel to slaves, baptized them, and invited them to the communion table, but their egalitarianism usually stopped at the church door." Immersed as they were in the hierarchical culture of eighteenth century society, few evangelicals saw any contradiction between offering slaves spiritual freedom through faith in Christ while at the same time denying them physical freedom in this life. After all, the Bible never categorically condemned the institution of slavery; it only regulated its practice with gospel principles. Thus, Whitefield saw no problem with owning a South Carolina plantation with slaves to support his Bethesda orphanage; the great evangelist even helped introduce slavery to the colony of Georgia. Edwards, too, owned slaves throughout his life, though he condemned the slave trade.[52]

Hart shared this paradoxical evangelical position. On the one hand, he ministered to the black citizens of Charleston with great energy and enthusiasm during the middle and later decades of the eighteenth century. One example is a young woman named Margaret Mageay, who appears to have been a slave in the Hart home at the time of the 1754 Charleston awakening. Hart took Margaret's soul concerns as seriously as he did those of a male Anglo church attender like Samuel Stillman. When Margaret opened up to Hart about her recent conversion experience, he listened intently, and afterward encouraged her that she had truly found Christ. When two other young ladies, struggling with sin, walked in, Hart urged Margaret to share her testimony. Hart's concern for African souls is further revealed in his investment in John Marrant, in the story related earlier in this chapter. While Marrant was literally sick over his guilt before God, Hart visited him in his home on multiple occasions, sitting beside his sickbed and persisting in prayer until Marrant's doubts were replaced by blessed assurance. Hart also would have ministered to black men and women on a weekly basis from the pulpit of the Charleston Baptist Church. He likely met the controversial black preacher David Margrett (n. d.) during his brief stay in Charleston, and may also have known black South Carolina preachers George Liele (c. 1750–1828) and David George (1742–1810).[53]

At the same time, Hart was a slave owner for most of his adult life. As early as in his 1754 diary, Hart refers to Margaret Mageay as "a Young Woman who hath liv'd in my House almost two years." On April 9, 1771, he records the purchase of a twenty-year-old slave named Dinah and her son Friday, for 356 pounds. In August of the following year, he reports that "Dinah was delivered of a daughter." When Hart married his second wife, wealthy Charleston native Anne Marie Sealy Grimball in 1774, he inherited several more slaves. Hart appears to have enjoyed an affectionate, if paternalistic, relationship with them. Once, when travelling, Anne wrote him that "the poor black members [of the household] hang about me and wish for Master," their love for Hart such that they "sometimes make me drop a tear." Of course, the quote should be evaluated in the context of the master-slave relationship. Yes, Hart appears to have been a benevolent master, conscientious of his spiritual responsibilities to the slaves in his household. As Hart said of his friend Francis Pelot, "He not only endeavored to train up his children in the paths of virtue and religion, but he also took much pains with his servants to teach them the fear of the Lord and the way of eternal happiness."[54] And yet, the inherently coercive nature of the master-slave relationship makes it difficult to assess what Hart's slaves truly thought of him or their status in his home, despite their ostensibly glowing comments about him to their mistress.

By the 1770s, the consciences of northern Baptists were awakening to the moral problem of slavery. Elhanan Winchester, briefly the pastor of the Philadelphia Baptist Church at the end of the decade, spoke openly of "the impropriety of the slave trade." Winchester denounced slavery as employing "every vice that degrades human nature." Antislavery sentiment gathered momentum among Baptists after the American Revolution. When the first abolition society was opened in Philadelphia, several local Baptists added their names to a petition to end the slave trade. The abolition cause received a fresh wave of converts in Philadelphia in 1787, through the reorganization of Pennsylvania Society for Promoting the Gradual Emancipation of Slavery. Prominent members included Benjamin Rush and Benjamin Franklin, as well as Hart's close friend William Rogers, who accepted the position of vice president of the society in 1790. Two of Hart's other friends and regular correspondents, Samuel Stillman and James Manning, joined an abolition society in Providence, Rhode Island. By 1789, the leaders of the Philadelphia Association publicly commended "the several societies formed in the United States and Europe, for the gradual abolition of slavery of the Africans, and for guarding against their being detained or sent off as slaves, after having obtained their liberty," and encouraged the Baptist people to form their own organizations for the same purpose.[55]

These developments made a profound impact on Hart. When he returned to the north in 1780, his friendships with Rogers, Manning, and Stillman, along with his active participation in the Philadelphia Association, undoubtedly drew him into serious conversations regarding slavery. Rogers's influence must have been especially instrumental, for Hart valued their relationship so highly that he named his youngest son "William Rogers Hart." Indeed, Rogers reported after Hart's death that he ultimately changed his position on the Atlantic slave system. "A mind like his was always open to conviction," Rogers remembered. "And although in the year 1780, he labored under some prejudices in favor of the slavery of the poor Africans and their descendants; his benevolent soul, soaring above every selfish motive, was soon brought to contemplate the whole with horror—and to wish, yea more, fervently to pray for success to attend the endeavours of those individuals or societies who are laudably engaged in promoting the happiness of the great human family!" In a footnote, Rogers filled in the details on Hart's actions regarding his slaves. "Mr. Hart, by his will, has left a young negro man free, after a few years service—who has since been disposed of to a good master for five years.—Mrs. Hart, since the death of her husband, has liberated a Negro Woman, with her youngest child, and disposed of her other two children, each till the age of 25—when they are to be free also." This comment indicates that even after embracing the cause of abolition, Hart retained slaves to the end of his life, though he and his wife made arrangements for their liberation by the age of twenty-five. These measures may strike contemporary readers as inadequate, even hypocritical. Yet evangelicals who favored such gradual emancipation believed that an incremental policy provided slaves the best opportunity to flourish in society as free men and women. Hart followed, on a much smaller scale, a similar path as his contemporary, George Washington (whom Hart greatly admired).[56] Still, the scene of Mrs. Hart's female slave and her baby being separated from the other two children is heartbreaking. It serves as a reminder of the inevitable tragedies accompanying the slave system.[57]

In the end, Hart was no revolutionary abolitionist. His Christian activism in the arena of slavery cannot compare to that of William Wilberforce in England, or even to that of his fellow American Baptist, John Leland. Still, Hart did not close his mind or heart to repenting of long-held beliefs and lifestyle choices. If Rogers's account is accurate, Hart ended his life a long way from his former proslavery position, which his friend Richard Furman continued to articulate from Charleston into the next generation. The changes Hart made in in the final decade of his life indicate a genuine humility of spirit and an honest desire to do the right thing. In this case, Hart was no pioneer but an ordinary Christian working through the ethical issues of his day with the aid of an open Bible and the counsel of trusted friends. Yet, in the arenas of evangelism, gospel partnerships, education, and politics, Hart embodied the energetic activism produced by the Great Awakening. As he liked to say, he often grew weary in the Lord's work, yet he never grew weary of it.[58]

CHAPTER 5

Revival Catholicity

On October 27, 1754, Richard Clarke, rector of St. Phillip's Anglican Church in Charleston, was taken ill. Scheduled to perform a funeral that afternoon and unable to attend, Clarke relayed a message to Oliver Hart. In an apparently unprecedented procedure, Clarke asked the Regular Baptist minister to conduct the service for him, and in his "own way." Though holding vastly different convictions regarding church order, Clarke recognized in Hart a fellow evangelical and trusted him to preach Christ to his people. Reflecting on this, Hart wrote, "In the Evening I Buried a Child in the Church Burying Ground, and Spoke Extempore, perhaps the first Instance of this Nature ever known in this Province. The Church Minister was sick and could not attend himself; therefore, gave me free Liberty to speak in my own way; which discovered an Extraordinary Catholick Spirit. Oh that all Bigotry was rooted out of the earth; then would there subsist a greater Harmony between persons persuasions, than what does; it is indeed a pity that our little outward Differences should cause such a shyness between us."[1]

The incident captures the spirit of evangelical "catholicity" that swept the north Atlantic Protestant world during the Great Awakening. The experience of the new birth, the hunger for gospel holiness, and the desire to see many converted to faith in Jesus Christ by the Spirit's power united Christians who differed over many issues of church order. Thomas S. Kidd and Barry G. Hankins have recently observed that Oliver Hart, along with most Regular Baptists, adopted the catholic spirit of the revival. "Like his mentor Whitefield, Hart took denominational boundaries lightly and focused primarily on promoting a vital relationship with God," they write. At the same time, Hart diligently promoted a distinctly Baptist church order throughout the colonial South. Hart's combination of warm-hearted catholicity and uncompromising Baptist conviction, characteristic of the Regular Baptists, stands out as a significant element of his evangelical spiritual legacy.[2]

The catholicity of the Great Awakening had its roots in a number of earlier movements across the Atlantic world. Among the most significant forerunners of Protestant ecumenism were the Continental Pietists, led by Philip Jacob Spener (1635–1705), August Herman Francke (1663–1727), and Gottfried Arnold

(1666–1714). The Pietists believed that heart devotion to Jesus Christ, rather than doctrinal formulations or worship forms, served as the true basis of unity for all Christians. They emphasized the priority of the invisible church of all regenerated souls over the visible church of any particular denomination. In the following generation, Moravian Pietist Count Nicholas Ludwig Von Zinzendorf (1700–60) argued that every Christian tradition offered a *tropos paideia*, or "type of teaching." Just as the beauty of a diamond can be fully appreciated only by viewing it from many angles, so the various traditions each offered their own needed and beautiful views of Christianity.[3]

Many English Puritans shared the Pietist burden to unite Christians around practical godliness. The nonconformist Richard Baxter (1615–91) famously referred to himself as a "meer Christian" and warned his readers of being "counfounded by the noise of sectaries, and divers opinions in religion." He prioritized the "one universal church of Christians in the world," which every believer entered "by being born of the Spirit." Like the Pietists, Baxter's chief concern was a life of vibrant holiness: "If then thou hast faith, and love, and the Spirit, thou art certainly a Christian, and a member of Christ, and of this universal church of Christians." Among American Puritans, Cotton Mather (1663–1728) was an outspoken proponent of "the unity of the godly" at the turn of the eighteenth century. In Richard F. Lovelace's words, Mather believed "the key of a vitalized Christian experience was sufficient to unlock all the doors built up between genuine Christians through misunderstanding." Indeed, to require precise doctrinal conformity of other believers was both unrealistic and uncharitable. "We must first forbear to impose one upon another. It is impossible for any but God who forms the Spirit of man within him, to form the understandings of men, into a belief of every Christian doctrine," Mather preached. He urged against "a Samaritan sort of crabbedenss, churlishness, forwardness, towards all that are not in everything just jumping with us," for this was "not the Spirit of the Gospel." Mather warned that "we must beware how we ever monopolize all godliness to our own little party . . . wherever we can see, *Alliquid Christi*, anything of Christ, let it be dear to us." For Mather, unity was an essential prerequisite for the worldwide revival that he believed would usher in the millennial reign of Christ. "There will be no revival unless there is unity," he said, "and the converse is equally true."[4]

By the late 1730s, Mather's dream appeared to have reached its fulfillment in the ministry of George Whitefield. Like his predecessors, Whitefield believed in the unifying power of heart religion over doctrine, the priority of the invisible communion of regenerate souls, and in evangelical harmony as essential to revival. What distinguished Whitefield was his unparalleled, firsthand experience of Christian diversity. In the course of his travels, Whitefield kneeled at the altar with Oxford Anglicans, preached in the fields to unlearned Methodists, served at the communion seasons of Scottish Presbyterians, and attended meetings of American

Congregationalists, Baptists, and Quakers. Historian D. Bruce Hindmarsh argues that Whitefield's unique experience as the grand itinerant raised his catholicity to previously unknown heights, causing him to "minimize church order, in order to maximize spiritual solidarity with individuals who had been born again." Whitefield himself wrote, "Though I profess myself a minister of the Church of England, I am of a catholic spirit; and, if I see any man who loves the Lord Jesus in sincerity, I am not very solicitous to what outward communion he belongs."[5]

In 1740, Whitefield explained his ecumenical policy to five Anglican interrogators in Boston, Massachusetts. When asked about his endorsement of non-Anglican ministers, Whitefield asserted that "a catholic spirit was best," and that "it was best to preach the new birth, and the power of godliness, and not to insist so much on the form: for people would never be brought to one mind as to that; nor did Jesus Christ ever intend it." Bishop Timothy Cutler pressed him here. Surely, Cutler argued, Christ's prayer "that all may be one, even as Thou Father and I are one [John 17:21]," demanded a single, visible church, namely the Church of England. But Whitefield offered a different interpretation. Echoing his Pietist forbears, Whitefield insisted that the reality of regeneration trumped all external expressions of the Christian faith. The unity Christ prayed for "was spoken of the inward union of the souls of the believers with Jesus Christ, and not of the outward Church," he countered. "I saw regenerate souls among the Baptists, among the Presbyterians, among the Independents, and among the Church folks—all children of God, and yet all born again in a different way of worship: and who can tell which is the most evangelical?"[6]

As Whitefield corresponded with a diverse range of Christians, he allowed differences of church communion to fade into insignificance before the all-important reality of the new birth. "What a divine sympathy and attraction is there between all those who by one spirit are made members of that mystical body, whereof Jesus Christ is the head! . . . Blessed be God that his love is so far shed abroad in our hearts, as to cause us to love one another, though we a little differ as to externals: for my part, I hate to mention them. My one soul question is, *Are you a Christian?* Are you sealed by Christ's spirit to the day of redemption? Are you hungering and thirsting after the perfect, everlasting righteousness of Jesus Christ? If so, you are my brother, my sister, and mother," he wrote. These remarks demonstrate Hindmarsh's observation that a major shift in Protestant spirituality took place in the dawn of the Great Awakening. Eighteenth-century evangelicals like Whitefield "abandoned the Puritan-Reformed question, 'what constitutes a true church?' for the Evangelical-Pietist question, 'What constitutes a true Christian?'"[7]

In some places, Whitefield almost treated church order as a taboo subject. In 1742, Whitefield wrote to John Oulton (1719–1804), the longtime Baptist minister of Liverpool. "If the Lord gives us a true catholic spirit, free from a party sectarian zeal, we shall do well. I am sorry to hear that there is so much narrowness among some of the brethren in Wales. Brother [Howell Harris] complains sadly of it," Whitefield remarked. Then he quickly turned to make application to Oulton. "I hope dear Mr. O. will be kept free, and not fall into disputing about baptism, or other non-essentials. For I am persuaded, unless we all are content to preach Christ, and to keep off from disputable things, wherein we differ, God will not bless us long," he warned. "If we act otherwise, however we may talk of a catholic spirit, we shall only be bringing people over to our own party, and there fetter them." To Whitefield, baptism was at best a "non-essential," at worst "a fetter" that bound people to a manmade party rather than to Christ. It seemed safest to the evangelical leader to "keep off" from such "disputable things," and to find contentment in proclaiming the simple gospel of Jesus. For Baptists like Oulton, who historically viewed baptism as an important matter of obedience to Christ, though not essential to salvation, Whitefield's remarks could be received as somewhat cavalier. Yet as the winds of revival blew across the transatlantic Protestant world, attitudes toward denominational distinctives began to change as a new, evangelical movement emerged.[8]

As the awakening wore on, however, Whitefield found the evangelical unity he so desired increasingly difficult to maintain. Despite his herculean efforts to rally all Christians around the essentials of the gospel, he found himself embroiled in painful, public conflicts with various groups who differed with him on secondary issues. This included his longtime friends John and Charles Wesley as well the Moravians. Still, Whitefield strove valiantly to hold evangelicals together, appealing to their common, heavenly destiny. "The divisions among the brethren sometimes grieve, but do not surprise me," he wrote. "O how do I long for heaven! Surely, *there* will be no differences, no strife there, but who shall sing with most affection to the Lamb that sitteth upon the throne."[9] Whitefield's promotion of evangelical catholicity for the sake of revival deeply influenced the Regular Baptists of the eighteenth century.

On the whole, Regular Baptists in the American colonies embraced the "catholic spirit" of the awakening. One early example is Jenkin Jones, pastor of the Pennepek and Philadelphia Baptist churches, leader in the Philadelphia Association, and Oliver Hart's boyhood minister for over twenty years. Whitefield sought Jones out on his first visit to Philadelphia on November 5, 1739, and quickly identified Jones as a fellow evangelical. "I was visited in the afternoon by the Presbyterian minister, and went afterward to see the Baptist teacher who seems to be a spiritual man," Whitefield wrote. The next night, Jones went to hear Whitefield in the Anglican Church, and was "much rejoiced to hear Jesus Christ preached in the Church." When Whitefield returned to Philadelphia in April of 1740, he was delighted to find that Jones had been promoting the revival in his absence. "It is impossible to express the joy many felt when they saw my face again," wrote Whitefield. "O how did they comfort my heart with the account of what God had done for their own and many other people's souls. The Baptist minister in particular, who has been instrumental in watering what God has planted, recounted to me many noble instances of God's power of free grace shown in the conviction and conversion of some ministers as well as common people."[10]

A few weeks later, it was Whitefield's turn to hear Jones. Greatly pleased, Whitefield reported that Jones "preached the truth as it is in Jesus." In fact, Whitefield called Jones "the only preacher that I know of in Philadelphia, who speaks feelingly and with authority. The poor people are much refreshed by him, and I trust the Lord will bless him more and more." For Jones, these experiences with Whitefield established sufficient grounds for an alliance. On May 9, he had Whitefield preach at the Pennepek meetinghouse, to over two thousand people. In the days to come, Jones extended similar invitations to other revivalists outside the Baptist circle, including Presbyterians Gilbert Tennent and John "Hell-fire" Rowland.[11]

The people of Jones's churches generally received the awakeners with enthusiasm, but Jones did meet resistance from his assistant minister, Ebenezer Kinnersley (1711–78). Kinnersley, who later taught English at the University of Pennsylvania and assisted Benjamin Franklin in his research of electricity, found the emotionalism of the awakening disgusting. When filling Jones's pulpit in his absence, Kinnersley sharply criticized Whitefield, Rowland, and the whole revival. The church was deeply offended. Many walked out on Kinnersley's sermon and later brought charges against him for undermining Jones's leadership. When Kinnersely refused to apologize, he was excluded from the Lord's Table. Matters turned uglier still when Kinnersley aired his grievances in Franklin's *Pennsylvania Gazette*. He accused Jones of lying and showing ungodly favoritism toward Rowland, a fellow Welshman, and attacked the church for ill-treating him. Incensed, the church responded by publishing its own letter, which exonerated Jones, condemned Kinnersley, and called the latter to repentance. Kinnerseley responded in print once more before the controversy died out. Kinnerseley was something of an outlier among Regular Baptists in his opposition to the revival, but the incident reveals the conflict that Baptist leaders like Jones could invite through their evangelical partnerships.[12]

Whitefield traveled south after leaving Pennsylvania in 1740 and by July 7 was in Ashley Ferry, South Carolina, fourteen miles outside of Charleston. He had been invited by Regular Baptist Isaac Chanler, whom Whitefield called "a gracious Baptist minister." Whitefield preached at the Ashley Ferry meetinghouse "to the conviction of some and the comfort of others," though he afterward collapsed from "the violent heat of the weather, and great expense of sweat." The next day he preached twice at the Independent Presbyterian Church before lodging with Chanler for the night, still "very weak." On July 9, Whitefield awoke weaker still but kept his appointment to preach for Chanler at ten in the morning. This time the meetinghouse could not contain the crowd, so Whitefield preached outside, under a tree. "People seemed to come from all parts, and the Word came with convincing power," he wrote. By July

20, Whitefield was convinced that revival had come to Charleston. "Though the heat of the weather, and frequency of preaching, have perhaps given an irrevocable stroke to the health of my body; yet I rejoice, knowing it has been for the conviction, and I believe conversion of many souls," Whitefield wrote. "Numbers are seeking after Jesus."[13]

Before leaving, Whitefield advised the local pastors to establish a weekly lecture to carry on the work of the revival. Chanler's first address at these meetings was published as *New Converts Instructed to Cleave to the Lord* (1740). It stands as a remarkable testimony of the Regular Baptists' revival catholicity. Chanler introduced the sermon by celebrating the revival, searching for adequate words to describe his "holy pleasure, as well as wonder" at God's "raising up and sending forth such eminent instruments of good to the souls of men, crowning their labour with so great and uncommon success." Here he could not restrain his enthusiasm over Whitefield, who he called "very dear unto all such as have felt the power of the word preached by him reaching their hearts." Chanler called his listeners to imitate Whitefield's virtues, particularly his catholic spirit. "Let our love like his be catholic, breathing in a free and open air, abstracted from all bigotry and party zeal, loving the image of God on whomever we may see it impressed . . . that is to say, all the regenerate sons and daughters of God, howsoever they may be distinguished by different denominations amongst men." The body of Chanler's sermon focused on the great evangelical themes Whitefield preached on both sides of the Atlantic: the sovereign grace of God in salvation, the priority of conversion, and the call to evangelical holiness. Chanler warned new believers against returning to their worldly ways, recommended sound Puritan books for their edification, and closed with a fervent evangelistic appeal for those who had not yet closed with Christ.[14] Interesting enough, Chanler at no point instructed the young converts on issues of baptism or proper church order.

A mutual friend of Chanler and Whitefield at this time was Regular Baptist William Tilly (1698–1744). A native of Salisbury, England, Tilly came to America in 1721, was called to ministry at the Charleston Baptist Church, and was ordained at Edisto Island Baptist Church (later Euhaw) in 1731. Tilly traveled to Whitefield's orphanage in Savannah with a group of friends on July 31, 1740. The following Sunday, Whitefield found himself so sick that "I was struck, as I thought, with death." Several guests had arrived, eager to hear Whitefield, but he was so weak that he asked Tilly to preach for him instead. Tilly did not consent, encouraging Whitefield that "God would strengthen [him] if [he] began." Whitefield began. As he prayed, one guest fell to the ground, "as though shot with a gun." From there, "the influence spread." As the congregation listened, "tears trickled down apace, and God manifested himself much amongst us at the Sacrament." To Whitefield's astonishment, Tilly partook of communion with the Anglican guests. In a letter the next week, Whitefield commented, "The word runs like lightning in Charles-Town. A serious lively Baptist minister, named *Tilly*, is here also; he has preached often for me, and last Sunday received the sacrament in our way—O bigotry, thou art tumbling down a-pace!" Jones, Chanler, and Tilly exemplify the catholicity that characterized Regular Baptists during the early days of the Protestant evangelical revival. They were willing to unite on the basis of evangelical piety to advance the gospel in the revival, though, as will be seen, this catholicity had limits. In the next generation, Oliver Hart carried on the Regular Baptist catholic spirit.[15]

Hart would have observed a remarkable example of evangelical catholicity in the city of Charleston during the mid-1750s. A monthly society formed for prayer and the discussion of "some literary or religious topic which had been previously agreed on." This ecumenical "holy club" counted among its members some of the leading figures of Charleston society, including the French Huguenot Gabriel Manigault (1704–81); Henry Laurens (1724–92) and Christopher Gadsden (1724–1805) of the Anglican church, both of whom would later serve the Continental Congress; and the eminent lawyer John Rattray (d.1761) of the Presbyterian Church. Among the ministers known to belong to the society were Richard Clarke, rector of St. Philip's, and the Presbyterians William Hutson (1720–61) and John J. Zubly (1724–81). Whether or not Hart participated in "Charleston's holy club" is unknown, though his prominence in the religious community and his friendship with virtually all of the above makes this plausible. At any rate, Hart certainly counted himself part of the transdenominational, international revival movement in the Atlantic Protestant world, one he had been immersed in from his childhood days in Jenkin Jones's Pennepek Baptist Church. This is evidenced by the "catholic" quality of his friendships in Charleston.[16]

Presbyterians represented the shortest theological leap for a Regular Baptist, whose own *Second London Confession* consciously followed the *Westminster Confession* so closely. So when two young Rhode Island College graduates were sent by their Presbytery "on a preaching excursion" to the Carolinas, Hart happily broke bread with them. One Presbyterian Hart especially admired was Samuel Davies (1723–61), who established an evangelical presence in Virginia from 1748 to 1759. In 1759, Davies accepted the presidency of New Jersey College, which had already trained several of Hart's Regular Baptist colleagues. Tragically, Davies died less than two years into his administration, at the age of thirty-seven. In a letter on April 27, 1761, Hart mourned Davies's death as a blow to the evangelical movement. The remarkable letter is worth quoting at length:

> I lament with you (and surely all the Friends of Zion must mourn) the Loss of the justly celebrated President Davies. Oh, what Floods of Sorrow must have overwhelmed the Minds of Many, when it was echoed from House to House and from Village to Village, as in the dismal Sound of hoarse thunder, *President Davies is no more!*—Oh, sad, and melancholy Dispensation! Arise, all ye Sons of Pity, and

> mourn with those that mourn.—And thou, my Soul, let drop the flowing Tear while commiserating the bereaved and distressed. Alas for the dear Woman, whose Beloved is taken away with a Stroke! May Jesus be Her Husband, Her Strength, and Her Stay.—Alas for the bereaved Children:—May their father's God be their God in covenant. Alas for the Church of Christ:—deprived of one of the principal Pillars, how grievous the Stroke to thee! But Jesus, thy Head, and Foundation, ever lives.
>
> And thou, Nassau Hall,—lately so flourishing, so promising, under the auspicious Management of so worthy a President—what might we not have expected from thee! But alas!—How is the Mighty fallen, in thee! How doth the large and beautiful House appear as a widow, in sable Weeds! And thy Sons, lately so gay and pleasant, as well as promising and contented—how do they retire into their apartments; and there with bitter sighs, heavy groans, and broken Accents, languish out:—My Father, my Father!—the Chariot of Israel, and the horsemen thereof! But I can no more.[17]

Hart also worked closely with Presbyterian William Tennent III (1740–77) during the American Revolution. They travelled the Back Country together in 1775 on a special mission from the South Carolina government and afterward petitioned the congress for religious liberty under the new constitution. These shared labors under such intense circumstances forged a strong friendship between the two men. When Tennent died on August 11, 1777, Hart preached a memorial sermon for him in the Baptist meetinghouse. He based his message on a popular eighteenth century funeral text, 2 Samuel 3:38, "Know ye not that there is—a great man fallen this day in Israel?" He considered how Tennent displayed five essential qualities of "a great man:" a distinguished pedigree, good natural parts and abilities, intelligence and learning, a benevolent heart, and devotion to religion. Hart dedicated the sermon, "preached from pure regard to his memory," to the bereaved mother, wife, and congregation, "with much affection."[18]

Hart also counted William Hutson among his Presbyterian friends. Hutson had been converted under Whitefield in 1740, while a stage player in New York. Hutson went on to teach in a slave school on the estate of Hugh Bryan (1689–1753), served a brief stint at Whitefield's Bethesda Orphan House, then helped pastor two Independent Presbyterian churches in the Charleston area. At every post, Hutson actively promoted revival, including publishing his late wife's letters and diaries under the title *Living Christianity, Delineated* (1760). Hart was often "much refreshed" by Hutson's visits. He invited Hutson to preach from his pulpit on several occasions and supported Hutson when he stood against Charleston's vices. Hart praised Hutson for his "Plain Excellent Discourse" from Matthew 22:5, as the former actor, now walking in evangelical holiness, "bore his testimony also against Stage Plays." The sermon stirred Hart, though Hutson's other listeners "made light of it."[19]

Hart and Hutson also shared a friendship with Swiss-born minister John J. Zubly of the Independent Presbyterian church. Zubly later gained infamy for switching to the Loyalist position during the Revolution, but Hart valued him as a trusted, ecumenical gospel partner in Charleston. In August of 1754, Hart spent a week at Zubly's home "very agreeably" and commented, "Oh how pleasant it is for Brethren to dwell in Unity!" The next month, Zubly returned the favor, staying with Hart and preaching several times, as "the Lord owned it for Comfort to many Souls." Zubly returned again the next month, proclaiming Christ from the Prodigal Son parable and bearing "a faithful and excellent Testimony against the Stage Plays." When Hart's congregation experienced revival that fall, Zubly helped Hart to discern it as a true work of God. Despite differences in ecclesiology, the mutual concern for conversion, revival, and holiness united Hart with many Presbyterians.[20]

In the fall of 1769, as Whitefield was preparing for his final journey to America, John Wesley's Methodists were also making plans to send their first missionaries to Britain's mainland settlements. To be technically accurate, Wesley never left the Anglican communion in his lifetime, and the Methodist church did not officially exist in America until 1784, or in England until after Wesley's death in 1790. Nevertheless, by 1769, Wesley was clearly the leader of a distinct, evangelical renewal movement within the Anglican church known to all as the Methodists. In the Conference at Leeds on August 3, 1769, Wesley announced that two of their number, Richard Boardman (1738–82) and Joseph Pilmoor (1739–1825), would soon depart for the colonies, and he took up a collection for them as "a token of brotherly love." After the Conference adjourned, Whitefield sent for the two young men; despite his stormy relationship with Wesley, he too wanted to send the missionaries off with a blessing. "As he had long been in America, he knew what directions to give us, and treated us with all the kindness and tenderness of a father in Christ," Pilmoor wrote. "Difference of sentiment made no difference in love and affection." After Whitefield "prayed heartily for us," the two men sailed for America on August 21, 1769, believing "we had full power, according to the New Testament, to preach the everlasting gospel and do all possible good to mankind."[21]

Pilmoor eventually journeyed south, arriving in Charleston after a "very rugged" passage on January 19, 1772. He received a dismal first impression when he inquired about family prayers in the house where he lodged. Pilmoor's host informed him that the practice "might not be agreeable" to "the mixed multitude" in his house, because "family prayer is very uncommon in Charleston." Taking his leave of these "sons of Belial," Pilmoor struck out for the General Baptist meetinghouse. Knowing they would share his Arminian theology, Pilmoor offered to preach for them, and the next day delivered his first sermon in Charleston. The crowd was small on short notice, but "two ministers were present all the time, and behaved very well." One was Oliver Hart. Pilmoor recorded that "the Baptist minister, Mr. Hart, returned me thanks for my sermon and invited me to preach in his pulpit." Hart's invitation encouraged Pilmoor that God had work prepared for him in the city. After preaching to the General Baptists the following Sunday morning, he travelled to Hart's meetinghouse. Pilmoor stuck with standard evangelical subjects: the salvation of God from Psalm 18 in the afternoon, and the unity of the regenerate from Romans 8:14, "As many as are led by the Spirit of God, they are the sons of God." Pilmoor reported the Baptist meetinghouse was "as full as it could hold" and that "the Lord was remarkably present." He preached several more times from Hart's pulpit before leaving Charleston, and even stayed in the home of a Baptist church member.[22]

Given Hart's commitment to Calvinism, his acceptance of the Arminian Pilmoor into his pulpit is striking. Their partnership was possible for the same reason that both Wesley and Whitefield could send Pilmoor out with their full blessing: all viewed themselves as part of the same international, transdenominational revival movement in the early modern Atlantic Protestant world. Pilmoor preached the gospel, called for conversions, and prayed for awakening just as Hart did. After addressing Hart's congregation on "the law as a schoolmaster to bring us to Christ," Pilmoor commented, "I am not so much satisfied with preaching the Law, as I am with the gospel; but it is necessary, and therefore I must submit for the good of mankind and glory of God." Hart could have made the same statement, and for this he received the young Methodist warmly. Pilmoor, in turn, left Charleston remembering Hart as "not only sensible, but truly evangelical, and very devout."[23]

Anglicanism historically represented the furthest stretch for a Baptist's ecumenism. In a 1751 tract *The Dissenters' Reasons for Separating from the Church of England*, English Baptist John Gill articulated eleven matters of conscience that kept Baptists and other dissenters from uniting with the established church. These included the Church of England's man-made constitution, its national rather than congregational form and order, its unregenerate membership, its corrupt and unbiblical doctrines, its wrongly administered ordinances, its creation of unbiblical ecclesiastical offices, its recognition of the King as head of the church, its pagan and Judaistic rites and ceremonies, its imposition of the Book of Common Prayer, and finally its "persecuting spirit" against all dissenters. Gill's pointed work left no doubt that disagreements between Baptists and Anglicans were numerous and significant. Indeed, Gill did not hesitate to announce, "We cannot think such a church is a true church of Christ." *Dissenters' Reasons* resonated with nonconformists of all stripes, seeing multiple editions in Gill's own lifetime. Baptists in Virginia, for instance, knew firsthand the "persecuting spirit" of established Anglicanism, as David Thomas's *The Virginian Baptist* (1774) clearly demonstrates.[24]

Despite the historic enmity between the two traditions, Hart was happy to work with clergymen who shared his evangelical commitments. We have already seen this in his long-term partnership with George Whitefield. But Hart also befriended Richard Clarke, who served St. Philip's in Charleston from 1753–59, during which time he strongly supported the revival. In later years, Clarke gained notoriety for his wild apocalyptic predictions, as when his "enthusiasm rose to such a height that he let his beard grow and ran about the streets crying, Repent, Repent, for the Kingdom of Heaven is at hand." Clarke sadly ended his life impoverished and espousing universalism, but in his Charleston years, Hart loved Clarke's evangelical fervor, and enjoyed a most cordial relationship with him. "Waited, this Afternoon, on the Rev. Mr. Clark, Rector of this place, who Receiv'd me with all possible Expressions of kindness; and after we had spent some time Agreeably together, he took me in his Chair to a funeral," Hart wrote. "I am heartily pleas'd to see the Catholic Spirit of which this man is possess'd; and I hope, and believe, he will be a Blessing to this Town." For the rector of St. Philip's to invite the Regular Baptist minister to ride in his carriage was unusual enough, but Clarke later outdid this gesture by inviting Hart to conduct a funeral at the church cemetery in his place. This, to Hart, "discovered an Extraordinary Catholick Spirit."[25]

The variety of personal friendships Hart maintained across the denominational spectrum testifies that the same "Extraordinary Catholick Spirit" resided in him. By focusing on a mutual commitment to the gospel and a shared experience of evangelical piety, Hart was able to establish effective gospel partnerships with Christians of sometimes vastly different doctrinal convictions. As historian David W. Bebbington has written, Hart's life demonstrates that the "experience of the revival brought Baptists closer to other Christian traditions. Evangelicals were sure that what united them, the gospel of salvation, was far more important than what divided them."[26] Hart's catholicity provides one clear signal of the revival's influence on Regular Baptist spirituality.

Hart's ecumenism had its limits. Thomas S. Kidd has called Hart "less a precisionist Baptist than a revivalist and moral reformer," but his Baptist convictions should not be trivialized. While Regular Baptists affirmed their solidarity with other evangelicals, they also remained passionate about maintaining biblical church order. This is evidenced by the Charleston Baptist Association's adoption of *A Summary of Church Discipline* (1774), which Hart and Francis Pelot had prepared. The Charleston Confession asserted that "the catholick or universal church, which (with respect to the internal work of the Spirit and truth of grace) may be called invisible" included "the whole number of the elect that have been, are, or shall be gathered into One, under Christ." Yet Hart also declared that membership in a local church, ordered according to the scriptures, was vital to Christian spirituality. He described "a particular gospel church" as consisting of "a company of saints, incorporated by a special covenant into one distinct body and meeting together in one place for the enjoyment of fellowship with each other and with Christ their Head in all his institutions to their mutual edification and the glory of God through the Spirit."[27] With other Regular Baptists, Hart continued to care deeply about biblically ordered local church life even as he cheerfully embraced Christians from other traditions to spread the revival. The ecclesiological issues that especially interested Hart were baptism, communion, and church membership.

The ordinance of baptism was "the defining rite of the Baptist religion" and represented the most obvious point of difference between Regular Baptists and their evangelical friends in Europe and America. Unlike virtually all other participants in the Great Awakening, Baptists rejected the sprinkling of infants as a sign of covenant membership, insisting instead that biblical baptism was only "by immersion, upon a profession of their faith, agreeable to the ancient practice of John the Baptist and the apostles of our Lord Jesus Christ."[28] Other traditions looked on immersion as a radical, offensive practice, as David Thomas wrote in *The Virginian Baptist*:

> Decency one might think, would constrain you to administer that ordinance, in a more agreeable and becoming manner than you do. What need dipping of people? Is not a drop or two of water as good as the whole ocean? And is not pouring or sprinkling much better modes of baptism, than plunging; especially in such a freezing cold country as this is? Why then are you so bigotted to such an obsolete, unfashionable, odious ceremony, as to differ with all the rest of the Christian world about it? It is your obstinate attachment to this ridiculous manner of baptizing your converts, that chiefly serves to render your sect odious, so contemptible in the eyes of every other denomination that practices water baptism at all. There is no peculiar mode essential to the ordinance, therefore one will answer as well as another, and it is very impudent not to choose that which is the easiest, the latest and of greatest reputation. How vain must you then be to persist in your odd way! When there are so many learned remonstrances made against it; since it exposes you to universal derision and makes your very name a laughing stock; surely it would be your wisest course to alter it immediately and bear the reproach of so needless a deviation from the common custom of Christians no longer.[29]

Baptists were unmoved by these scoffs. As they saw it, only the immersion of a confessing believer conformed to scripture's pattern of baptism and communicated the rich symbolism "of our fellowship with Christ, in his death, burial, and resurrection—of the remission of our sins, and of our resurrection from the death of sin to new and holy life." And so Hart rejoiced with Richard Furman over the significance of the baptisms of his wife and daughter: "But when you had the Happiness of leading a Wife and a Daughter into the Water and burying them with Christ in Baptism; and having thus symbolically washed away their Sins, of receiving them into Christ's Sheepfold, methinks your soul was in Raptures." Baptism was precious to Regular Baptists.[30]

Hart did not shrink from trying to persuade non-Baptists of his position. In 1780, Hart preached for several weeks to the people of Stone River Presbyterian Church. One night, Captain John Stephenson, a member of the church, told Hart he was "convinced of the Invalidity of Infant Sprinkling and the Validity of Believers Baptism, to which he desired to submit." Hart examined Stephenson, who satisfied Hart with his "gracious Experience & Knowledge of Gospel Doctrines." A few weeks later, Hart gathered "a large Congregation" for a service "under the shade of trees, near the banks of N. River." Though all were "professed Presbyterians," Hart preached for half an hour from Mark 16:16, "from which first I endeavoured to prove that Believers are the only proper Subjects of Baptism, and that Dipping is the Mode of Administration." He confessed that "How the People felt I don't know," though they all "behaved decently, and heard with much attention." After the sermon, Hart stepped down into the river. There, "in the face of the whole congregation, I baptized Capt. John Stephenson, a man of good character, and member of the Presbyterian Church." The ritual held the pedobaptist crowd spellbound: Stephenson was "the first Person ever Baptized in these Parts or in this River, hope Numbers may follow the Example, though a new and strange Thing to almost all who saw it. Never did I see people behave with more Decorum and Solemnity at the Administration of Baptism, in all my Life." Afterward Hart added, "I hope he will not disgrace the Baptists by embracing their Principles."[31]

Hart's convictions regarding baptism carried significant implications for his views of local church membership. As he noted in the *Summary of Church Discipline*, all who are received into church communion "ought to be truly baptized in water, i.e. by immersion, upon a profession of their faith, agreeable to the ancient practice of John the Baptist and the apostles of our Lord Jesus Christ." Requiring baptism before membership and communion at the Lord's table was not unique to Baptists; it was a fact "allowed by all," Baptist and pedobaptist alike. Baptists simply did not recognize pedobaptists to have been "truly baptized in water," and were convinced that "there is not one instance in the Word of God of any being admitted without it." Thus, while Hart felt free to invite the Methodist Joseph Pilmoor or the Presbyterian John Zubly to preach in his pulpit, he could not admit them to church membership or to the Lord's table.[32]

This position tended to blunt the force of the ecumenical ethos of the transatlantic Protestant revival, and Whitefield regularly confronted his Baptist friends over their "narrowness." He pleaded with Jenkin Jones, "Oh admit of a *mixed communion*. I think the glory of God requires this at your hands. May the Lord give you a right understanding in all things." The Philadelphia Association would, in fact, speak to this issue at their meeting just months later. Prompted by the catholicity of the revival, the Cohansey Baptist Church inquired if a pious pedobaptist may be admitted to communion without baptism, and, furthermore, "doth not refusing admittance to such an one, discover want of charity in a church so refusing?" The association unanimously answered in the negative, citing three reasons for their ruling. First, they found in the commission of Christ no unbaptized persons admitted to communion (Matt 28:19–20; Mark 16:16; Acts 2:41; 1 Cor 12:13); second, it is the church's duty to maintain the ordinances as delivered in Scripture (2 Thess 2:15; 1 Cor 11:2; Isa 8:20); and third, "because we cannot see it agreeable, in any respect, for the procuring that unity, unfeigned love, and undisturbed peace, which is required, and ought to be in and among Christian communities (1 Cor 1:10; Eph 4:3)."[33]

The discussion was not new in Baptist life, as Whitefield pointed out in a 1767 preface to the *Works of John Bunyan*. Bunyan, beloved by all evangelicals for his *Pilgrim's Progress*, had served as a Baptist pastor in Bedford, England, in the late seventeenth century. Yet he invited controversy in 1672 by publishing *A Confession of my Faith, and A Reason of my Practice; or With who and who not, I can hold church-fellowship, or the communion of saints.* Here Bunyan announced that while he dared not fellowship with the openly profane, he would happily commune with "those that are visible saints by calling: with those that, by the word of the gospel, have been brought over to faith and holiness." In classic Pietist fashion, Bunyan prioritized the invisible church of all the regenerate over any visible church form. Differences over water baptism should not bar God's children from communion in the local church, for "the edification of souls in the faith and holiness of the gospel, is of greater concernment, than an agreement in outward things." When Christians differed over baptism, Bunyan advised, "love them still, forgive them, bear with them, and maintain church communion with them. Why? Because they are new creatures, because they are Christ's: for this swallows up all distinctions." Bunyan even accused those who made baptism grounds for separation in church communion of being "carnal," "babyish Christians." Several Particular Baptist ministers immediately "fell with might and main" upon Bunyan. Unmoved, he responded with *Differences in Judgment About Water Baptism No Bar to Communion*, and *Peaceable Principles and True*. He maintained that "baptism with water, is neither a bar nor bolt to communion of saints, nor a door nor inlet to communion of saints." He prayed, "God, banish bitterness out of the churches and pardon them that are the maintainers of schisms and divisions among the godly."[34]

Whitefield praised Bunyan for his big-hearted ecumenism. "But this, I must own, more particularly endears Mr. Bunyan to my heart," Whitfield wrote.

> He was of a catholic spirit, the want of water adult baptism with this man of God, was no bar to outward Christian communion. And I am persuaded that if, like him, we were more deeply and experimentally baptized in to the benign and gracious influences of the blessed Spirit, we should be less baptized into the waters of strife, about circumstances and non-essentials. For being thereby rooted and grounded in the love of God, we should necessarily be constrained to think, and let think, bear with and forbear one another in love; and without saying "I am of Paul, Apollos, or

> Cephas," have but one grand, laudable, disinterested strife, namely who should live, preach and exalt the ever-loving, altogether lovely Jesus most.

While Hart celebrated the unity of the universal church, he did not believe scripture permitted him to adopt these more liberal standards of local church communion. In 1782, Hart and the rest of the Philadelphia Association responded to the question, "What measures ought to be taken with a sister church who holds and actually admits unbaptized persons to the Lord's Supper?" Again, their response was unequivocal: "We observe, that such a church may and ought in the first instance, to be written to by a sister church, exhorting them to desist from such a practice, and to keep the ordinances as they were delivered to them in the word of God."[35]

Hart expressed himself warmly on the subject in a 1790 letter to Richard Furman. The Charleston Association, led by Furman, had recently approved the admittance of some Baptists into membership in a pedobaptist congregation. From his home in Hopewell, New Jersey, Hart vigorously objected to this decision, showing once again how he was both a precisionist Baptist and an evangelical revivalist. He noted that both Baptists and pedobaptists agreed that baptism was "essential to Church Membership and Communion." With this point established, Hart believed "it naturally follows that no Society of Christians, however pious, can impose a regular orderly Church, upon a Gospel Plan, without baptism." From this ground, Hart concluded that "it cannot be consistent with *good order* to dismiss our Members to any Church whatever which is so disorderly as to set aside an Ordinance, which Christ in his Gospel holds as essentially necessary to Church Communion and Fellowship." Hart believed that pedobaptists were consistent in their position, and that Baptists should be, too. Pedobaptists would "never do" what the association had done, and dismiss their members into communion with a Baptist church. This would legitimize believer's baptism, which "would end to bring down their Infant-Sprinkling." In the same way, Hart argued, the association's approval of its members joining pedobaptist churches comprised "a tacit Acknowledgement that Infant Sprinkling is equally valid with Believers Baptism" and opened the door for its members to "slide into the Bosom of Pedobaptist Churches." He closed by emphatically stating that "there need be no dismissing of members to churches with whom we are not in communion; for we ought to hold communion with all *True Christian Churches*."

Hart realized that his strong ecclesiological statements did not savor of the "catholic spirit" he exhibited on so many other occasions. Hart did not intend to be sectarian, simply obedient to Christ's commands: "I hope nothing that I have said will be construed into Bigotry, or the want of Christian Regard to Pedobaptists. I think the whole Tenor of my Conduct acquits me from such a Charge. I sincerely declare, that I esteem a number of Pedobaptists as Christians, in Preference to many Baptists, and could freely commune with them at the Lord's Table, if my Master did not forbid by making Baptism an *essential* Prerequisite to Church Membership; and we are to walk by this. With regard to our Pedobaptist Brethren I wish them well and forbid them not, though they walk not with us." Hart's letter to Furman supplies valuable insight into the ecumenical tensions Regular Baptists experienced in the wake of the revival. Evangelical piety provided sufficient grounds for cooperation in preaching the gospel and spreading the revival. Yet sincere piety did not set aside what to them were clear biblical directives regarding "a regular orderly church, upon a Gospel Plan." Regular Baptists held church order to be far more significant than did Whitefield or Bunyan. On the other side of the new birth, both Baptists and pedobaptists must walk in obedience to Christ as best they both knew how, even if they could not walk together.[36]

Though Hart enjoyed a wide acceptance in Charleston society, he understood that both a religious and a social stigma were attached to being Baptist. He wrote to Furman, "I wish for the Interest of the Religion we profess, [that] we may all grow in Grace, Knowledge, and Understanding, that the Baptists may be distinguished by Something superior to Folly and Meanness" This negative perception was more pronounced in Virginia, but Baptists everywhere occupied a lower rung on the social ladder. This is clearly demonstrated in the journals of Charles Woodmason (1720?–89). In 1766, Woodmason took ordination vows in the Anglican Church and accepted an itinerant mission to the Carolina backcountry. During this mission, Woodmason regularly skewered the "New Light Baptists" in his journal, including Regulars and Separates alike. He condemned Baptists for revival enthusiasm: "They set about effecting in an instant, what requires both labour and time—they apply to the passions, not the understanding of the people." He also accused them of hypocrisy and immorality: "does your assembling together to see a few worthless wretches dipp'd in water, and viewing their nakedness (which some have purposely expos'd to your view) tend to edification?" he asked his congregation. The Baptists did not help the relationship. Among other abuses he suffered, Woodmason reported, "The people took up two others for entering the house where I was when in bed—stealing my gown—putting it on—and then visiting a woman in bed, and getting to bed to her, and making her give out next day, that the Parson came to bed to her—this was a scheme laid by the Baptists—and man and woman prepared for the purpose." Still, Woodmason did not condemn all Baptists. "I know, and greatly respect, many worthy persons among them and I wish that there were many more such," he admitted; "it is very plain that the errors of some of our neighbors do not so much proceed from a bad heart (as is the case with another sect) as from a wrong head."[37]

Hart appears to be one of the wrongheaded Baptists Woodmason tolerated, for he records delivering a parcel of letters and books to "the Reverend Mr. Hart" in Charleston on September 7, 1766. Nevertheless, Hart happily identified himself with the frontier Baptists Woodmason despised, and accepted the scorn that came along with it. He remembered his hero, Whitefield, scoffing at immersion. "The great and good Mr. Whitfield exclaim'd—'These Anabaptists are stealing Sheep, they wash my Sheep and they fleece my Sheep,'" Whitefield clearly intending "'Washing'" as "a term of aspersion." On one occasion, Hart mentioned a young woman whom he feared was "perhaps raised too high to associate with the humble Baptists." In reflecting on the young lady's hesitancy, he remembered a similar case from his past experience: a lady who became convinced of Baptist principles yet remained unwilling to hold communion with the Baptists. She "wished me to baptize her, that she might join the Church of England. I could not find a Freedom to do it," Hart recalled. "It is a pity that Grandeur should have so much Influence on the Minds of those who would be deem'd Followers of that humble Jesus, who had nowhere to lay his Head." Like other Baptists of his day, Hart viewed the sneer of the culture that his piety attracted as a badge of honor, a mark of his separation from the world.[38]

In the end, Richard Furman was right to remember Hart as "a consistent, liberal Baptist." In his relationships with other believers, Hart sought to avoid both a narrow sectarianism that sacrificed Christian charity as well as a careless sentimentality that compromised the truth as he understood it. Hart described his own principled ecumenism when he praised his friend William Tennent III. "It may not be amiss to observe, that his religious sentiments were open, free and generous, built upon principles of true catholocism [*sic*]; not influenced by bigotry or party spirit. He thought that religion should be left entirely free, and that there should be no manner of constraint upon the conscience," Hart said. "He was of opinion, that there was a wise providence in permitting people to think differently about modes of worship, and therefore valued good men of every denomination." The evangelical catholicity of Oliver Hart and his Regular Baptist friends stands as a further testimony to their participation in the international Protestant evangelical awakening. Without apology, they maintained their commitment to Baptist principles wherever they found them in the Bible, for they viewed obedience even in "nonessentials" as a matter of loyalty to Jesus. At the same time, the stories of Hart, Jenkin Jones, Isaac Chanler, William Tilly, and other eighteenth-century Regular Baptists reveal that their "religious sentiments were free, open, and generous," and that they indeed "valued good men of every denomination" as they together worked to advance the evangelical revival in their time.[39]

Conclusion

Revival Legacy

Oliver Hart was delighted to receive a note from Isaac Backus at the beginning of 1777. For over twenty-five years, both ministers had labored for revival among the Baptist people, Backus in Middleborough, Massachusetts, and Hart in Charleston, South Carolina. Yet the two men, among the leading American Baptist figures of their generation, had never met. Hart was pleased that Backus had "opened the door" for correspondence. He complimented Backus on several of his recent publications and expressed interest in his forthcoming history of the Baptists in New England. Eventually, Hart turned to the spiritual condition of his Charleston congregation. "I have resided in this Town, and had the pastoral Charge of the Baptist Church here, upwards of twenty seven years, in which time have seen many Changes, and passed through many Tryals, personal and relative. The Church at some Times has flourished, at others declined. At present it is at a low Ebb, and can hardly be looked upon in any other Light than as a *little sister* among the Daughters of Zion. My Soul longs for the downpouring of the Spirit amongst us, that we may have an ingathering of many Souls; for this, I crave your Interest at the Throne of Grace." These lines exemplify the piety of the Great Awakening. The meteoric rise of the Separate Baptist movement in the mid-1750s has generally overshadowed the contribution that Regular Baptists made to the eighteenth-century evangelical revival. By analyzing the spirituality of South Carolina Regular Baptist Oliver Hart, we have seen that revival played a far greater role in Regular Baptist identity than historians have recognized. Indeed, the transoceanic evangelical revival of the eighteenth century profoundly shaped Hart's entire life and ministry.[1]

The findings of this book are significant on at least three levels. At the broadest level, the thesis confirms current scholarly work on the pervasive influence of the Great Awakening in colonial South Carolina and the lower South. For decades, American religious historians assumed that, compared to New England and the Middle Colonies, the South was little impacted by the evangelical revival until later in the eighteenth century. More recently, Kidd, Thomas J. Little, and

Samuel C. Smith have all shown the extensive influence of the revival in South Carolina from an early date. The present study contributes to this growing body of literature by demonstrating the revival spirituality of Regular Baptist pastor Oliver Hart of Charleston.[2]

This book has also exposed the weaknesses of a popular model of Southern Baptist identity. In the latter half of the twentieth century, William L. Lumpkin and Walter B. Shurden credited the Separate Baptists with bringing the spiritual "ardor" of the Great Awakening to the Baptists of the South. In his influential study of the Separate Baptists, Lumpkin made numerous, sweeping, dismissive statements regarding Regular Baptist participation in the revival. "The Baptist awakening was not in any primary sense the concern or achievement of the 'regular' Baptist groups already resident in the South prior to 1755," Lumpkin insisted. He claimed that "the Regulars stood aloof" from the evangelical awakening, "wary of its theology, its enthusiasm, and its connections with established churches." He further opined that the Regular Baptists "could never have won the South. They lacked the enthusiasm, the vision, and the leadership required for so formidable an undertaking." In the generation following Lumpkin, Shurden solidified this perception at both the academic and the popular levels, by assigning the pithy labels of "order" to the Regular Baptists and "ardor" to the Separates. As this book has demonstrated, Lumpkin and Shurden offered an oversimplified and misleading presentation of the Regular Baptists, which has widely mischaracterized the movement. Lumpkin's failed assessment of the Regular Baptists appears to have stemmed from his exclusive focus on colonial Virginia, where the movement was admittedly weaker than in the middle colonies or in the lower South. Lumpkin and Shurden failed to account for the abundant primary source material that attests to the revival spirituality of the Regular Baptists in colonial South Carolina. Beginning in the late seventeenth century, Particular and Regular Baptists like William Screven, Gilbert Ashley, Isaac Chanler, and William Tilly all practiced a vigorous, revival spirituality in the lower South long before the Separate Baptist movement emerged under the ministry of George Whitefield. In the following generation, Oliver Hart, Francis Pelot, Samuel Stillman, Edmund Botsford, Evan Pugh, and Joseph Reese also actively participated in the transatlantic Protestant awakening. While Lumpkin and Shurden rightly identify some of the significant cultural and stylistic differences that existed between the Regulars and Separates, their overall portrayal of sharp discontinuity in their theology and spirituality is ultimately unhelpful and should be discarded.[3]

Finally, this study represents the first book-length treatment of Oliver Hart, a giant among eighteenth-century American Baptists. With all due respect to the unparalleled achievements of Separate Baptists Shubal Stearns and Daniel Marshall, our study suggests that it is Hart, the Regular Baptist revivalist, who should be credited with laying the foundations of Baptist life in the South. As historian Loulie Latimer Owens remarked over fifty years ago, Southern Baptists have no more important pioneer. The potent spiritual mixture of Particular Baptist order and Great Awakening ardor produced in him one of the most dynamic and fascinating lives of his remarkable generation.[4]

NOTES

INTRODUCTION

1. Hart, diary, August 25, 1754; August 27, 1754; September 1, 1754; August 23, 1754; Hart MSS, James B. Duke Memorial Library, Furman University, Greenville, South Carolina (hereafter JBDL); Kidd, *Great Awakening,* xix.

2. Baker, Craven, and Blalock, *First Baptist Church,* 33–71; Burrage, *History,* 18–19, 13–14. Historians debate whether the year of the church's migration was 1682 or not until 1696. Hirsch, *Huguenots,* 309; Lincoln et al., eds., "The Hinkley Papers," 305; Tupper, *Two Centuries,* 58; Talbert and Farish, *Antipedo Baptists,* 19–26; Townsend, *South Carolina Baptists,* 12.

3. Chanler, *Doctrines of Glorious Grace;* Kegley and Little, "The Records of the Ashley River Baptist Church, 1736–1769," 3–4, 10, 11; Whitefield, *Journals,* 440–41; Chanler, *New Converts Exhorted;* Little, *Southern Evangelicalism,* 154–57, 174; Edwards, *History of the Baptists,* 2:125; Townsend, *South Carolina Baptists,* 20, 38, 63.

4. Townsend, *South Carolina Baptists,* 8; Benedict, *General History,* 703; Whitefield, *Journals,* 447; George Whitefield to Mr. N., August 15, 1740, in *Works,* 1:203.

5. Little, *Southern Evangelicalism,* i–xv; Hill, "A Survey of Southern Religious History," 383; Heyrman, *Southern Cross,* 9; Little, *Southern Evangelicalism,* xii–xiii; examples of fine studies on the Great Awakening in Virginia include Gewehr, *Great Awakening in Virginia;* Isaac, *Transformation of Virginias;* and Mulder, *Controversial Spirit.*

6. Lumpkin, *Baptist Foundations,* v–vi.

7. Ibid., v–vi, 20–21, 147, 29, 157, 70–71, 154.

8. Shurden, "Southern Baptist Synthesis," 2–11. Shurden later credited Claude L. Howe, his major church history professor at New Orleans Baptist Theological Seminary, for introducing him to the designations of "order" and "ardor" in the discussion of the Charleston and Sandy Creek Traditions. Shurden, *Not an Easy Journey,* 204n5.

9. Shurden later referred to this address as a "precture," or "a dab of lecturing and a dab of preaching." He adds, "I have done a good bit of precturing in my life. It is one of my favorite things to do. A 'precture' both frees one from the formality of an academic article while holding one accountable for what is said." Shurden, *Not an Easy Journey,* iv; Shurden, "Southern Baptist Synthesis," 11, emphasis original.

10. Matthews, *Religion in the Old South,* 23; McBeth, *Baptist Heritage,* 227–34; Leonard, *Baptist Ways,* 120, 122; Leonard, "Southern Baptist Confessions: Dogmatic Ambiguity," 164; Fletcher, *Southern Baptist Convention,* 31–32; Wardin, *Tennessee Baptists,* 34; Flynt, *Alabama Baptists,* 26n60.

11. Caner, "The Forgotten Hour"; Tomlin, "Sandy Creek."

12. Smith, "Prayer Language Debate"; the "Our History" page on the First Baptist Waynesboro website reads, "FBC Waynesboro is a church that was born out of the Charleston

Tradition and maintained that tradition tenaciously for a long time. The church has known intermittent seasons of Sandy Creek saturation and has become the kind of church in which these streams have merged mightily, a church where the mind can be challenged and the heart can be 'strangely warmed,' where the holiness of God is honored and the love of God is celebrated, a church where genuine emotional expression in worship is encouraged in the context of biblically directed decorum," "Our History," *First Baptist Church, Waynesboro, Georgia,* accessed 10 December 2014, http://fbcwaynesboro.org/about/history/.

13. Lumpkin, *Baptist Foundations,* 60–63; Nettles, "Shubal Stearns," 26–31; Smith, "Prayer Language Debate"; Wills, "Whosoever Will: A Review Essay," 10–11; Ascol, "Happy Birthday Sandy Creek."

14. Loftis, "Factors in Southern Baptist Identity," xxi, 257.

15. Owens, "South Carolina Baptists and the American Revolution," 31–45; McGloughlin, *Isaac Backus;* Rogers, *Richard Furman;* Owens, *Oliver Hart, 1723–1795;* Owens, "Hart, Oliver," in *Encyclopedia of Southern Baptists,* 601; Owens, "Oliver Hart and the American Revolution," 2–17; Clayton and Owens, eds., "Oliver Hart's Diary of the Journey to the Backcountry," 18–30; Owens, "South Carolina Baptists and the American Revolution"; Baker, Craven, and Blalock, *First Baptist Church;* Davies, *Transatlantic Brethren;* Rogers, *Richard Furman;* McKibbens, "Over Troubled Waters: Baptist Preachers Who Were Bridge Builders," 58–63; Nettles, *The Baptists: Beginnings in America;* Kidd, *Great Awakening,* 264–66; Kidd and Hankins, *Baptists in America;* Little, *Origins of Southern Evangelicalism.*

16. Hart, *Character of a Truly Great Man;* Hart, *Dancing Exploded;* Hart, *Humble Attempt;* Hart, *Gospel Church Portrayed;* Hart, *America's Remembrancer;* Hart, "Circular Letter," in Gillette, ed., *Minutes,* 181–91; Guild, *Early History;* Brackney, "James Manning (1738–1791)," in *A Noble Company,* 3:511–38; Davies, *Transatlantic Brethren;* Mallary, *Edmund Botsford;* Stillman, *Select Sermons;* Broome, *Hezekiah Smith.*

CHAPTER 1: SHAPED BY REVIVAL

1. Furman, *Rewards of Grace,* 21.

2. Hart co-wrote this essay with another Quaker named Thomas Budd. The Hart family historian, writing in 1877, noted, "We have never seen a copy of this work, and do not know that one is in existence"; Davis, *Bucks County,* 215; Butler, "Gospel Order Improved," 431–52; Whitefield, *Journals,* 341; Davis, *Hart Family,* 22–23.

3. Davis, *Hart Family,* 31–32.

4. Lindman, *Bodies of Belief;* McLoughlin, *Baptist Beginnings in Education,* 23; Gillette, *Minutes,* 60–63; McBeth, *Baptist Heritage,* 243–46; Lumpkin, *Baptist Confessions of Faith,* 348–55; Furman, *Rewards of Grace,* 24; Rogers, *Death of the Rev. Oliver Hart,* 22.

5. Hart, *Character,* 24; Ray, "Jenkin Jones," 203; Kidd, *Great Awakening,* 36–39; Maxson, *Great Awakening,* 62.

6. Whitefield, *Journals,* 310, 420; Oliver Hart to Richard Furman, June 1, 1791, Hart MSS, JBDML.

7. Davis, *Hart Family,* 32, 101, 102.

8. Davis, *Hart Family,* 103; Hart, *Original Diary,* 2.

9. Edwards, *Materials,* 2:123; Baker, Craven, and Blalock, *First Baptist Church,* 101–3.

10. Townsend, *South Carolina Baptists,* 36–38; Manly, *Mercy and Judgment,* 23, 27; Baker, Craven, and Blalock, *First Baptist Church,* 115–19.

11. Furman, *Charleston Association,* 7; Manly, *Mercy and Judgment,* 31.

12. "Poem by Captain Martin," quoted in Edgar, *South Carolina,* 155.

13. Whitefield, *Journals,* 384; Edgar, *South Carolina,* 161–62; Oliver Hart to John Hart, September 1755, South Caroliniana Library, University of South Carolina, Columbia (hereafter SCL); Oliver Hart to Samuel Jones, June 30, 1769, McKesson MSS, Historical Society of Pennsylvania (hereafter HSP); Oliver Hart to John Hart, March 24, 1778, Hart MSS, SCL; Hart, diary, June 10, 1780, SCL.

14. Whitefield, *Journals,* 444; Edgar, *South Carolina,* 171–73; Hart, diary, September 8, 1754, JBDML.

15. Edgar, *South Carolina,* 156–61; the children Hart lost were Seth (1748–1750), Hannah (1750–1753), Joseph (1760–1761), Sarah (October 16, 1772–October 19, 1772), and Silas, a child of his second marriage (August 30, 1775–September 21, 1775); Oliver Hart to Samuel Jones, July 15, 1765, McKesson MSS, HSP; Hart, *Original Diary,* 2–5; Fraser, *Charleston!,* 83–85; Hart, *Dancing Exploded,* 1–2.

16. Wood, *Black Majority,* 132.

17. Woodmason, *Carolina Backcountry,* 6–7.

18. Hart, diary, August 19, 1754, Hart MSS, Furman; Baker, Craven, and Blalock, *First Baptist Church,* 136–37; Hart, sermon on 1 Timothy 4:16, Hart MSS, SCL, emphasis original.

19. Furman, *Rewards of Grace,* 24; Hart, *Humble Attempt,* 14–15.

20. Hart, sermon on 1 Timothy 4:16, Hart MSS, SCL; Mallary, *Edmund Botsford,* 14.

21. Hart, diary, August 24, 1754, Hart MSS, JBDML.

22. Furman, *Rewards of Grace,* 24; Mallary, *Edmund Botsford,* 16; Botsford, Diary 1769–1770, JBDML.

23. Hart, diary, October 6, 1754, Hart MSS, JBDML; Lumpkin, *Baptist Foundations,* v.

24. Hart, sermon on 1 Timothy 4:16, Hart MSS, SCL; Oliver Hart to John Hart, March 10, 1757, Hart MSS, SCL; Oliver Hart to Richard Furman, November 26, 1793, Hart MSS, JBDML.

25. Oliver Hart to James Manning, August 30, 1765, Manning MSS, John Hay Library, Brown University, Providence, Rhode Island (hereafter JHL). In a letter to Samuel Jones from the same period, Hart wondered if the Bedgegood debacle was not a sign of God's judgment: "We are, I am persuaded, guilty before God, in bringing Mr. Bedgegood from a numerous, well-affected people, where he was greatly useful, to serve us, who were not so much in need of help. Hence God has frowned upon us ever since; so that from step to step, our case has been growing worse and worse, until it is almost become desperate." Oliver Hart to Samuel Jones, July 15, 1765, McKesson MSS, HSP.

26. Oliver Hart to Samuel Jones, March 7, 1766, McKesson MSS, HSP.

27. Hart, *Original Diary,* 7; Anne Hart, *Narrative,* HSP.

28. Oliver Hart to John Hart, September 1755, Hart MSS, SCL; Edwards, *Materials Towards a History of the Baptists,* 1:98; Basil Manly, *Mercy and Judgment,* 34; Hart, *Original Diary,* 12; Baker, Craven, and Blalock, *First Baptist Church,* 143.

29. Oliver Hart to Samuel Jones, June 30, 1769, Mckesson MSS, HSP. Hart's attitude toward the Separates certainly does not reflect Lumpkin's blanket statement that "the Regulars were suspicious of the Separates' enthusiasm and irregularity in permitting women and illiterate men to preach." He also records Fristoe as saying that "the Regular Baptists were jealous of the Separate Baptists." Lumpkin, *Baptist Foundations,* 69. This attitude appears to have been far more prominent among Regular Baptists in Virginia than among those in

South Carolina. Lumpkin fails to give Hart and his Regular Baptist cohorts the credit they deserve in laying foundations for Baptist life in the South. Examples of his faint praise for the Regular Baptists include: "The Separates soon were made to realize, however, that there were other Baptist groups in the South beside themselves, all rather small, struggling companies," and "The Regular Baptists, in a word, could never have won the South. They lacked the enthusiasm, the vision, and the leadership required for so formidable an undertaking. To be sure, the Regulars experienced a renewed vigor during the southern Awakening, but this renewal came chiefly from the Separates. The Regulars then made a real contribution to the Awakening, but it was limited in scope." Lumpkin, *Baptist Foundations*, 63, 157.

30. Hart's backcountry journals, decoded, are published in Clayton and Owens, eds., "Journey to the Backcountry," 18–30.

31. Hart, diary, December 16, 1780, Hart MSS, SCL. Hart's first order of business upon moving into the parsonage was to retrieve his niece, Nelly Thomas, as his housekeeper. "I trust Providence will favor me in sending her," he wrote, "for I know not how to manage without her," Hart, diary, December 26, 1780, Hart MSS, SCL. In several entries, Hart mentions the church mending his fences, plowing his fields, cutting his wood, and otherwise working to make him comfortable. Six of Anne's letters to Oliver from this period have survived, all in Hart MSS, SCL. From these letters, Owens suggests, "Nancy must have been quite spoiled. She chided her husband for leaving her, and she whined over her health and bad fortunes with an excess of self-pity." Owens, *Oliver Hart, 1723–1795*, 19. Oliver Hart to Anne (Nancy) Hart, June 12, 1781, Hart MSS, SCL; Hart, diary, September 2, 1781, Hart MSS, SCL.

32. Hart, diary, February 10, 1782, Hart MSS, SCL. In a letter dated August 27, 1790, Furman refers to a "hint" that Hart had dropped that he was interested in returning to the area. Though Furman expressed excitement over the prospect, he also reported that there was simply no suitable place of ministry for him at that time. Richard Furman to Oliver Hart, August 27, 1790, Richard Furman and James C. Furman Collection, JBDML. Hart, diary, April 8, 1781, Hart MSS, SCL. Hart's writing from this period mentions travels to Baltimore, Frederick Town, Philadelphia, and New York City. Hart has left a detailed account of one such trip in the spring of 1788, when he supplied the pulpit of the First Baptist Church of New York City for his friend John Gano.

33. Gillette, *Minutes*, 169–70, 181–91.

34. Oliver Hart to Isaac Backus, February 16, 1777, Gratz Collection, HSP; Gillette, *Philadelphia Baptist Association*, 174; Oliver Hart to Warren Baptist Association, April 22, 1781, Backus MSS, Franklin-Trask Library, Andover Newton Theological Seminary, Newton Centre, Massachusetts (hereafter FTL); Oliver Hart to Isaac Backus, July 25, 1781, Backus MSS, FTL.

35. Gillette, *Minutes*, 256; Oliver Hart to Richard Furman, May 30, 1793, Furman MSS, JBDML; Oliver Hart to Richard Furman, August 27, 1793, Hart MSS, SCL; Talbert and Farish, *Antipedo Baptists*, 36–37.

36. Hart, *Original Diary*, 2; Oliver Hart, diary, July 15, 1781, Hart MSS, SCL. Hart had written to Furman on October 9, 1784: "Hitherto I have been detailed in this place, and whether I shall ever return to Charleston or not is a matter yet undetermined. I have my health so well here am so well settled, and the situation of this church is such, that I scarce know how to leave the Place. Yet wish my old charge to be supplied. I understand they have had an eye upon you. I have wrote to them to give you a call, which hope you will accept, if you can see

your way clear, as I know not of anyone that I should choose in preference, to fill up that place. I hope God will direct you in this great affair, for his own glory, and the good of his church. The struggles I have had in my own mind, to know duty, perhaps have not often been experienced. I now leave it with Him whose I am, [whom] I desire to serve and who can guide all my ways." Oliver Hart to Richard Furman, October 9, 1784, Hart MSS, JBDML.

37. Hart, diary, September 23, 1788, SCL; poem cited in William Rogers, *Death of Rev. Oliver Hart,* 21–22.

38. Oliver Hart to Richard Furman, July 15, 1790, Hart MSS, JBDML; Oliver Hart to Richard Furman, May 30, 1793, Richard Furman and James C. Furman MSS, JBDML; Oliver Hart to Richard Furman, June 15, 1791, Hart MSS, JBDML; Oliver Hart to Richard Furman, August 26, 1791, Hart MSS, JBDML; Oliver Hart for Charleston Baptist Association to Warren Baptist Association, February 16, 1777, Backus MSS, FTL.

39. Rogers, *Death of Rev. Oliver Hart,* 28–29, 19, 35; Furman, *Rewards of Grace,* 27; Hart, diary, October 1788, Hart MSS, SCL.

CHAPTER 2: REVIVAL PIETY

1. Hart, *Gospel Church,* 37–38.

2. Kidd, *Great Awakening;* Semple, *Rise and Progress,* 68, emphasis original.

3. Noll, *Rise of Evangelicalism,* 127–28.

4. Rogers, *Death of the Rev. Oliver Hart,* 22; *Second London Confession* 5.1–2; Gillette, *Minutes,* 182; Hart, *Gospel Church,* 19.

5. Wesley, *Free Grace,* 12–13, 14, 17–18, 18–23, 23–30; Oliver Hart to Samuel Jones, November 1, 1764, McKesson Collection, HSP; Oliver Hart, sermon on 1 Timothy 4:16, Hart MSS, SCL.

6. Gill, *Body of Divinity,* 203; Oliver Hart to Samuel Jones, December 1, 1763, McKesson MSS, HSP.

7. Hart, *Humble Attempt,* 15–16, emphasis original.

8. Hart, sermon on 1 Timothy 1:15, Hart MSS, SCL; Mallary, *Edmund Botsford,* 29, 45; Stillman, *Select Sermons,* x–xi; Whitefield, *A Letter to the Reverend John Wesley,* 12.

9. Whitefield, *Indwelling of the Spirit,* 16; Hart, sermon on 2 Timothy 1:9, sermon on 1 Timothy 2:5, Hart MSS, SCL; *Second London Confession* 6.4; Botsford, Diary 1769–1770, JBDML; Gillette, *Minutes,* 181.

10. Oliver Hart to Richard Furman, June 1, 1791, Hart MSS, JBDML; Hart, sermon on 1 Timothy 4:16, Hart MSS, SCL; Owens, *Oliver Hart, 1723–1795,* 26; Oliver Hart to Richard Furman, June 20, 1793, Hart MSS, SCL; Oliver Hart, diary, August 5, 1754, Hart MSS, JBDML, emphasis original; Oliver Hart, diary, October 15, 1781, Hart MSS, SCL.

11. Hart, *Dancing Exploded,* 5–6.

12. Ibid., 15, 16, 19, 24.

13. Hart, sermon on 1 Timothy 2:5, Hart MSS, SCL; Hart, sermon 1 Timothy 1:15, Hart MSS, SCL.

14. Oliver Hart to Richard Furman, May 8, 1790, Hart MSS, JBDML; Kidd, *Great Awakening,* 323; Whitefield, *A Sermon on Regeneration,* 5; Hart, diary, August 4, 1754, Hart MSS, JBDML.

15. Anne Hart, *Narrative of Anne Maria Sealy Grimball Hart, born 1741, South Carolina,* HSP.

16. Hart, sermon on 2 Timothy 1:9, Hart MSS, SCL; Hart, sermon on 1 Timothy 4:16, Hart MSS, SCL.

17. Hart, sermon on 2 Timothy 1:9, Hart MSS, SCL; Hart, diary, February 10, 1782, Hart MSS, SCL; Hart, diary, August 20, 1754, Hart MSS, JBDML.

18. Botsford, Diary 1769–1770, JBDML; Oliver Hart, Sermon Register 1773–1794, Hart MSS, SCL; Gillette, *Minutes,* 186–87; the poem can be found in Hart MSS, SCL.

19. Hart, sermon on 1 Timothy 1:9, Hart MSS, SCL; Edwards, "A Divine and Supernatural Light" in *Sermons,* 121–40; Hart, sermon on 1 John 3:2, in Edmund Botsford, Diary 1769–1770, JBDML.

20. Whitefield, *A Sermon on Regeneration,* 18; Hart, *Gospel Church,* 37–38.

21. Hart, sermon on 1 Timothy 1:15, Hart MSS, SCL; Hart, *Gospel Church,* 23.

22. Botsford, Diary 1769–1770, JBDML; Hart, sermon on 1 Timothy 1:15, Hart MSS, SCL.

23. Hart, sermon on 1 Timothy 1:9, Hart MSS, SCL; Hart, *Gospel Church,* 37.

24. Gillette, *Minutes,* 191; Hart, *Gospel Church,* 38; Whitefield, *Indwelling of the Spirit,* 6, 11; Chauncy, *Seasonable Thoughts,* i–xxx.

25. Botsford, Diary 1769–1770, JBDML.

26. Botsford, Diary 1769–1770, JBDML.

27. Hart, sermon on 1 Timothy 4:16, SCL; *Second London Confession* 13.2; Hart, sermon on 2 Timothy 2:3, SCL; see Ephesians 6:12; Hebrews 12:1; 1 Corinthians 9:24; 1 Timothy 6:12; 2 Timothy 4:7; 2 Timothy 2:3.

28. Oliver Hart to John Hart, September 1755, Hart MSS, SCL; Hart, sermon on 1 Timothy 4:16, Hart MSS, SCL; Whitefield, Letter MCMXII to Lady Huntingdon, December 31, 1755, in *Works,* 3:153; *Minutes of the Charlestown Association, February 6, 1775* (Charleston, 1775), 4; *Minutes of the Charlestown Association, October 19, 1778,* 4; Hart, sermon on 1 Timothy 4:16, Hart MSS, SCL.

29. Owen, *On the Mortification of Sin in the Believer* in *Works,* 6:8; Gill, *Body of Practical and Doctrinal Divinity,* 388; *Minutes of the Charleston Association, February 2, 1778* (Charleston, 1778), 4; Botsford, Diary 1769–1770, JBDML.

30. *Second London Confession* 15; Botsford, Diary 1769–1770, JBDML.

31. Hart, sermon on 1 Timothy 4:16, Hart MSS, SCL.

32. Botsford, Diary 1769–1770, JBDML; Hart, *Dancing Exploded,* 32.

33. Hart, diary, September 24, 1788, Hart MSS, SCL; Oliver Hart to Richard Furman, June 15, 1791, Hart MSS, JBDML; Oliver Hart to Richard Furman, May 7, 1792, Hart MSS, JBDML.

34. Whitefield, *Walking with God,* in *Works,* 5:27–31; Whitefield, *Sermon on Regeneration,* 17; Hart, diary, August 5, 1754, Hart MSS, JBDML.

35. *Second London Confession* 1.1; Hart, *Humble Attempt,* 35–36. Rogers, Hart, diary, August 19, 1754; October 23, 1754, Hart MSS, JBDML. Hart, diary, September 23, 1788, Hart MSS, SCL; *Death of the Rev. Oliver Hart,* 22.

36. Hart, *Original Diary,* 8; *Minutes of the Charleston Baptist Association, February 1775,* 4; Hart, diary, November 8, 1769–February 2, 1770, January 31, 1780, Hart MSS, SCL.

37. Haykin, "Shaping of English Puritan Piety," 38; Lovelace, *Cotton Mather,* 131; Hart, *Gospel Church,* 33–34.

38. Hart, *Humble Attempt,* 16; Hart, *Gospel Church,* 14; Hart, diary, August 3, 1780, SCL; Hart, diary, January 24, 1789, Hart MSS, SCL.

39. Hart, *Humble Attempt*, 17–18; Hart, *Gospel Church*, 27; Hart, diary, August 11, 1754, Hart MSS, JBDML; Hart, diary, January 20, 17, Hart MSS, SCL.

40. Furman, *Rewards of Grace*, 24; Hart, *Original Diary*, 8.

41. Hindmarsh, *John Newton*, 240–50; Davies, *Transatlantic Brethren*, 98; Oliver Hart to Samuel Jones, November 1, 1764, McKesson MSS, HSP; Mallary, *Edmund Botsford*, 52–53; Oliver Hart to Samuel Jones, December 1, 1763, McKesson MSS, HSP.

42. Oliver Hart to Samuel Jones, June 30, 1769, McKesson MSS, HSP; Oliver Hart to James Manning, December 23, 1767, Manning MSS, JHL.

CHAPTER 3: REVIVAL NARRATIVE

1. Hart, *Original Diary*, 3.

2. Edwards, *Great Awakening*, 176.

3. Ibid., 146–48, 151, 210.

4. Ibid., 130, 131, 134.

5. Wesley, *Journal*, 2:84; Hindmarsh, "Reception of Jonathan Edwards," 204–6; Robe, *Extraordinary Work*; Ward, *Protestant Evangelical Awakening*, 322; Noll, *Rise of Evangelicalism*, 91.

6. Hindmarsh, *Evangelical Conversion Narrative*, 68–69; Blair, *A Short and Faithful Narrative*, 3; Kidd, *Great Awakening*, 23.

7. Blair, *A Short and Faithful Narrative*, 44, 3–5.

8. Ibid., 15–16.

9. Ibid., 10–11, 15–18, 44.

10. Furman, *Rewards of Grace*, 25.

11. Spener, *Pia Desidera*, 45, 46; Kidd, *Great Awakening*, 39.

12. Gordon, *Evangelical Spirituality*, 5.

13. Hart, diary, August 5, 1754, Hart MSS, JBDML, emphasis original.

14. Hart, diary, August 19, 1754, Hart MSS, JBDML.

15. Bebbington, *Evangelicalism in Modern Britain*, 12–14; Edwards, *Great Awakening*, 184; Edwards, *Letters and Personal Writings*, 753–59, 741–52, 790–804.

16. Hart, diary, September 2, 1754, Hart MSS, JBDML, emphasis original; Manly, *Mercy and Judgment*, 35; Marsden, *Jonathan Edwards*, 158.

17. Hart, diary, August 4, 1754, Hart MSS, JBDML.

18. Hart, diary, August 23, 1754; August 25, 1754; September 20, 1754; October, 1754; September 1, 2, 3, 13, 1754; August 23, 1754; October 13, 1754; September 11, 22, August 25, 1754, Hart MSS, JBDML; Whitefield, "Blind Bartimaeus" in *Sermons*, 1:456–66.

19. Hart, diary, August 18, 20; September 16, 29, 1754, Hart MSS, JBDML.

20. Edwards, *Great Awakening*, 388; Hart, diary, August 4, 25, 1754, Hart MSS, JBDML.

21. Hart, diary, September 1, 11, August 11, October 2, August 27, September 4, 16, October 6, 1754, Hart MSS, JBDML.

22. Stillman, *Select Sermons*, vi.

23. Ibid.

24. Edwards, *Materials*, 2:93.

25. Stoeffler, *The Rise of Evangelical Pietism*, 19; Spener, *Pia Desideria*, 90; Noll, *Rise of Evangelicalism*, 67–69; Edwards, *Great Awakening*, 155–56, 161.

26. Hart, diary, August 20, 1754, Hart MSS, JBDML.

27. Oliver Hart, sermon on 1 Timothy 4:16, SCL; Hart, diary, August 20, 1754, Hart MSS, JBDML.

28. Hart, diary, August 21–23, 1754, Hart MSS, JBDML.

29. Hart, diary, August 24, 25, 26, 1754, Hart MSS, JBDML.

30. Edwards, *Great Awakening*, 176, 149, 190; Timothy Cutler to Zachary Grey, June 5, 1735, in Marsden, *Jonathan Edwards*, 161; Edwards, *Great Awakening*, 191.

31. Hart, diary, October 1, 1754, Hart MSS, JBDML; Outler, *John Wesley*, 67.

32. Hart, diary, September 5, 1754, Hart MSS, JBDML; Outler, *John Wesley*, 67, emphasis original; Edwards, *Great Awakening*, 172.

33. Bebbington, *Evangelicalism in Modern Britain*, 43, 47.

34. Hart, diary, September 5, 1754, Hart MSS, JBDML.

35. Edwards, *Religious Affections*, 101.

36. Hart, diary, August 26, 1754, Hart MSS, JBDML.

37. Ibid.

38. Hart, diary, September 16, 1754, Hart MSS, JBDML; Edwards, *Great Awakening*, 196; Hart, diary, August 27, 29, September 4, 1754, Hart MSS, JBDML.

39. Dickinson, *A display*; McClymond and McDermott, "Theology of Revival," 424–47; Edwards, *Great Awakening*, 226; Hart, diary, September 1, 1754, Hart MSS, JBDML.

40. Hart, diary, September 17, 22, 3, 1754, Hart MSS, JBDML.

41. Hart, diary, September 9, September 16, August 30, 1754, Hart MSS, JBDML.

42. Hart, diary, August 30, 1754, Hart MSS, JBDML.

43. Hart, diary, September 27, October 10, 1754, Hart MSS, JBDML.

44. Kidd, *Great Awakening*, xix; Lumpkin, *Baptist Foundations*, 20–21.

CHAPTER 4: REVIVAL ACTIVISM

1. Hart, diary, September 12, August 4, 1754, Hart MSS, JBDML; Bebbington, *Evangelicalism in Modern Britain*, 10–12; Gordon, *Evangelical Spirituality*, 59, 63; Hart, *Humble Attempt*, 41.

2. Hart, *Humble Attempt*, 4, 37–39.

3. Oliver Hart to Samuel Jones, December 1, 1763, McKesson MSS, HSP; Oliver Hart to John Hart, March 10, 1757, Hart MSS, SCL; Hart, *Gospel Church*, 23.

4. Hart, *Original Diary*, 3, 10–11; the other two soldiers were led to believe they would be executed with Malcolm but were instead reprimanded and returned to the ranks. Hart knew of this plan.

5. Hart, sermon on 1 Timothy 4:16, Hart MSS, SCL.

6. Lindman, *Bodies of Belief*, 169–72; Oliver Hart to John Hart, March 10, 1757, Hart MSS, SCL; Broome, *Hezekiah Smith*, 223–25; Hart, *Original Diary*, 5, 14–15; Hart, diary, July 5, 1780, Hart MSS, SCL.

7. Wolever, *John Gano*, 60.

8. Whitefield, *Works*, 2:116.

9. Marrant, *Narrative*, 12–13.

10. Oliver Hart to Richard Furman, November 26, 1793, Hart MSS, JBDML.

11. Owens, *Oliver Hart 1723–1795*, 1; Phillip James had been ordained by Isaac Chanler and Thomas Simmons in 1743. John Brown, ordained in May, 1750, left Welsh Neck soon

afterward, apparently due to some strange beliefs about the last things. He preached at large in the region for the next forty years; see Townsend, *South Carolina Baptists*, 64.

12. Hart, *Original Diary*, 2, 8.

13. Owens, *Oliver Hart, 1723–1795*, 10; Baker, Craven, and Blalock, *First Baptist Church*, 150–51.

14. Hart, Sermon on Associations, Hart MSS, SCL.

15. Lindman, *Bodies of Belief*, 24–25.

16. Hart, Sermon on Associations, Hart MSS, SCL.

17. Baker, Craven, and Blalock, *First Baptist Church*, 147.

18. For Gano's account of these events, see Wolever, *John Gano*, 40–49.

19. Many historians have criticized Gano for this. For a negative evaluation, see Mulder, *A Controversial Spirit*, 38–44; for a positive evaluation, see Benedict, *A General History*, 2:98–100, and Nettles, *Baptists*, 2:111–13, 460n19.

20. Hart, *Original Diary*, 3; Furman, *Charleston Association*, 10–11; Rogers, *Richard Furman*, 135–68.

21. Semple, *Rise and Progress*, 101, 67, emphasis original; Mallary, *Edmund Botsford*, 42–43.

22. Leland, *Writings*, 105; the "strict Calvinism" Leland refers to is their strict adherence to the *Sceond London Confession*; Semple, *Rise and Progress*, 67.

23. Leland, *Writings*, 105.

24. Isaac, *Transformation of Virginia*, 162; for a Separate Baptist defense of "serious living," see Thomas, *Virginian Baptist*, 59–60; Semple, *Rise and Progress*, 67; Furman, *Charleston Association*, 33.

25. Furman, *Charleston Association*, 33; Semple, *Rise and Progress*, 68, emphasis original; Furman, *Charleston Association*, 33.

26. Oliver Hart to Samuel Jones, June 30, 1769, McKesson MSS, HSP; Hart, "Journey to the Backcountry," 22; Hart, *Original Diary*, 14; Oliver Hart to Isaac Backus, February 16, 1777, Gratz MSS, HSP.

27. Townsend, *South Carolina Baptists*, 150–53; Furman, *Charleston Association*, 72; Hart, *Original Diary*, 6; Oliver Hart to Richard Furman, February 12, 1777, Hart MSS, JBDML.

28. Oliver Hart to Richard Furman, October 9, 1784, Hart MSS, JBDML; Townsend, *South Carolina Baptists*, 150; Furman, *Rewards of Grace*.

29. Owens, *Biography*, 41; Furman, *Rewards of Grace*, 23; Rogers, *Death of the Rev. Oliver Hart*, 24; Furman, *Rewards of Grace*, 23–24; Nettles writes, "One of the remarkable features of this sermon is the number of times Hart quotes verbatim from the *Baptist Catechism* as a foundation for his theological exposition. He does this at least on seven occasions," Nettles, *Baptists*, 2:459n68; Rumburg, *Southern Documents*, 211–38; Oliver Hart to Samuel Jones, December 1, 1763, McKesson MSS, HSP; Hart, *Humble Attempt*, 46.

30. Hart, Sermon on Associations, Hart MSS, SCL; Oliver Hart to John Hart, September 1755, Hart MSS, SCL; Furman, *Rewards of Grace*, 26; Furman, "Rules for the Society for Promoting Christian Knowledge and Practice, entered to at Charleston, 1755," Furman MSS, JBDML; Baker, Craven, and Blalock, *First Baptist Church*, 161; Owens, *Biography*, 13.

31. Evan Pugh to unknown recipient, April 23, 1762, McKesson Collection, HSP; Hart, *Original Diary*, 3; Leah Towsend, *South Carolina Baptists*, 86–87; Hart, *Original Diary*, 6; Furman, *Charleston Association*, 72–75; Hart, sermon on 1 Timothy 4:16, Hart MSS, SCL.

32. Oliver Hart to Richard Furman, March 2, 1790, Hart MSS, Furman; Hart, *Gospel Church*, 16–17; Boyce (1827–1888), prominent Southern Baptist denominational leader and theologian of the nineteenth century, founded The Southern Baptist Theological Seminary in 1859; see Wills, *Southern Baptist Theological Seminary*, 14–16; McBeth, *Baptist Heritage*, 237.

33. Guild, *James Manning*, 7; Oliver Hart to Samuel Jones, February 7, 1764, McKesson MSS, HSP; Oliver Hart to James Manning, April 17, 1770, Manning MSS, JHL.

34. Guild, *Brown University*, 22, 80; Rogers, *A Sermon*, 25; Oliver Hart to Richard Furman, May 30, 1793, Hart MSS, JBDML.

35. Mallary, *Edmund Botsford*, 48–49, emphasis original; James Manning, "Public admonition of a number of students," Manning MSS, JHL; Oliver Hart to James Manning, November 27, 1773, Manning MSS, JHL.

36. Owens, *Biography*, 41. Furman, *Rewards of Grace*, 26.

37. Hart, *America's Remembrancer*, 9; Hart, *Original Diary*, 9.

38. From a copy of Hart's commission, printed in the *Baptist Courier*, March 9, 1793, and cited in Owens, *Biography*, 16.

39. Hart, *Original Diary*, 9.

40. Hart, "Journey to the Back-Country," 19–20.

41. Ibid., 23.

42. Oliver Hart to James Manning, December 23, 1767, Manning MSS, JHL; Edwards, *Materials*, 2:141; Townsend, *South Carolina Baptists*, 125.

43. Hart, "Journey to the Back-Country," 20–26; Owens, "Hart and the American Revolution," 5–12.

44. Loulie Latimer Owens, "Oliver Hart and the American Revolution," 14, 2.

45. Furman, *Rewards of Grace*, 26. Hart; *America's Remembrancer*, 15; Hart, *Character*, 29–30; Oliver Hart to Richard Furman, February 12, 1777, Hart MSS, JBDML.

46. Edgar, *South Carolina*, 237–38; Hart, *Original Diary*, 9.

47. Hart, diary, May 21, 1780, Hart MSS, SCL; Hart, *Original Diary*, 13; Hart, diary, October 24, 1781, Hart MSS, SCL.

48. Brekus, *Sarah Osborn's World*, 237.

49. Young, *Domesticating Slavery*, 20; Weir, *Colonial South Carolina*, 205; Olwell, *Masters, Slaves & Subjects*, 20; DeWolfe Howe, ed., "Journal of Josiah Quincy, Junior, 1773," 455.

50. Young, *Domesticating Slavery*, 21; Olwell, *Masters, Slaves, & Subjects*, 21–25; Hart, March 4, 1779, *Original Diary*.

51. Kidd, *Great Awakening*, 215; Jonathan Edwards, *Great Awakening*, 159; Jonathan Edwards, *A History of the Work of Redemption*, 472, 480; Marsden, *Jonathan Edwards*, 258; Whitefield, *Journals*, 20–21; Whitefield, *A Letter to the Inhabitants of Maryland, Virginia, and South Carolina*, in *Works*, 4:37–41, 39.

52. Brekus, *Sarah Osborn's World*, 243; Kidd, *George Whitefield*, 188–90; Marsden, *Jonathan Edwards*, 255–58.

53. Hart, diary, August 26, 1754, Hart MSS, Furman; Marrant, *Narrative*, 12–13; Lockley, "David Margrett," 729–45; Carretta, ed., *Unchained Voices*, 325–50.

54. Hart, diary, August 26, 1754, Hart MSS, JBDML; Hart, *Original Diary*, 6; Anne Hart to Oliver Hart, July 19, 1781, Hart MSS, SCL; Gallay, *Masters and Slaves*, 1–18; Hart, *Original Diary*, 8.

55. Winchester, *Reigning Abominations;* Nash, *Forging Freedom*, 103–6; Sprague, *American Pulpit*, 6:147; Nash, *Forging Freedom*; McLoughlin, *New England Dissent*, 2:768; Gilette, *Minutes*, 247.

56. Rogers, *A Sermon*, 24; for Washington's provision for his slaves upon his death, see Hirschfield, *George Washington and Slavery*, esp. 209–23; for Hart's admiration of Washington, see Hart, *America's Remembrancer*, 11.

57. Rogers, *A Sermon*, 24.

58. Leland, *Writings*, 174; Rogers, *Richard Furman*, 221–30; Hart, diary, September 2, 1754, JBDML, emphasis original.

CHAPTER 5: REVIVAL CATHOLICITY

1. Hart, diary, October 27, 1754, Hart MSS, JBDML.

2. Kidd and Hankins, *Baptists in America*, 28–29.

3. Freeman, "Count Nicholas Ludwig Von Zinzendorf," 297.

4. The memorable "meer Christian" quotation in Baxter, *Church-History*, [xiv]; Baxter, *Christian Directory*, 52–53; Lovelace, *Cotton Mather*, 274; Mather, *Blessed Unions*, 72–79; Mather advances his ideas regarding revival and the millennium in his *Shaking Dispensations*.

5. Hindmarsh, "Spirituality of George Whitefield;" George Whitefield to Ralph Erskine, January 16, 1740, in *Works*, 1:140.

6. Whitefield, *Journals*, 458.

7. George Whitefield to Mr. P., November 28, 1739, in *Works*, 1:126, emphasis original; Hindmarsh, *John Newton*, 322.

8. George Whitefield to Mr. [John] O[ulton], May 27, 1742, in *Works*, 1:394.

9. George Whitefield to Mr. J. H., in *Works*, 1:224, emphasis original.

10. Whitefield, *Journals*, 342, 406.

11. Ibid., 419.

12. *Pennsylvania Gazette*, July 15, 1740; *Pennsylvania Gazette*, August 14, 1740, appendix D; Ray, "Jenkin Jones," in *A Noble Company*, 200–210.

13. Whitefield, *Journals*, 440–44.

14. Chanler, *New Converts*, 1–2, 4–5, 38–42. Whitefield wrote to Chanler the following year, sending his love to the flock at Ashley Ferry, George Whitefield to Isaac Chanler, February 17, 1741, in *Works*, 1:237–38.

15. Townsend, *South Carolina Baptists*, 38; Benedict, *General History*, 703; Whitefield, *Journals*, 447; George Whitefield to Mr. N., August 15, 1740, in *Works*, 1:203.

16. See Ramsay, *History of South Carolina*, 2:452–53; Dalcho, *Protestant Episcopal Church*, 180–83; Smith, *Cautious Enthusiasm*, 94–107.

17. Hart, *Original Diary*, 12; Oliver Hart to James Manning, April 27, 1761, Manning MSS, JHL.

18. Hart, *Character*, 4.

19. Hutson, *Living Christianity*; Hart, diary, October 16, 18, 1754, Hart MSS, JBDML.

20. See Miller, *"A Warm & Zealous Spirit"*; Hart, diary, August 17, 30, September 17–18, October 17–18, 1764, Hart MSS, JBDML.

21. Shipp, *History of Methodism*, 123–24.

22. Ibid., 127–29.

23. Pilmoor's diary during this period is reproduced in Shipp, *History of Methodism*, 128–34.

24. Gill, *Dissenters' Reasons*, 14; Thomas, *Virginian Baptist;* Isaac, *Transformation of Virginia*, 161–77.

25. Little, *Southern Evangelicalism*, 148; Dalcho, *Protestant Episcopal Church*, 183; Hart, diary, September 23, October 27, 1754, Hart MSS, JBDML.

26. Bebbington, *Baptists through the Centuries*, 80–81.

27. Kidd, *Great Awakening*, 257; *A Confession of Faith*, 71; *Summary of Church Discipline*, 2.

28. *Summary of Church Discipline*, 17.

29. Thomas, *Virginian Baptist*, 50.

30. Hart, *Humble Attempt*, 16; Oliver Hart to Richard Furman, November 26, 1793, Hart MSS, JBDML.

31. Oliver Hart, diary, July 14, August 3, 1780, Hart MSS, SCL.

32. *Summary of Church Discipline*, 17. Hart and Pelot cited Acts 2:41, 8:12, 16:15, 18:8, 19:5; Rom 6:3–4; Gal 3:27; and Col 2:12 as establishing the biblical pattern of baptism preceding church membership.

33. George Whitefield to Jenkin Jones, May 12, 1740, in *Works*, 1:175; Gillette, *Minutes*, 42–43.

34. Bunyan, *Works*, 2:604, 611, 612, 613, 656, 657.

35. Whitefield, *Works*, 4:307–8; Gillette, *Minutes*, 200.

36. Oliver Hart to Richard Furman, March 2, 1790, Hart MSS, JBDML, emphasis original.

37. Oliver Hart to Richard Furman, March 2, 1790, Hart MSS, JBDML; Isaac, *Transformation of Virginia*, 161–71; Thomas, *Virginian Baptist*; Hooker, "Introduction," in Woodmason, *Carolina Backcountry*, xi–xxxix, 117, 45.

38. Woodmason, *Carolina Backcountry*, 6; Oliver Hart to Richard Furman, March 2, 1790, Hart MSS, JBDML; Oliver Hart to Richard Furman, November 9, 1791, Hart MSS, JBDML.

39. Furman, *Rewards of Grace*, 24; Hart, *Great Man*, 26.

CONCLUSION: REVIVAL LEGACY

1. Backus published the first of his three-volume project in 1777 under the title *A Story of New England, with particular reference to the Denomination of Christians called Baptists* (Boston: Edward Draper, 1777); Oliver Hart to Isaac Backus, Feb. 16, 1777, Gratz MSS, HSP.

2. Kidd, *Great Awakening*; Little, *Southern Evangelicalism*; Smith, *Cautious Enthusiasm*.

3. Lumpkin, *Baptist Foundations*, v–vi, 63, 155, 157; Shurden, "Southern Baptist Synthesis," 2–11.

4. Owens, *Oliver Hart, 1723–1795*, 1.

BIBLIOGRAPHY

ARCHIVAL MATERIAL

Backus, Isaac. Papers. Franklin-Trask Library, Andover Newton Theological Seminary, Newton Centre, Mass.

Botsford, Edmund. Papers. James B. Duke Memorial Library, Furman University, Greenville, S.C.

Furman, Richard. Papers. James B. Duke Memorial Library, Furman University, Greenville, S.C.

Hart, Anne. *Narrative of Anne Maria Sealy Grimball Hart, born 1741, South Carolina.* Historical Society of Pennsylvania, Philadelphia.

Hart, Oliver. *A Copy of the Original Diary of Rev. Oliver Hart of Charlestown, Pastor of the Baptist Church of Charlestown.* Mimeographed Copy. James P. Boyce Centennial Library, Southern Baptist Theological Seminary, Louisville.

———. Letters. Gratz Collection. Historical Society of Pennsylvania, Philadelphia.

———. Letters. McKesson Collection. Historical Society of Pennsylvania, Philadelphia.

———. Papers. James B. Duke Memorial Library. Furman University, Greenville, S.C.

———. Papers. South Caroliniana Library, University of South Carolina, Columbia, S.C.

Manning, James. Papers. John Hay Library, Brown University, Providence, R.I.

Pugh, Evan. Letters. Gratz Collection. Historical Society of Pennsylvania, Philadelphia.

PRIMARY SOURCES

Backus, Isaac. *A Story of New England, with particular reference to the Denomination of Christians called Baptists.* Boston: Edward Draper, 1777.

Baxter, Richard. *A Christian Directory.* Grand Rapids: Soli Deo Gloria, 2008.

———. *Church-History of the Government of Bishops and their Councils Abbreviated.* London: John Kidgell, 1680.

Blair, Samuel. *A Short and Faithful Narrative of the late remarkable revival of religion in the congregation of New Londonderry, and other parts of Pennsylvania, as the same was sent in a letter to the Rev. Mr. Prince of Boston.* Philadelphia: William Bradford, 1744.

Broome, John David. *The Life, Ministry, and Journals of Hezekiah Smith: Pastor of the First Baptist Church of Haverhill, Massachusetts, 1765 to 1805 and Chaplain in the American Revolution, 1775 to 1780.* Springfield, Mo.: Particular Baptist Press, 2004.

Bunyan, John. *Works of John Bunyan.* 3 vols. Edited by George Offor. Edinburgh: Banner of Truth, 1991.

Chanler, Isaac. *The Doctrines of Glorious Grace Unfolded, defended, and practically improved.* Boston: S. Kneeland and T. Green, 1744.

———. *New Converts Exhorted to Cleave to the Lord. A Sermon on Acts XI 23 Preach'd July 30, 1740 at a Wednesday Evening-lecture, in Charlestown, Set Up at the Motion, and the Desire of the Rev. Mr. Whitefield; With a Brief Introduction Relating to the Character of that Excellent Man . . . With Preface by the Reverend Mr. Cooper of Boston, N.E.* Boston: D. Fowle for S. Kneeland and T. Green, 1740.

Charleston Association. *A Confession of Faith, Put Forth by the Elders and Brethren of Many Congregations of Christians (Baptized upon Profession of their Faith) in London and the Country. Adopted by the Baptist Association in Charlestown, South-Carolina. To which is annexed, A Summary of Church Discipline.* Charleston: David Bruce, 1774.

———. *Minutes of the Charleston Association, February 7, 1774.* Charleston, 1774.

———. *Minutes of the Charleston Association, February 6, 1775.* Charleston, 1775.

———. *Minutes of the Charleston Association, February 3, 1777.* Charleston, 1777.

———. *Minutes of the Charlestown Association, February 2, 1778.* Charleston, 1778.

———. *Minutes of the Charleston Association, October 19, 1778.* Charleston, 1778.

Chauncy, Charles. *Seasonable Thoughts on the State of Religion in New-England.* Boston: Rogers and Fowle, 1743.

Dickinson, Jonathan. *A display of God's special grace. In a familiar dialogue between a minister & a gentleman of his congregation, about the work of God, in the conviction and conversion of sinners, so remarkably of late begun and going on in these American parts.* Boston: Rogers and Fowle, 1742.

Edwards, Jonathan. *The Great Awakening.* Edited by C. C. Goen. Vol. 4 of *The Works of Jonathan Edwards.* New Haven, Conn.: Yale University Press, 2009.

———. *Letters and Personal Writings.* Edited by George S. Claghorn. Vol. 16 of *The Works of Jonathan Edwards.* New Haven, Conn.: Yale University Press, 1998.

———. *Religious Affections.* Edited by John E. Smith. Vol. 2 of *The Works of Jonathan Edwards.* New Haven, Conn.: Yale University Press, 1959.

———. *The Sermons of Jonathan Edwards: A Reader.* Edited by Wilson H. Kimnach, Kenneth P. Minkema, and Douglas A. Sweeney. New Haven, Conn.: Yale University Press, 1999.

Edwards, Morgan. *The Customs of Primitive Churches, or A Set of Propositions Relative to the Name, Materials, Constitution, Power, Officers, Ordinances, Rites, Business, Worship, Discipline, Government, &c. of a Church; to Which Are Added Their Proofs from Scripture; and Historical Narratives of the Manner in Which Most of Them Have Been Reduced to Practice.* Philadelphia: Andrew Stuart, 1768.

———. *Materials Towards A History of the Baptists.* 2 vols. Edited by Eve B. Weeks and Mary B. Warren. Danielsville, Ga.: Heritage Papers, 1984.

Furman, Richard. *Rewards of Grace Conferred on Christ's Faithful People: A Sermon, Occasioned by the Decease of the Rev. Oliver Hart, A.M.* Charleston: J. McIver, 1796.

Garden, Alexander. *Take heed how ye hear.* Charleston: Peter Timothy, 1741.

Gillette, A. D., ed. *Minutes of the Philadelphia Baptist Association, from A.D. 1707 to A.D. 1807.* Philadelphia: American Baptist Publication Society, 1851.

Gill, John. *A Body of Doctrinal and Practical Divinity.* Atlanta: Turner Lassetter, 1950.

———. *The Dissenters' Reasons for Separating from the Church of England. Which were published at the end of Dr. Gill's Answer to a Welch Clergyman, and Occasioned by the said writer.* 4th ed. London: 1760.

Hart, Oliver. *America's Remembrancer, with Respect to her Blessedness and Duty*. Philadelphia: Dobson, 1791.

———. The Character of a Truly Great Man Delineated, and His Death Deplored as a Public *Loss: A Funeral Sermon, Occasioned by the Death of the Rev. William Tennent, A.M.* Charleston: David Bruce, 1777.

———. *Dancing Exploded: A Sermon Shewing the Unlawfulness, Sinfulness, and Bad Consequences of Balls, Assemblies, and Dances in General.* Charleston: David Bruce, 1778.

———. *A Gospel Church Portrayed, and Her Orderly Service Pointed Out—A Sermon, Delivered in the City of Philadelphia at the Opening of the Baptist Association, October 4, 1791.* Trenton, N.J.: Isaac Collins, 1791.

———. *An Humble Attempt to Repair the Christian Temple, Shewing The Business of Officers and Private Members in the Church of Christ, and How Their Work Should Be Performed; with Some Motives to Excite Professors Ardently to Engage in It.* Philadelphia: Aitken, 1785.

Hutson, William. *Living Christianity, delineated, in the Diaries and Letters of two Eminently pious Persons, lately deceased; vis. Mr. Hugh Bryan, and Mrs. Mary Hutson, Both of South Carolina. With a Preface by the Reverend Mr. John Conder, and the Reverend Mr. Thomas Gibbons*. London: J. Buckland, 1760.

Leland, John. *The Writings of the Late Elder John Leland*. New York: G. W. Wood, 1845.

Lumpkin, William L. *Baptist Confessions of Faith*. Valley Forge, Pa.: Judson Press, 1969.

Mallary, Charles D. *The Memoirs of Elder Edmund Botsford*. Springfield, Mo.: Particular Baptist Press, 2004.

Marrant, John, and William Aldridge. *A Narrative of the Lord's Wonderful Dealings with John Marrant, a Black, now Going to Preach the Gospel in Nova-Scotia, born in New-York, in North America*. London: Gilbert and Plummer, 1785.

Mather, Cotton. *Blessed Unions*. Boston: B. Green and J. Allen, 1692.

———. *Shaking Dispensations*. Boston: B. Green, 1715.

Outler, Albert C., ed. *John Wesley*. New York: Oxford, 1964.

Owen, John. *Works*. 6 vols. Edited by William H. Goold. Edinburgh: Banner of Truth, 1966.

Robe, James. *A Short Narrative of the Extraordinary Work at Cambuslang, in a letter to a friend*. Boston: Kneeland and Green, 1742.

Rogers, William. *A Sermon Occasioned by the Death of the Rev. Oliver Hart*. Philadelphia: Lang and Ustick, 1796.

Spener, Philip Jacob. *Pia Desidera*. Translated by Theodore G. Tappert. Philadelphia: Fortress Press, 1964.

Stillman, Samuel. *Select Sermons on Doctrinal and Practical Subjects, by the Late Samuel Stillman, D. D., Comprising Several Sermons Never Before Published to Which Is Prefixed A Biographical Sketch of the Author's Life*. Boston: Manning & Loring, 1808.

Tennent, Gilbert. *The Danger of an Unconverted Ministry, Considered in a Sermon on Mark 6:34*. Philadelphia: Benjamin Franklin, 1740.

Thomas, David. *The Virginian Baptist: or A view and defence of the Christian religion, as it is professed by the Baptists of Virginia*. Baltimore: Enoch Story, 1774.

Wesley, John. *Free Grace, a sermon preached at Bristol*. Boston: T. Fleet, 1741.

Whitefield, George. *The Duty and Interest of an Early Piety set forth in a sermon from Eccl xii, i*. Boston: Kneeland and Green, 1739.

———. *The Indwelling of the Spirit, the Common Privilege of all Believers.* Boston: Kneeland and Green, 1739.

———. *Journals.* Edinburgh: Banner of Truth, 1978.

———. *A Letter from the Reverend George Whitefield, to the Reverend John Wesley, in answer to his sermon, entitled Free Grace.* Boston: Kneeland and Green, 1740.

———. *A Sermon on Regeneration, preach'd to a numerous audience in England.* Boston: T. Fleet, 1739.

———. *The Sermons of George Whitefield.* Edited by Lee Gattis. Wheaton, Ill.: Crossway, 2012.

———. *Works of the Reverend George Whitefield.* 4 vols. London: Edward and Charles Dilly, 1771.

Winchester, Elhanan. *The Reigning Abominations: Especially the Slave Trade, Considered as Causes of Lamentation; Being the Substance of a Discourse Delivered in Fairfax County, Virginia, December 30, 1774.* London: H. Trapp, 1788.

Woodmason, Charles. *The Carolina Backcountry on the Eve of the Revolution: The Journal and Other Writings of Charles Woodmason, Anglican Itinerant.* Edited by Richard J. Hooker. Chapel Hill: University of North Carolina Press, 1953.

SECONDARY SOURCES

Books

Alexander, Archibald. *Biographical Sketches of the Founder, and Principal Alumni of the Log College.* Princeton, N.J.: J. T. Robinson, 1845.

Bailyn, Bernard. *Atlantic History: Concept and Contours.* Cambridge, Mass.: Harvard University Press, 2005.

Baker, Robert A., Paul J. Craven, and Marshall A. Blalock. *History of the First Baptist Church of Charleston, South Carolina, 1682–2007.* Springfield, Mo.: Particular Baptist Press, 2007.

Bebbington, D. W. *Baptists through the Centuries: A History of a Global People.* Waco, Tex.: Baylor University Press, 2010.

———. *Evangelicalism in Modern Britain: A History from the 1730s to the 1980s.* New York: Routledge, 2005.

Benedict, David. *A General History of the Baptist Denomination in America, and Other Parts of the World.* 2 vols. Boston: Lincoln and Edmonds, 1813.

Bolton, S. Charles. *Southern Anglicanism: The Church of England in Colonial South Carolina.* Westport, Conn.: Greenwood Press, 1982.

Brekus, Catherine A. *Sarah Osborn's World: The Rise of Evangelical Christianity in Early America.* New Haven, Conn.: Yale University Press, 2013.

Burrage, Henry S. *History of the Baptists in Maine.* Portland, Maine: Marks, 1904.

Butler, Jon. *Awash in a Sea of Faith: Christianizing the American People.* Cambridge, Mass.: Harvard University Press, 1990.

Carretta, Vincent, ed. *Unchained Voices: An Anthology of Black Authors in the English-Speaking World of the 18th Century.* Lexington, Ky.: University of Kentucky, 1996.

Clarke, Erskine: *Our Southern Zion: A History of Calvinism in the South Carolina Low Country, 1690–1990.* Tuscaloosa: University of Alabama Press, 1996.

———. *Wrestlin' Jacob: A Portrait of Religion in Antebellum Georgia and the Carolina Lowcountry.* Tuscaloosa: University of Alabama Press, 2000.

Coalter Michael J., Jr. *Gilbert Tennent, Son of Thunder: A Case Study of Continental Pietism's*

Impact on the First Great Awakening in the Middle Colonies. Westport, Conn.: Greenwood Press, 1986.

Dalcho, Frederick. *An Historical Account of the Protestant Episcopal Church in South Carolina, from the first settlement of the province, to the war of the Revolution.* Charleston: E. Thayer, 1820.

Davis, W. W. H. *History of Bucks County, Pennsylvania, From the Discovery of the Delaware to the Present Time.* Doylestown, Pa.: Democrat Book and Job, 1876.

———. *History of the Hart Family of Warminster, Bucks County, Pennsylvania. To Which Is Added the Genealogy of the Family, from Its First Settlement in America.* Doylestown, Pa.: W. W. H. Davis, 1867.

Davies, Hywel. *Transatlantic Brethren: Rev. Samuel Jones (1735–1814) and his Friends: Baptist in Wales, Pennsylvania, and Beyond.* Bethlehem, Pa.: Lehigh University Press, 1995.

Edgar, Walter B. *South Carolina: A History.* Columbia: University of South Carolina Press, 1998.

Flynt, Wayne. *Alabama Baptists: Southern Baptists in the Heart of Dixie.* Tuscaloosa: University of Alabama Press, 1998.

Fraser, Walter J. *Charleston! Charleston! The History of a Southern City.* Columbia: University of South Carolina Press, 1991.

Frey, Sylvia R., and Betty Wood. *Come Shouting Zion: African American Protestantism in the American South and the British Caribbean to 1830.* Chapel Hill: University of North Carolina Press, 1998.

Furman, Wood. *History of the Charleston Association of Baptist Churches in the State of South-Carolina; with an appendix containing the principal circular letters to the churches.* Charleston: J. Hoff, 1811.

Garrett, James Leo. *Baptist Church Discipline: A Historical Introduction to the Practices of Baptist Churches, with Particular Attention to the Summary of Church Discipline Adopted in 1773 by the Charleston Association.* Paris, Ark.: Baptist Standard Bearer, 2004.

Gewehr, Wesley M. *The Great Awakening in Virginia, 1740–1790.* Durham, N.C.: Duke University Press, 1930.

Gordon, James. *Evangelical Spirituality.* Eugene, Oreg.: Wipf & Stock, 2002.

Greene, Jack P. and Philip D. Morgan, eds. *Atlantic History: A Critical Appraisal.* New York: Oxford University Press, 2009.

Guild, Reuben Aldridge. *Life, Times, and Correspondence of James Manning, and the Early History of Brown University.* Boston: Gould and Lincoln, 1864.

Haykin, Michael A. G., and Kenneth J. Stewart, eds. *The Advent of Evangelicalism: Exploring Historical Continuities.* Nashville: B&H Academic, 2008.

Heyrman, Christine Leigh. *Southern Cross: The Beginnings of the Bible Belt.* New York: Alfred A. Knopf, 1997.

Hindmarsh, D. Bruce. *The Evangelical Conversion Narrative: Spiritual Autobiography in the Eighteenth Century.* New York: Oxford University Press, 2005.

———. *John Newton and the English Evangelical Tradition.* Grand Rapids: Eerdmans, 1996.

Hirsch, Arthur Henry. *The Huguenots of Colonia South Carolina.* Durham, N.C.: Duke University Press, 1928.

Hirschfield, Fritz. *George Washington and Slavery: A Documentary Portrayal.* Columbia, Mo.: University of Missouri Press, 1997.

Holifield, E. Brooks. *Theology in America*. New Haven, Conn.: Yale University Press, 2003.

Howe, George. *History of the Presbyterian Church in South Carolina*. 2 vols. Columbia: Duffie & Chapman, 1870.

Isaac, Rhys. *The Transformation of Virginia, 1740–1790*. Chapel Hill: University of North Carolina Press, 1982.

Kidd, Thomas S. *George Whitefield: America's Spiritual Founding Father*. New Haven, Conn.: Yale University Press, 2014.

———. *God of Liberty: A Religious History of the American Revolution*. New York: Basic Books, 2010.

———. *The Great Awakening: The Roots of Evangelical Christianity in America*. New Haven, Conn.: Yale University Press, 2007.

Kidd, Thomas S., and Barry G. Hankins. *Baptists in America: A History*. New York: Oxford University Press, 2015.

Krawczynski, Keith. *William Henry Drayton: South Carolina Revolutionary Patriot*. Baton Rouge: Louisiana State University Press, 2001.

Lambert, Frank. *"Peddlar in Divinity": George Whitefield and the Transatlantic Revivals*. Princeton, N.J.: Princeton University Press, 1994.

Lemay, J. A. Leo. *Ebenezer Kinnersley, Franklin's Friend*. Philadelphia: University of Pennsylvania Press, 1964.

Lewis, A. J. *Zinzendorf the Ecumenical Pioneer*. Philadelphia; Westminster, 1962.

Lindberg, Carter, ed. *The Pietist Theologians*. New York: Blackwell, 2005.

Lindman, Janet Moore. *Bodies of Belief: Baptist Community in Early America*. Philadelphia: University of Pennsylvania Press, 2008.

Little, Thomas J. *Origins of Southern Evangelicalism: Religious Revivalism in the South Carolina Lowcountry, 1670–1760*. Columbia: University of South Carolina Press, 2013.

Lovelace, Richard. *F. The American Pietism of Cotton Mather: Origins of American Evangelicalism*. Grand Rapids: Christian University Press, 1979.

———. *Dynamics of Spiritual Life: An Evangelical Theology of Renewal*. Downers Grove, Ill.: IVP Academic, 1979.

Lumpkin, William L. *Baptist Foundations in the South: Tracing through the Separates the Influence of the Great Awakening, 1754–1787*. Nashville: Broadman Press, 1961.

Manly, Basil. *Mercy and Judgment: A Discourse, Containing Some Fragments of the History of the Baptist Church in Charleston, S.C.* Providence, R.I.: Knowles, Vose and Co., 1837.

Marsden, George M. *Jonathan Edwards: A Life*. New Haven, Conn.: Yale University Press, 2003.

Matthews, Donald G. *Religion in the Old South*. Chicago: University of Chicago Press, 1977.

Maxson, Charles Hartshorn. *The Great Awakening in the Middle Colonies*. Chicago: University of Chicago Press, 1920.

McBeth, H. Leon. *The Baptist Heritage: Four Centuries of Baptist Witness*. Nashville: Broadman Press, 1987.

McCurry, Stephanie. *Masters of Small Worlds: Yeoman Households, Gender Relations, the Political Culture of the Antebellum South Carolina Low Country*. New York: Oxford, 1995.

McLoughlin, William J. *Baptist Beginning in Education: A History of Furman University*. Nashville: Sunday School Board, Southern Baptist Convention, 1926.

———. *Isaac Backus and the American Pietistic Tradition*. Boston: Little, Brown, 1967.

McKibbens, Thomas R., and Kenneth L. Smith. *The Life and Works of Morgan Edwards*. New York: Arno Press, 1980.

Miller, Randall M. *"A Warm and Zealous Spirit": John J. Zubly and the American Revolution, a Selection of his Writings*. Macon: Mercer University Press, 1982.

Mulder, Philip N. *A Controversial Spirit: Evangelical Awakenings in the South*. New York: Oxford University Press, 2002.

Nettles, Tom J. *The Baptists: Key People Involved in Forming a Baptist Identity: Beginnings in America*. Fearn, Scotland: Christian Focus Publications, 2005.

Nash, Gary B. *Forging Freedom: The Formation of Philadelphia's Black Community, 1720–1840*. Cambridge, Mass.: Harvard University Press, 1988.

Noll, Mark. *The Rise of Evangelicalism: The Age of Edwards, Whitefield, and the Wesleys*. Downers Grove, Ill.: IVP Academic, 2010.

Olwell, Robert. *Masters, Slaves & Subjects: The Culture of Power in the South Carolina Lowcountry, 1740–1790*. Ithaca, N.Y.: Cornell University Press, 1998.

Owens, Loulie Latimer. *Oliver Hart, 1723–1795: A Biography*. Greenville, S.C.: South Carolina Baptist Historical Society, 1966.

Ramsay, David. *The History of South Carolina, from its first settlement in 1670, to the year 1808*. Charleston: David Longworth, 1809.

Semple, Robert Baylor. *A History of the Rise and Progress of the Baptists in Virginia*. Richmond, Va.: Pitt and Dickinson, 1894.

Shipp, Albert Micajah. *The History of Methodism in South Carolina*. Nashville: Southern Methodist Publishing House, 1834.

Shurden, Walter B. *Not an Easy Journey: Some Transitions in Baptist Life*. Macon: Mercer University Press, 2005.

Smith, Samuel C. *A Cautious Enthusiasm: Mystical Piety and Evangelicalism in Colonial South Carolina*. Columbia: University of South Carolina Press, 2013.

Sprague, William B. *Annals of the American Pulpit*, 6 vols. New York: Robert Carter & Brothers, 1860.

Rogers, James A. *Richard Furman: Life and Legacy*. Macon: Mercer University Press, 2001.

Talbert, Roy, Jr., and Meggan A. Farish. *The Antipedo Baptists of Georgetown, South Carolina, 1710–2010*. Columbia: University of South Carolina Press, 2013.

Townsend, Leah. *South Carolina Baptists, 1670–1805*. Baltimore: Clearfield Publishing, 2003.

Tupper, H. A., ed. *Two Centuries of the First Baptist Church of South Carolina, 1683–1883*. Baltimore: R. H. Woodward and Company, 1889.

Ward, William R. *The Protestant Evangelical Awakening*. New York: Cambridge University Press, 1992.

Wardin. Albert W. *Tennessee Baptists: A Comprehensive History, 1779–1999*. Brentwood, Tenn.: Executive Board of the Tennessee Baptist Convention, 1999.

Weir, Robert M. *Colonial South Carolina: A History*. Columbia: University of South Carolina Press, 2007.

Wills, Gregory A. *Southern Baptist Theological Seminary, 1859–2009*. New York: Oxford University Press, 2009.

Wolever, Terry. *The Life and Ministry of John Gano, 1727–1804*. Springfield, Mo.: Particular Baptist Press, 1998.

Wood, Peter H. *Black Majority: Negroes in Colonial South Carolina from 1670 through the Stono Rebellion*. New York: W. W. Norton, 1996.

Young, Jeffrey Robert. *Domesticating Slavery: The Master Class in Georgia and South Carolina, 1670–1837*. Chapel Hill: University of North Carolina Press, 2005.

Articles

Allen, Wm. Loyd. "The Peculiar Welsh Piety of The Customs of Primitive Churches." In *Distinctively Baptist: A Festschrift in Honor of Walter B. Shurden*, edited by Marc A. Jolley, 171–92. Macon, Ga.: Mercer University Press, 2005.

Ascol, Thomas K. "Happy Birthday, Sandy Creek." At *Tom Ascol*, November 8, 2005. Accessed December 10, 2014. http://tomascol.com/happy-birthday-sandy-creek/.

———. "Sandy Creek Revisited." *Founders Journal* 66 (Fall 2006): 1.

Brackney, William H. "James Manning (1738–1791)." In vol. 3 of *A Noble Company: Biographical Essays on Notable Particular-Regular Baptists in America*, edited by Terry Wolever, 511–38. Springfield, Mo.: Particular Baptist Press, 2013.

Brewster, Paul. "Who Forgot What? A Reply to Emir Caner." *Journal of Baptist Studies* 4 (2010): 30–45.

Bridges, Gene M. "The Raw Calvinism of the North Carolina Separate Baptists of the Sandy Creek Tradition." *Founders Journal* 66 (Fall 2006): 2–25.

Burrage, Henry S. "The Baptist Church in Kittery." *Collections and Proceedings of the Maine Historical Society*, 2nd ser., 9 (1898): 382–91.

———. "Memoir of William Screven." *Collections and Proceedings of the Maine Historical Society*, 2nd ser., 1 (1889): 45–56.

———. "Some Added Facts Concerning William Screven." *Collections and Proceedings of the Maine Historical Society*, 2nd ser., 5 (1894): 275–84.

Caner, Emir. "The Forgotten Hour of How the South Was Won: The Legacy of Daniel Marshall, Pioneer Georgia Baptist." *The Christian Index*, September 24, 2009.

Clayton, J. Glenwood, and Loulie Latimer Owens, eds. "Oliver Hart's Diary of the Journey to the Backcountry." *Journal of the South Carolina Baptist Historical Society* 1 (November 1975): 2–17.

Dockery, David S. "Southern Baptists and Calvinism: A Historical Look." In *Calvinism: A Southern Baptist Dialogue*, edited by E. Ray Clendenen and Brad J. Waggoner, 29–46. Nashville: B&H Academic, 2008.

Finn, Nathan A. "The Making of a Baptist Universalist: The Curious Case of Elhanan Winchester." Paper presented to the Baptist Studies Group at the Evangelical Theological Society, San Francisco, California, 2011.

Freeman, Arthur. "Count Nicholas Ludwig Von Zinzendorf: An Ecumenical Pioneer." *Journal of Ecumenical Studies* 36, nos. 3–4 (Summer-Fall 1999): 287–302.

Gallay, Allan. "Planters and Slaves in the Great Awakening." In *Masters and Slaves in the House of the Lord*, edited by John Boles, 1–18. Lexington: University of Kentucky Press, 1988.

Haykin, Michael A. G. "'His Soul-Refreshing Presence': The Lord's Supper in Baptist Thought & Experience in the 'Long' Eighteenth Century." In *Baptist Sacramentalism*, edited by Anthony R. Cross, 177–93. Waynesboro, Ga.: Paternoster Press, 2003.

———. "Word And Space, Time And Act: The Shaping of English Puritan Piety." *Southern Baptist Journal of Theology* 14, no. 4 (Winter 2010): 38–47.

Hill, Samuel S. "A Survey of Southern Religious History." In *Religion in the Southern States: A Historical Study*, edited by Samuel S. Hill, 383–85. Macon: Mercer University Press: 1983.

Hindmarsh, D. Bruce. "The Reception of Jonathan Edwards by Early Evangelicals in England." In *Jonathan Edwards at Home and Abroad: Historical Memories, Cultural Moments, Global Horizons*. Edited by David W. Kling and Douglas A. Sweeney, 201–20. Columbia: University of South Carolina Press, 2003.

———. "The Spirituality of George Whitefield." Paper presented at "Whitefield and the Great Awakening," Andrew Fuller Conference, The Southern Baptist Theological Seminary, Louisville, October 22, 2014.

Hutson, R. W., ed. "Register Kept by the Rev. Wm. Hutson, of Stoney Creek Independent Congregational Church and (Circular) Congregational Church in Charles Towen, S.C. 1743–1760." *South Carolina Historical Magazine* 38 (January 1937): 21–36.

Jackson, Harvey H. "Hugh Bryan and the Evangelical Movement in Colonial South Carolina." *William and Mary Quarterly* 43, no. 4 (1986): 594–614.

Johnson, Walter E. "Isaac Eaton (1725?–1772)." In vol. 3 of *A Noble Company: Biographical Essays on Notable Particular-Regular Baptists in America*, edited by Terry Wolever, 217–33. Springfield, Mo.: Particular Baptist Press, 2013.

Kegley, Sarah E., and Thomas J. Little, "The Records of the Ashley River Baptist Church, 1736–1769," *Journal of the South Carolina Baptist Historical Society*, 27 (November 2001:3–32.

Lockley, Tim. "David Margrett: A Black Missionary in the Revolutionary Atlantic." *Journal of American Studies* 46, no. 3 (2012): 729–45.

Lovelace, Richard F. "Evangelical Spirituality: A Church Historian's Perspective." *Journal of the Evangelical Theological Society* 31, no. 1 (March 1988): 25–35.

McKibbens, Thomas R. "Disseminating Biblical Doctrine through Preaching." *Baptist History and Heritage* 19, no. 3 (Fall 1984): 42–52.

———. "Over Troubled Waters: Baptist Preachers who were Bridge Builders." *Baptist History and Heritage* 40, no. 2 (Spring 2005): 58–63.

Nettles, Tom J. "John Gill and the Evangelical Awakening." In *The Life and Thought of John Gill (1697–1771): A Tercentennial Appreciation*, edited by Michael A. G. Haykin, 131–70. Leiden: Brill, 1997.

———. "Shubal Stearns and the Separate Baptist Tradition." *Founders Journal* 66 (Fall 2006): 26–31.

Owens, Loulie Latimer. "Hart, Oliver." In *Encyclopedia of Southern Baptists*, 601. Nashville: Broadman Press, 1958.

———. "Oliver Hart and the American Revolution." *Journal of the South Carolina Baptist Historical Society* 1 (November 1975): 2–17.

———. "South Carolina Baptists and the American Revolution." *Journal of the South Carolina Baptist Historical Society* 1 (November 1975): 31–45.

Ray, Thomas. "Jenkin Jones (c.1686–1760)." In vol. 2 of *A Noble Company: Biographical Essays on Notable Particular-Regular Baptists in America*, edited by Terry Wolever, 179–212. Springfield, Mo.: Particular Baptist Press, 2006.

Shurden, Walter B. "The Southern Baptist Synthesis: Is It Cracking?" *Baptist History and Heritage* 16, no. 2 (April 1981): 2–11.

Smith, James A. "Prayer Language Debate: Whose History is Correct?" *Baptist Press News*, February 26, 2007.

Tomlin, Gregory. "Sandy Creek: Tributary of Baptist Life Celebrates 250 Years." *Baptist Press News*, November 7, 2005.

Ward, William R. "Philip Jacob Spener." In *Biographical Dictionary of Evangelicals*. Edited by Timothy Larsen, 622–24. Downers Grove: IVP, 2003.

Wills, Gregory A. "Whosoever Will: A Review Essay." *Journal for Baptist Theology and Ministry* 7 (Spring 2010): 10–11.

Dissertation

Loftis, John Franklin. "Factors in Southern Baptist Identity as Reflected by Ministerial Role Models, 1750–1925." Ph.D. diss., The Southern Baptist Theological Seminary, 1987.

INDEX